THE WHO ENDLES

This publication is not authorised for sale in
the United States of America and / or Canada

WISE PUBLICATIONS
part of The Music Sales Group
London / New York / Paris / Sydney / Copenhagen / Berlin / Madrid / Tokyo

Published by
Wise Publications
14-15 Berners Street, London, W1T 3LJ, UK.

Exclusive distributors:
Music Sales Limited
Distribution Centre, Newmarket Road,
Bury St Edmunds, Suffolk, IP33 3YB, UK.

Music Sales Pty Limited
120 Rothschild Avenue, Rosebery,
NSW 2018, Australia.

Order No. AM989120
ISBN 13: 978-1-84609-902-1
This book © Copyright 2007 Wise Publications,
a division of Music Sales Limited.

Unauthorised reproduction of any part
of this publication by any means including
photocopying is an infringement of copyright.

Edited by Tom Farncombe.
Music arranged by Matt Cowe.
Music processed by Paul Ewers Music Design.

Cover Design: © Richard Evans Design & Art Direction.

Printed in the EU.

Your Guarantee of Quality:
As publishers, we strive to produce every book
to the highest commercial standards.

The running order of the songs matches the recorded album
and the music has been freshly engraved.

Particular care has been given to specifying
acid-free, neutral-sized paper made from pulps
which have not been elemental chlorine bleached.
This pulp is from farmed sustainable forests
and was produced with special regard for the environment.

Throughout, the printing and binding have
been planned to ensure a sturdy, attractive
publication which should give years of enjoyment.

If your copy fails to meet our high standards,
please inform us and we will gladly replace it.

www.musicsales.com

FRAGMENTS

Words & Music by
Pete Townshend & Lawrence Ball

Capo 3rd fret

© Copyright 2006 Eel Pie Publishing Limited/Copyright Control.
BMG Music Publishing Limited (75%)/Copyright Control (25%).
All Rights Reserved. International Copyright Secured.

Verse

G5*
(E5*)

We are a bil - lion frag - ments ex - plod - ing out - ward.

Like bro - ken glass,___ we da - mage, ev - en in de - feat.

We are ti - ny pie - ces fall - ing___ now and set - tling

like snow flake cry - stal, build - ing on the ci - ty street.

6

A MAN IN A PURPLE DRESS

Words & Music by
Pete Townshend

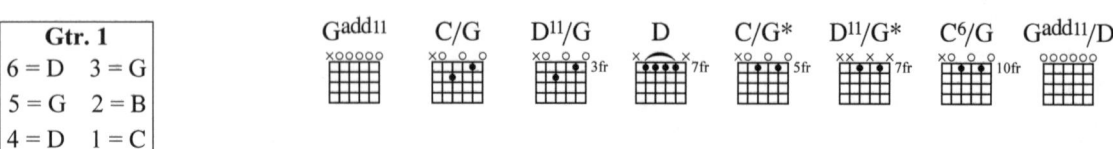

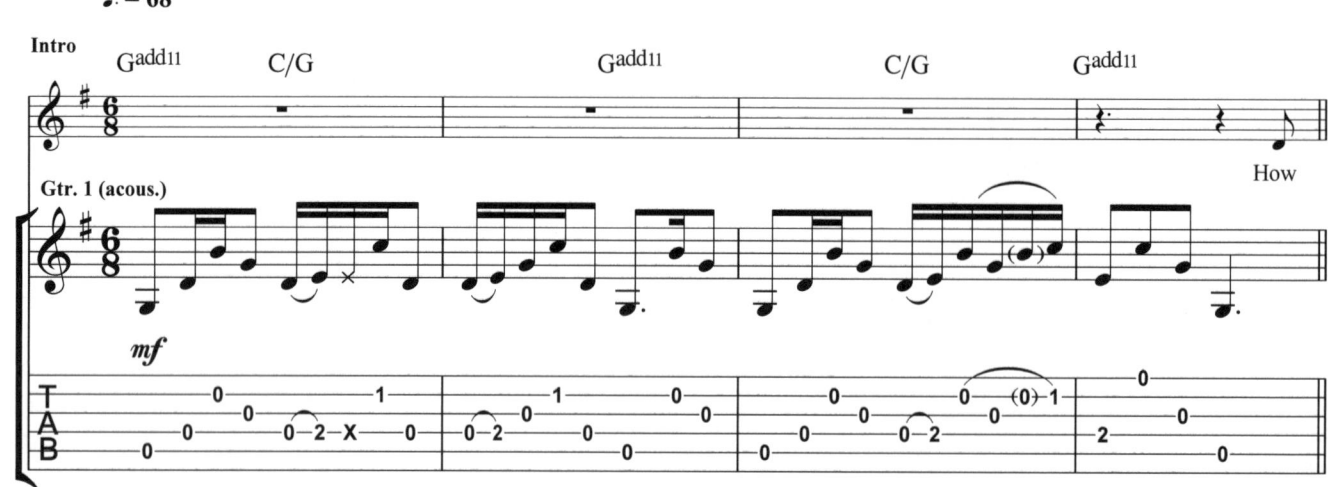

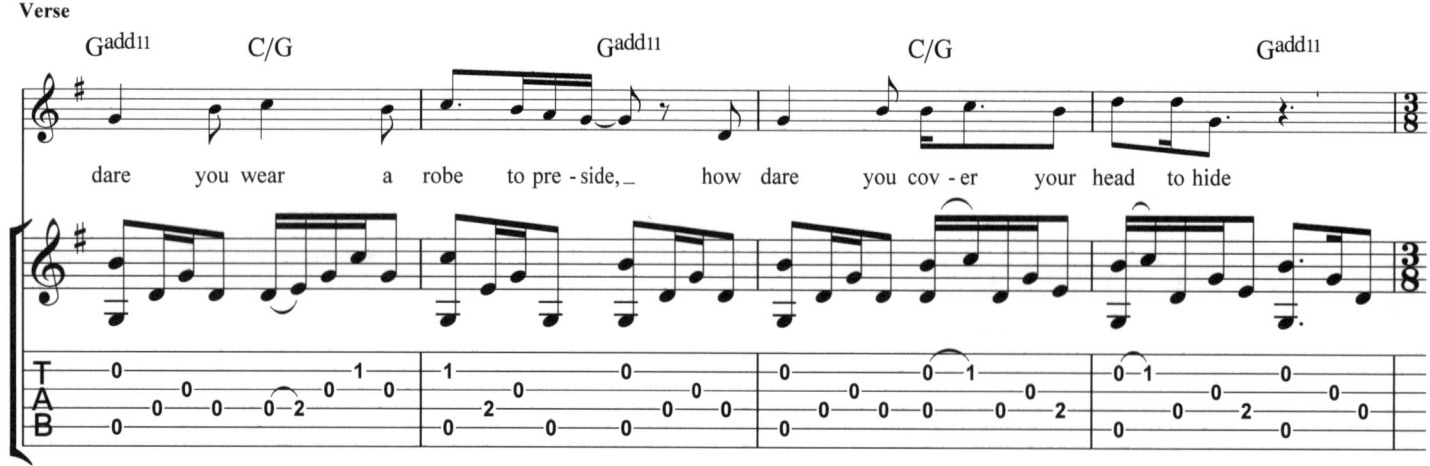

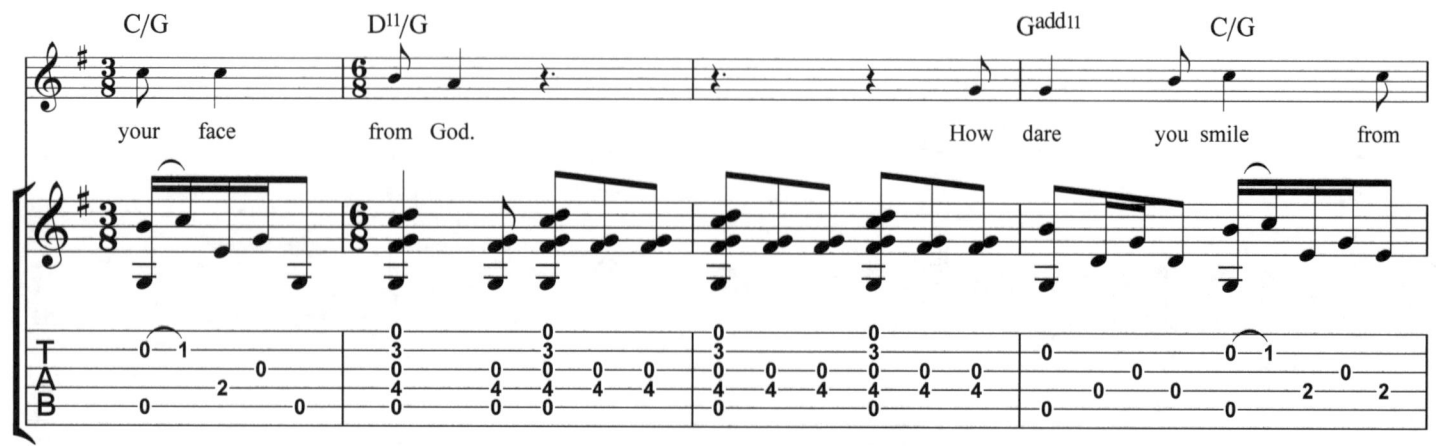

© Copyright 2006 Eel Pie Publishing Limited.
BMG Music Publishing Limited.
All Rights Reserved. International Copyright Secured.

be-hind your beard,_ to hide the fact_ your heart's a-feared,_ and wave your

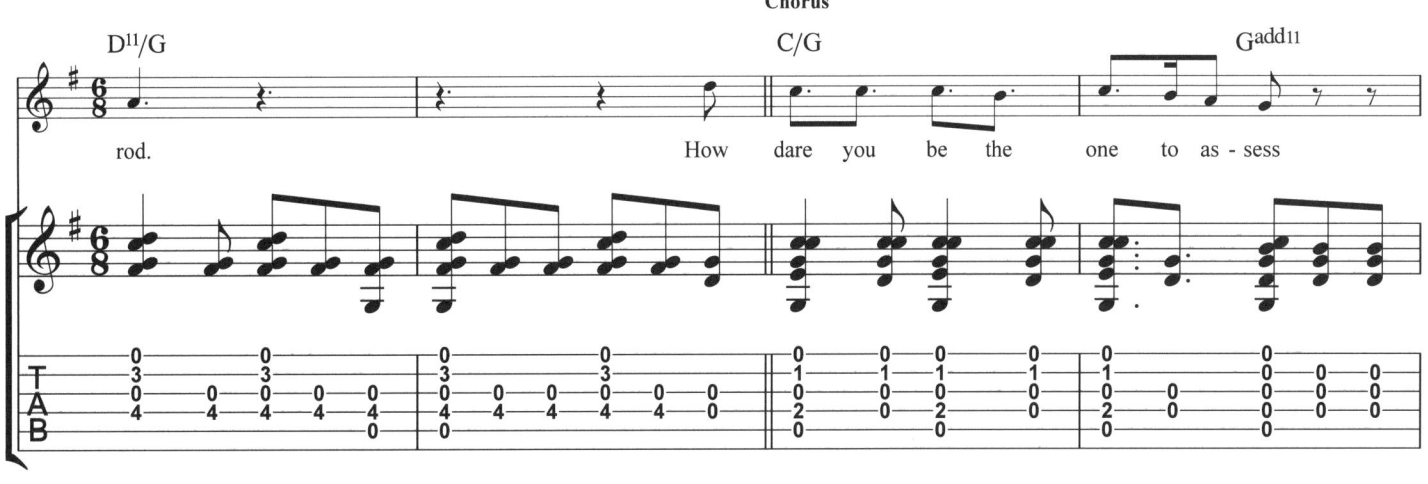

Chorus

rod. How dare you be the one to as-sess

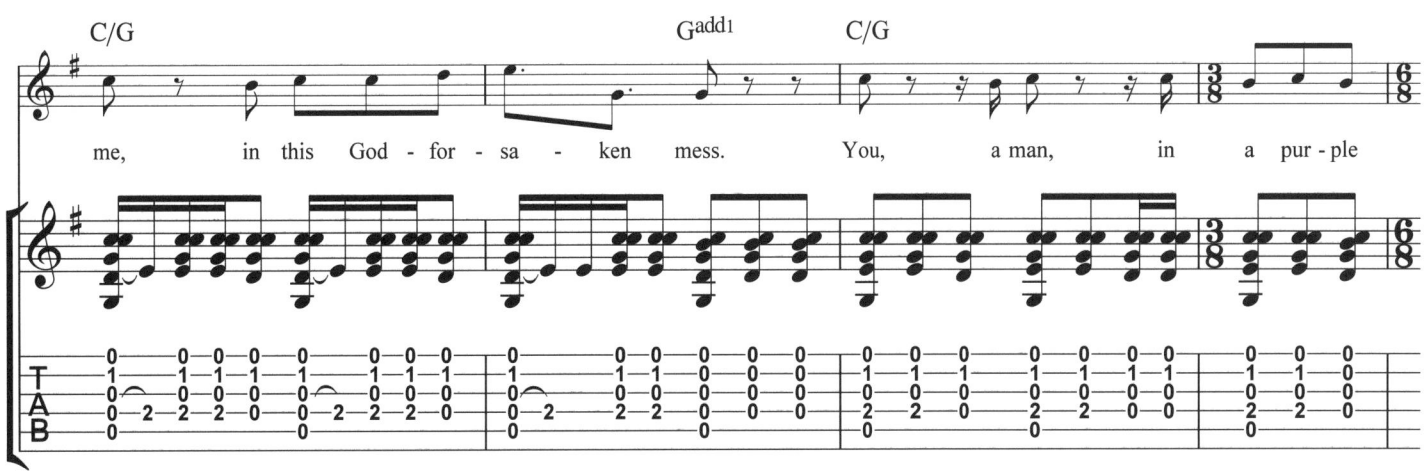

me, in this God-for-sa-ken mess. You, a man, in a pur-ple

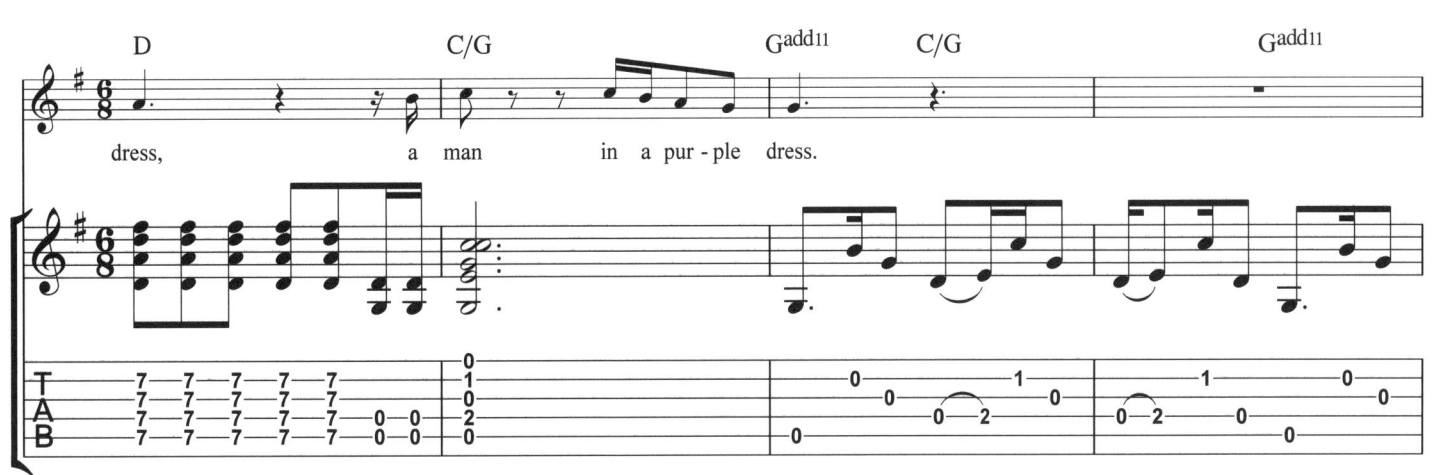

dress, a man in a pur-ple dress.

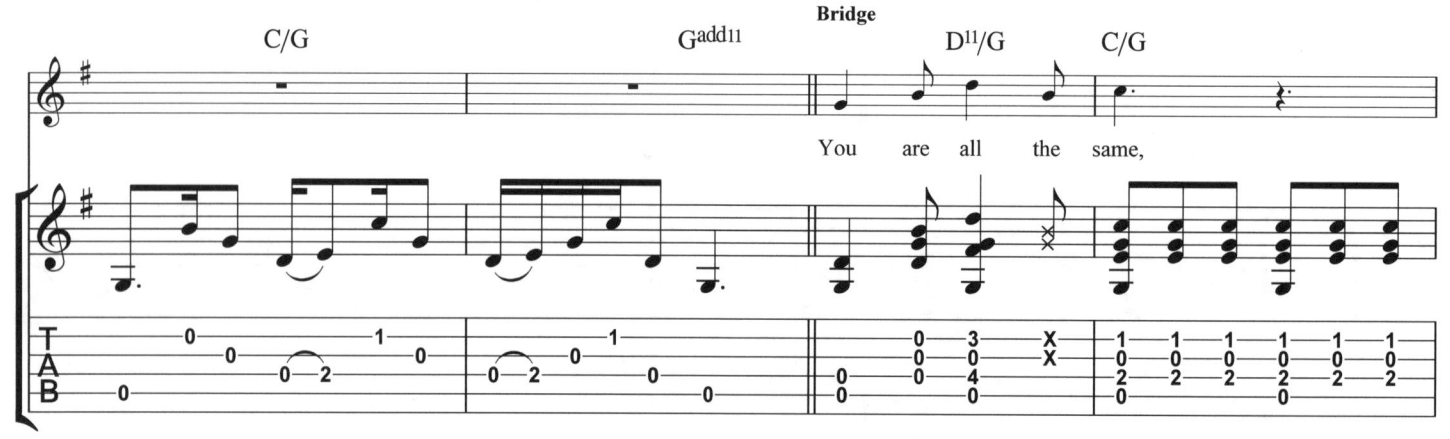

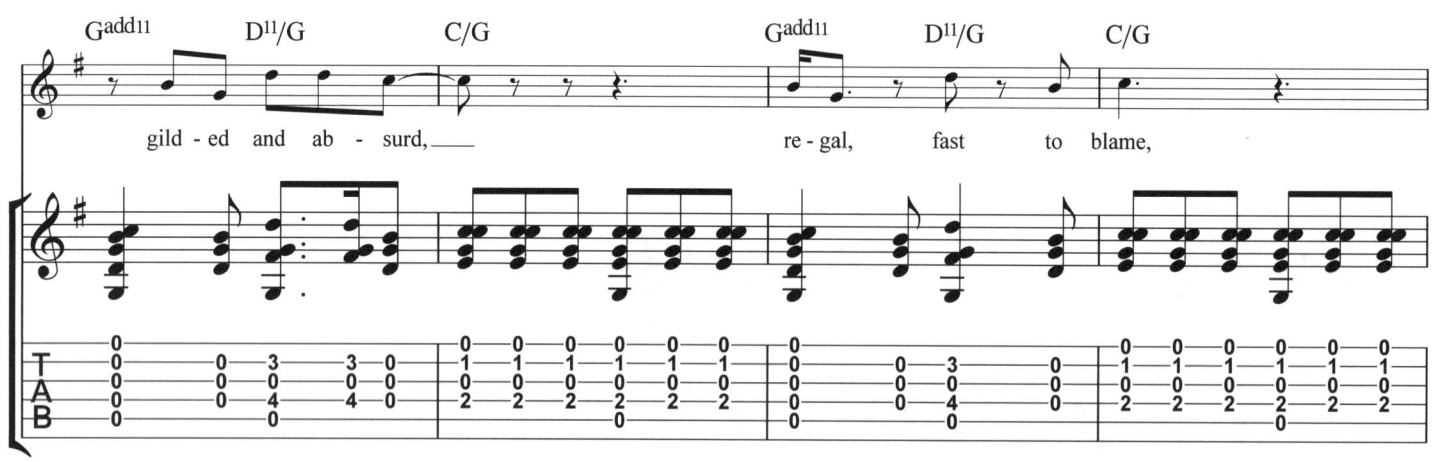

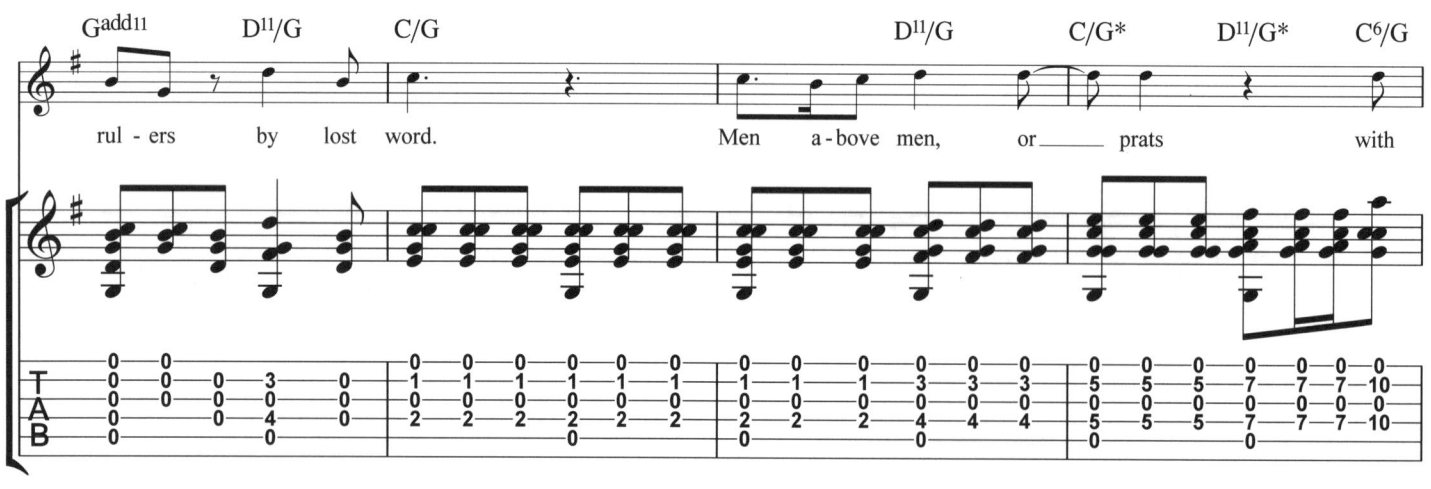

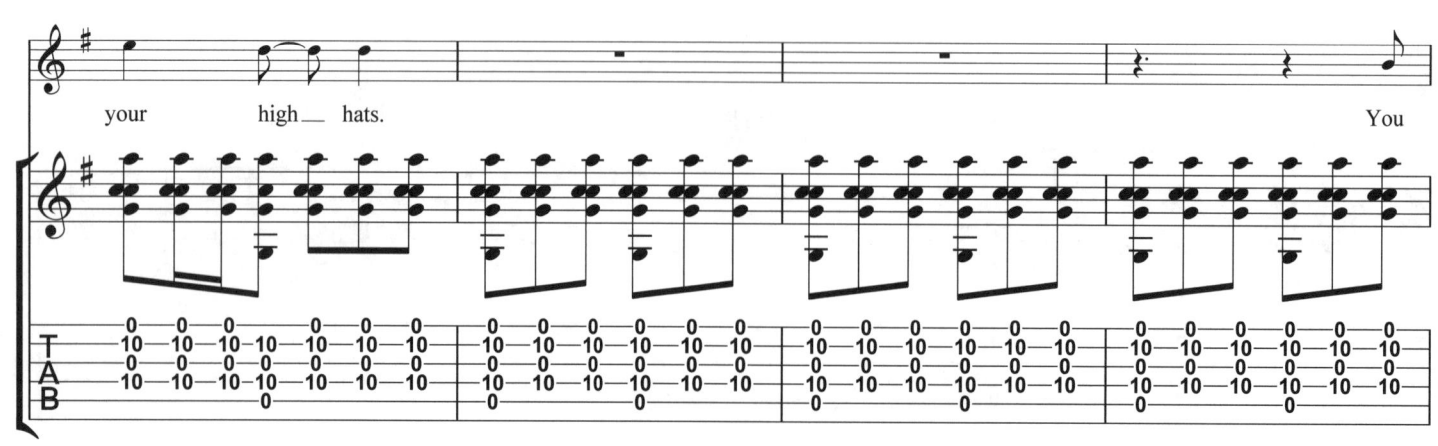

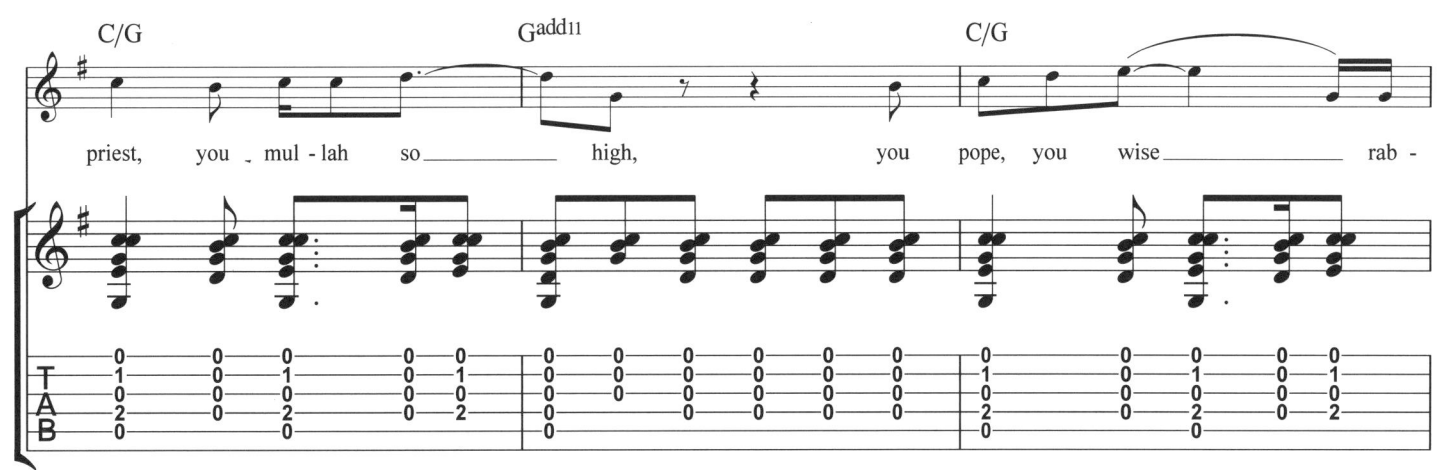

priest, you mul-lah so high, you pope, you wise rab-

-bi. You're in-vi-si-ble to me, like va-pour from the

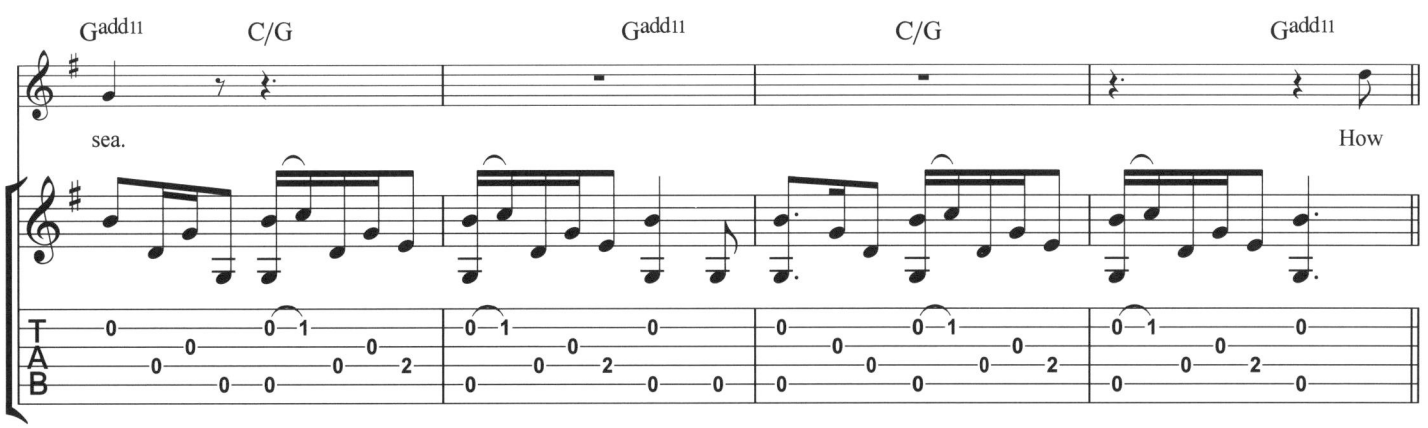

sea. How

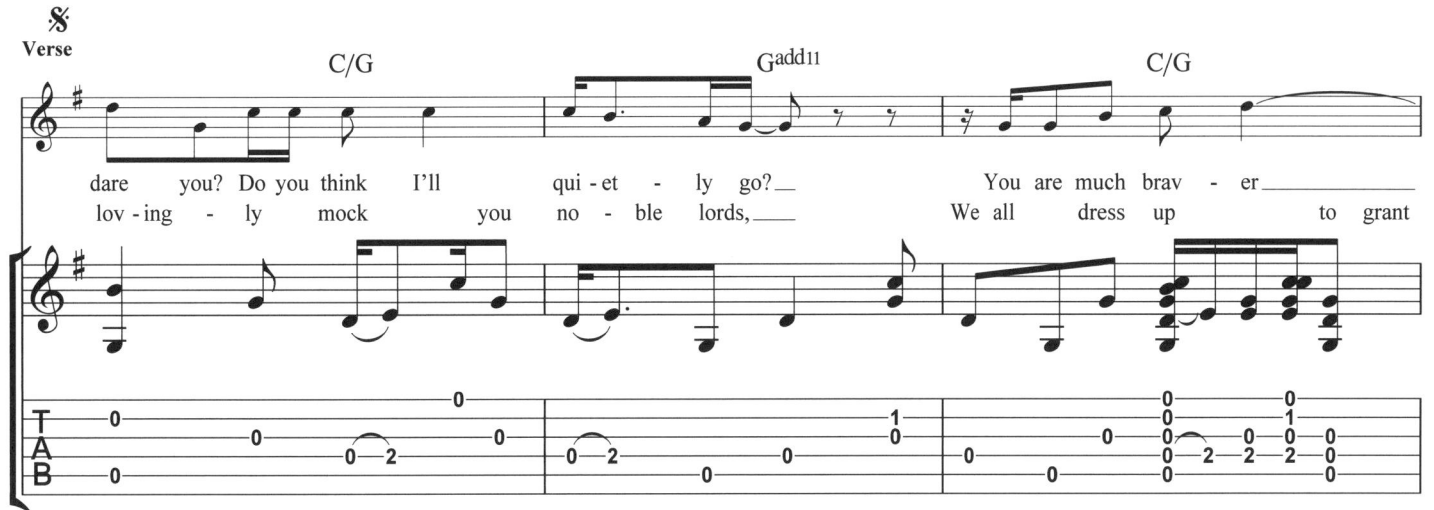

dare you? Do you think I'll qui-et-ly go?
lov-ing-ly mock you no-ble lords, We all dress up to grant

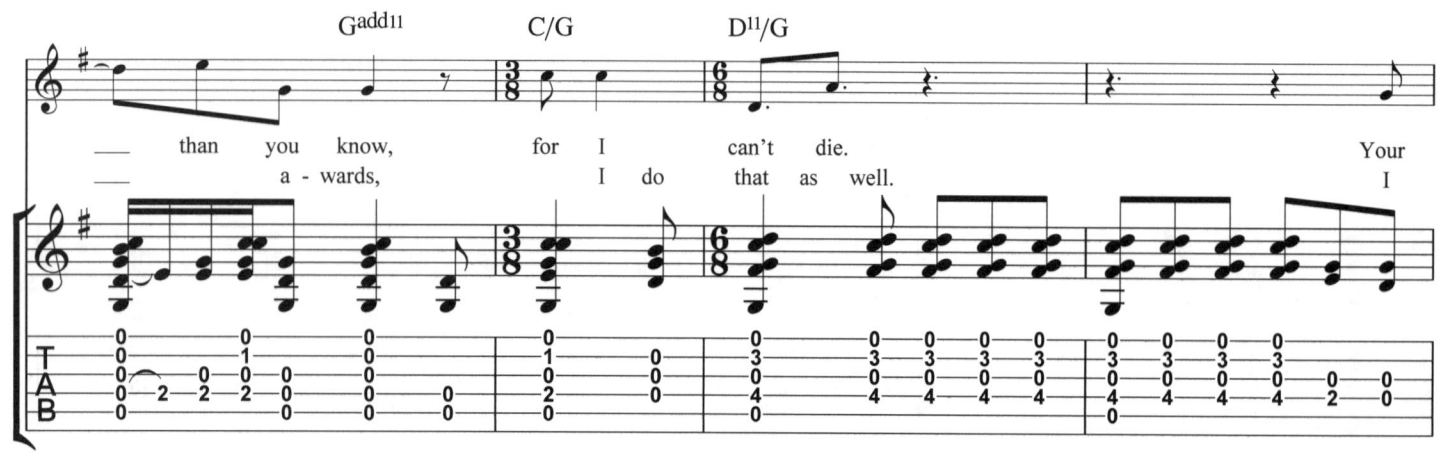

than you know, for I can't die.
a - wards, I do that as well.

Your
I

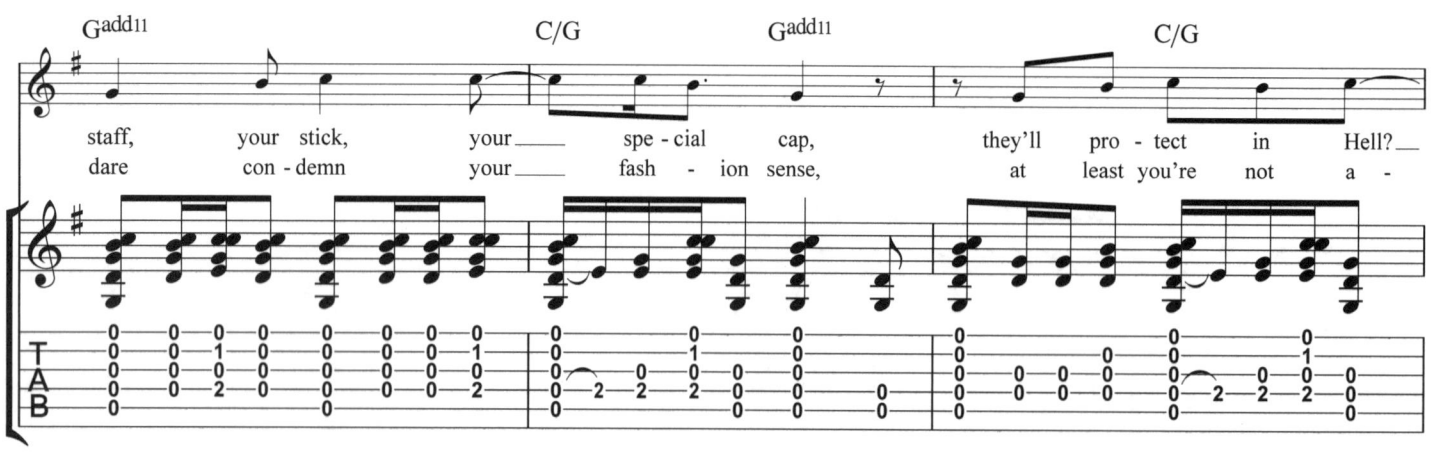

staff, your stick, your_____ spe - cial cap, they'll pro - tect in Hell?_____
dare con - demn your_____ fash - ion sense, at least you're not a -

What_ crap! Be - lieve the lie.
- stride a fence, that would not sell.

How
But I

Chorus

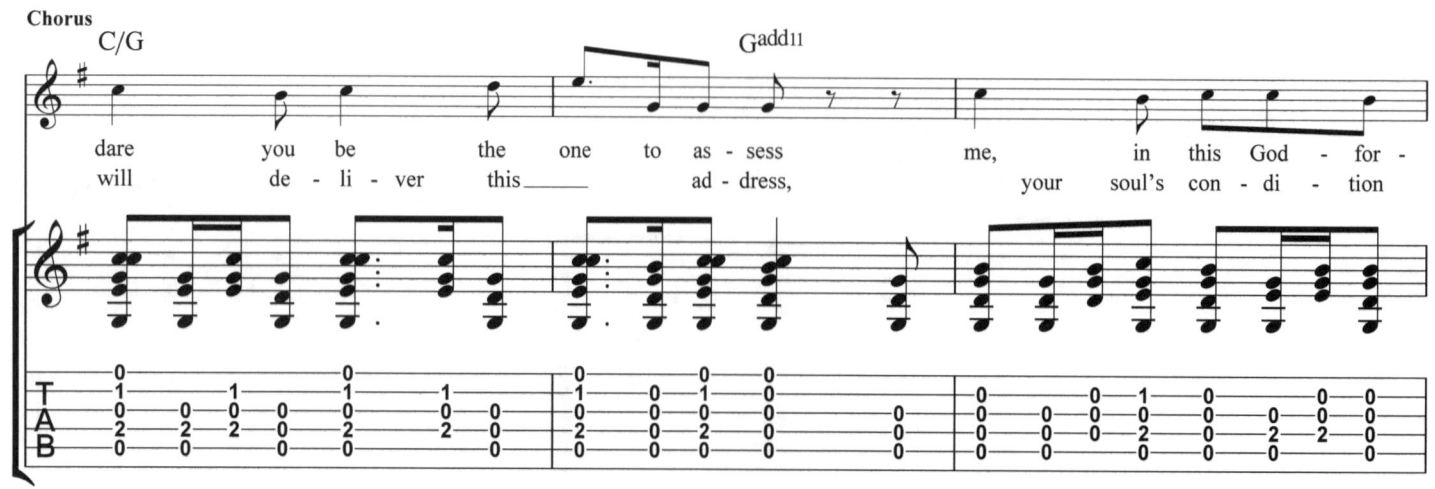

dare you be the one to as - sess me, in this God - for -
will de - li - ver this_____ ad - dress, your soul's con - di - tion

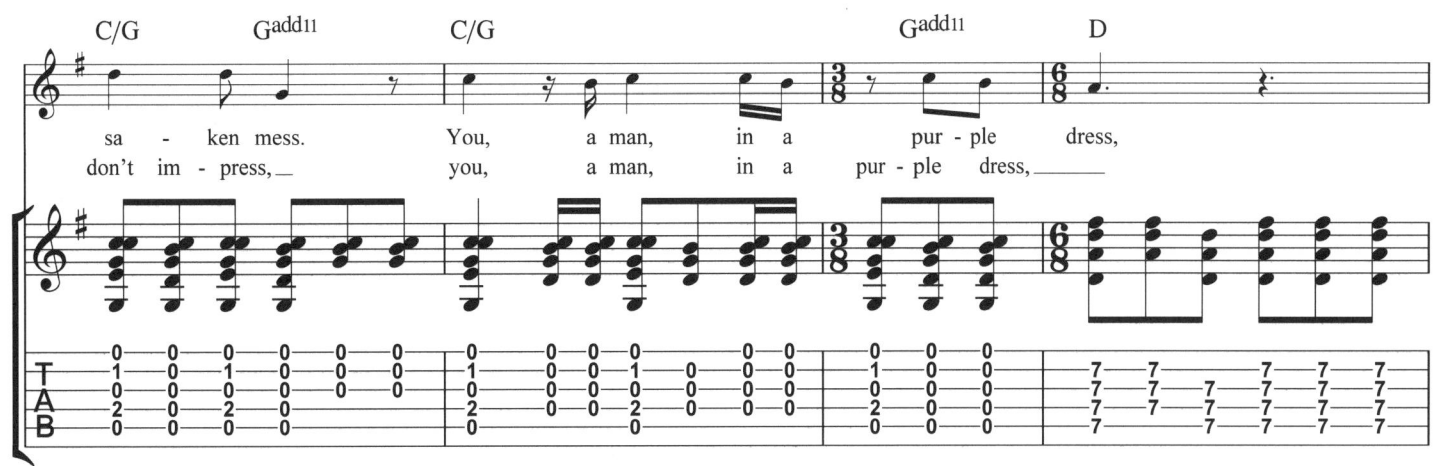

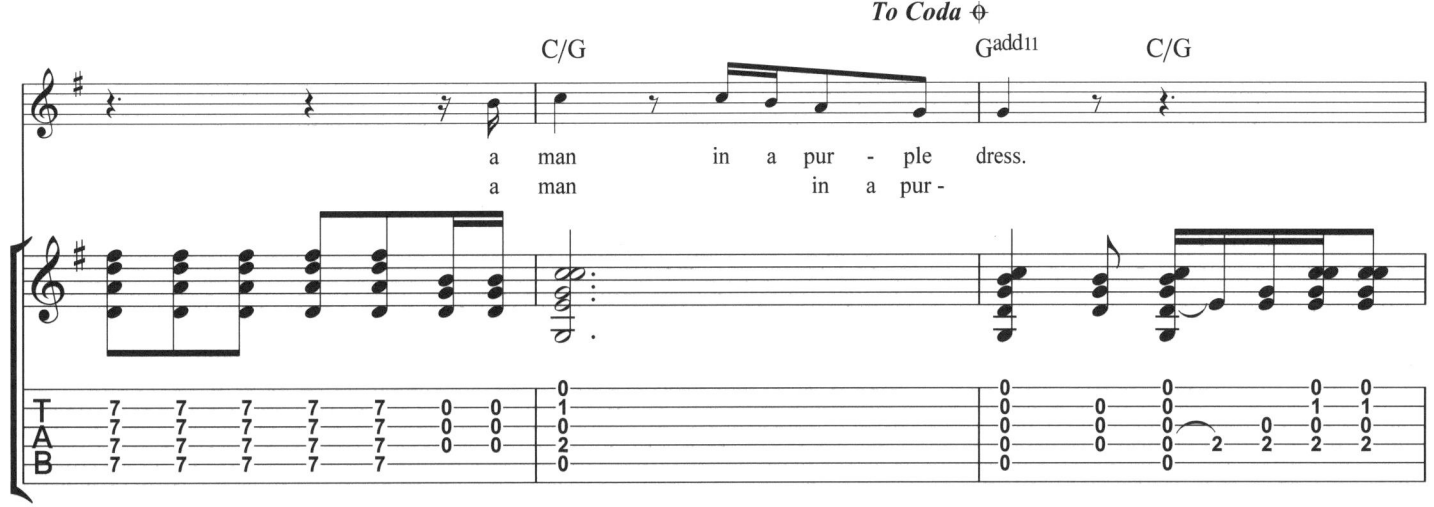

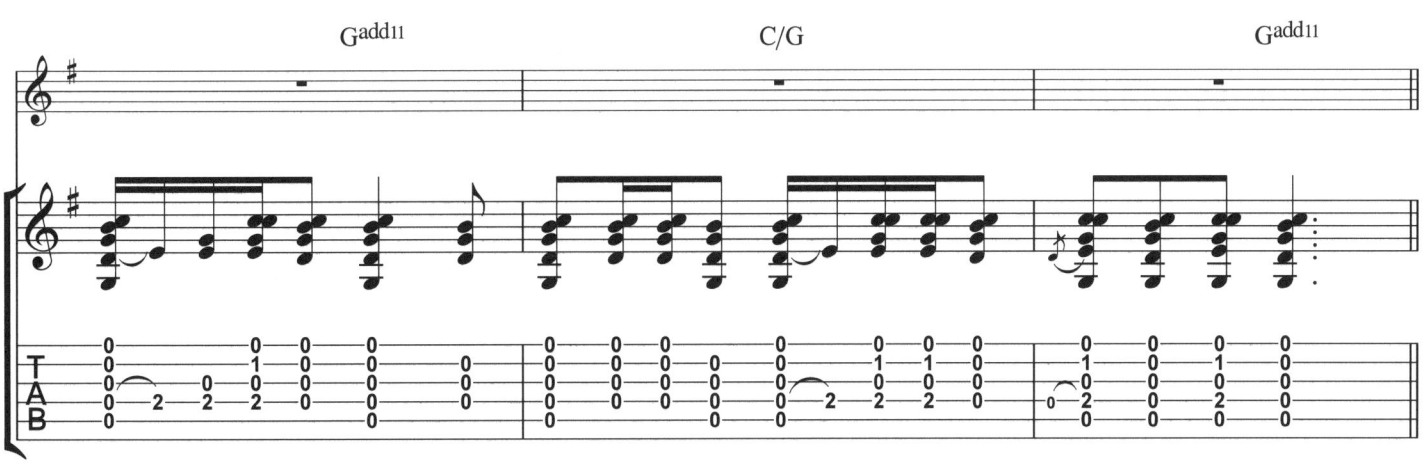

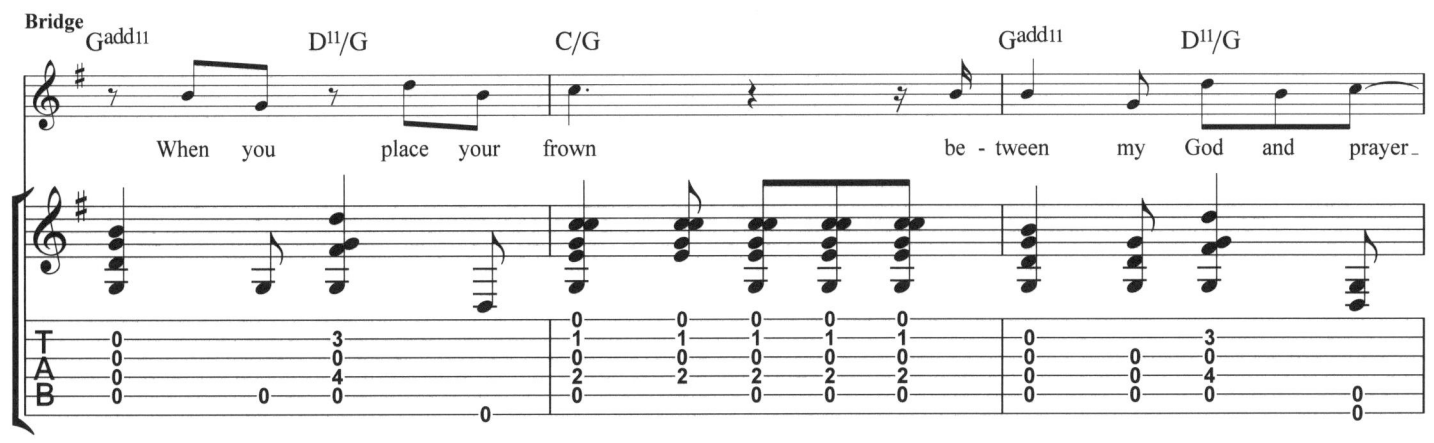

15

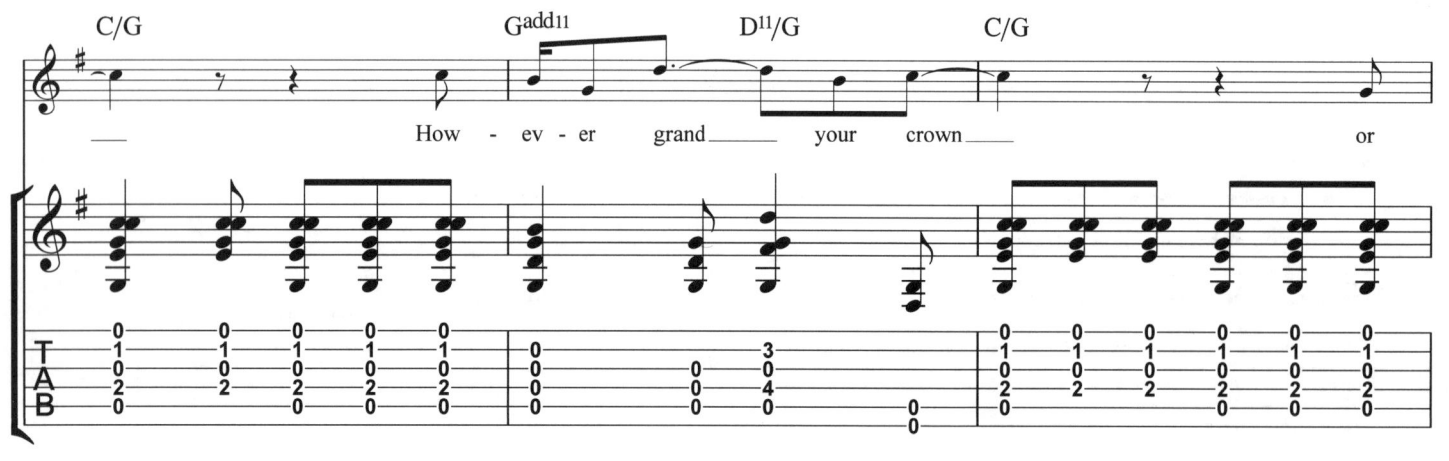

How - ev - er grand____ your crown____ or

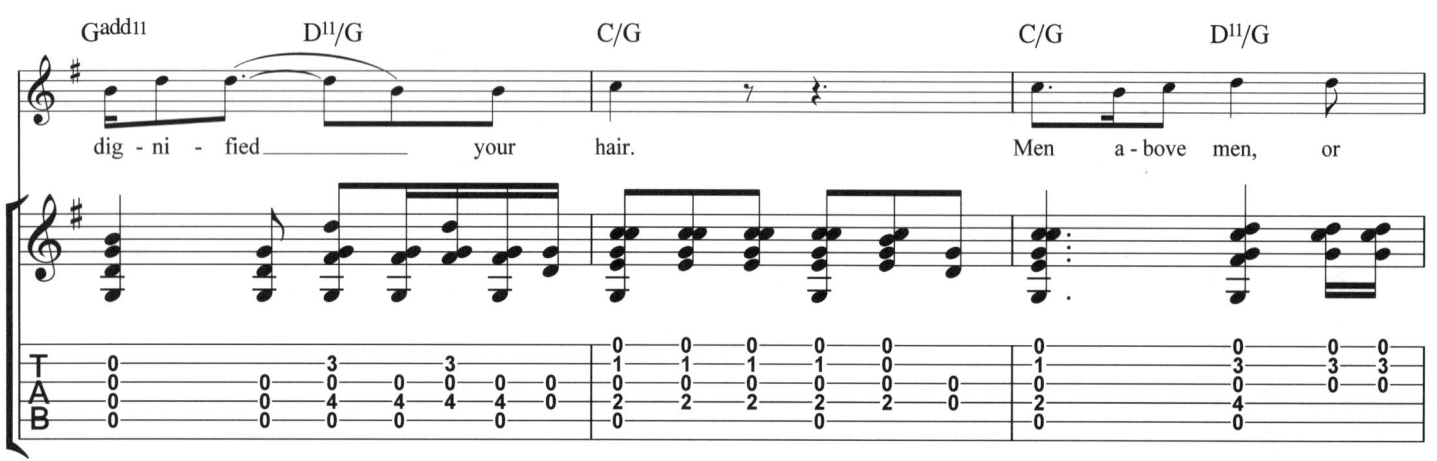

dig - ni - fied____ your hair. Men a - bove men, or

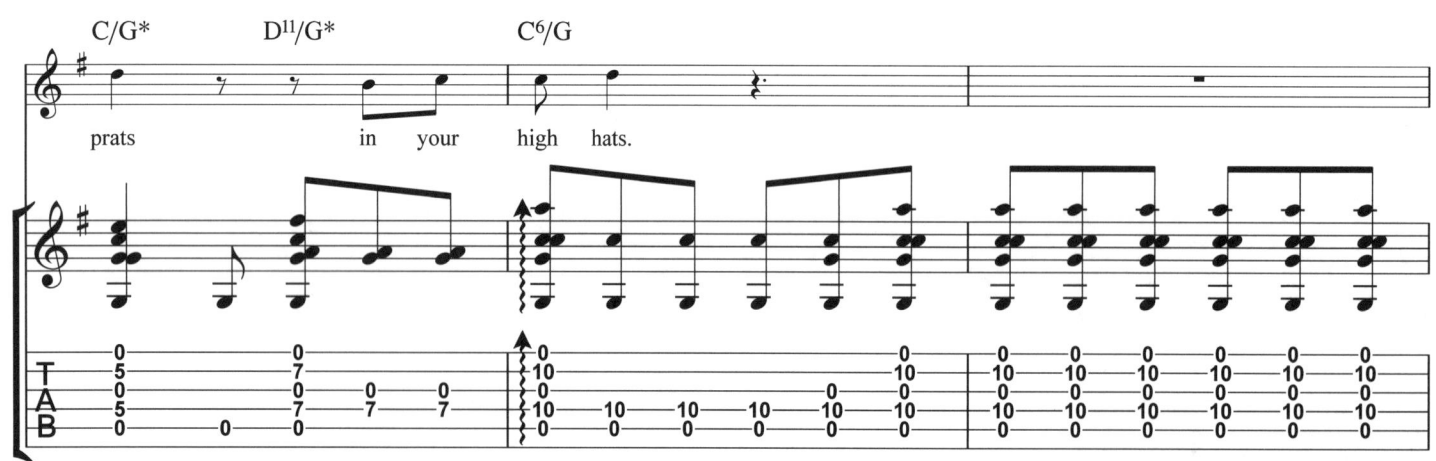

prats in your high hats.

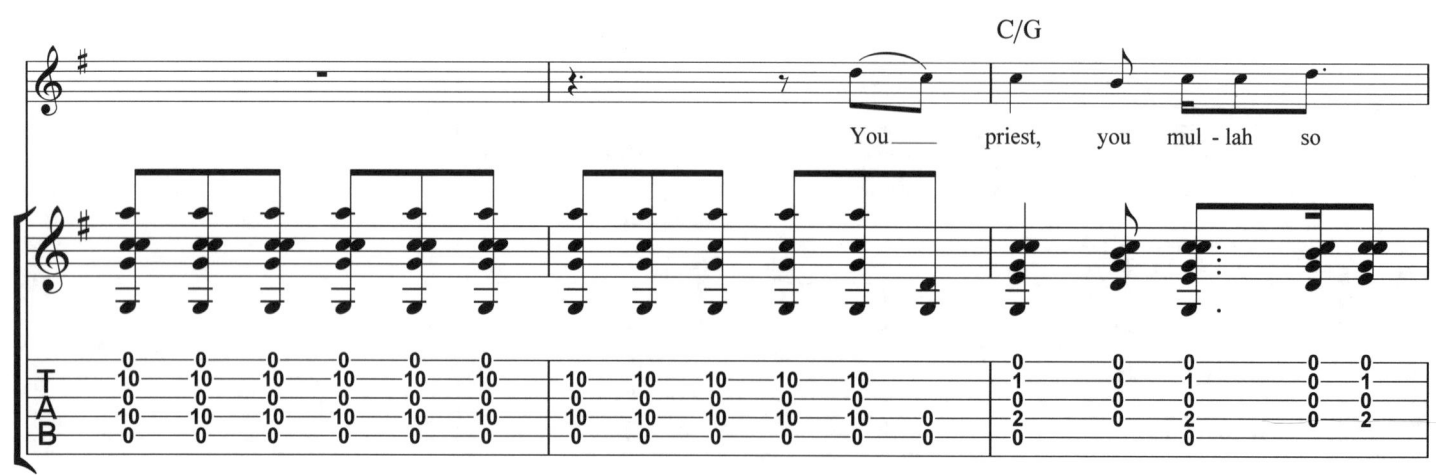

You____ priest, you mul - lah so

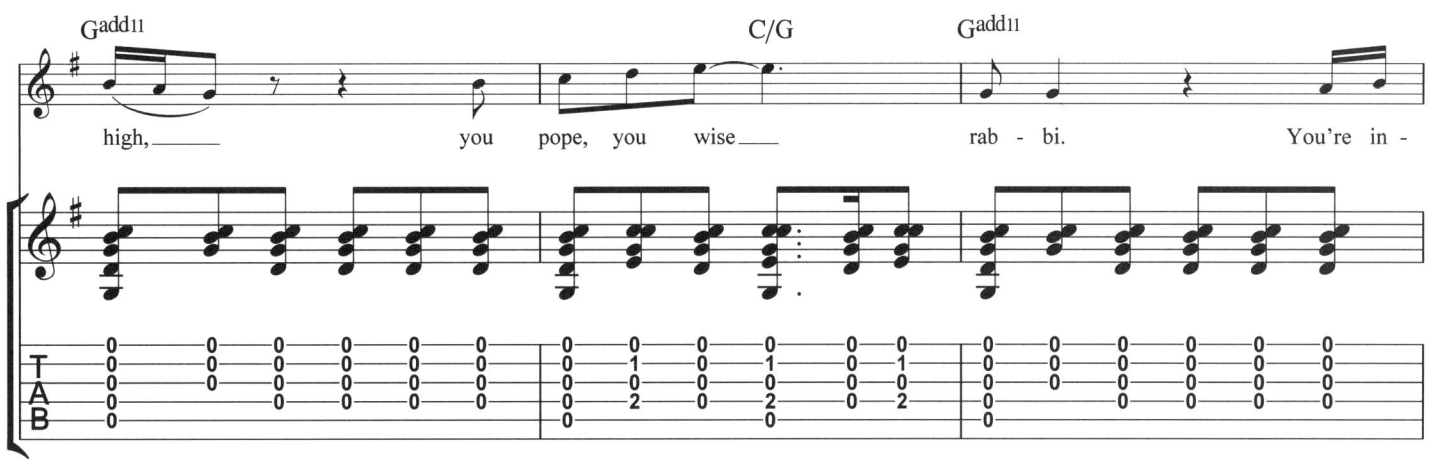

high,_____ you pope, you wise_____ rab - bi. You're in -

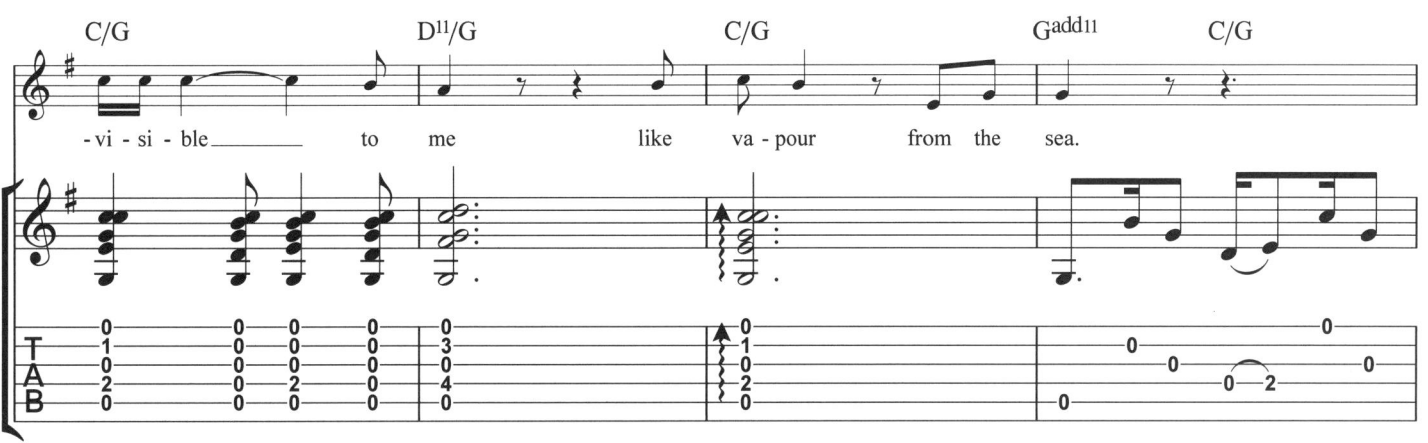

-vi - si - ble_____ to me like va - pour from the sea.

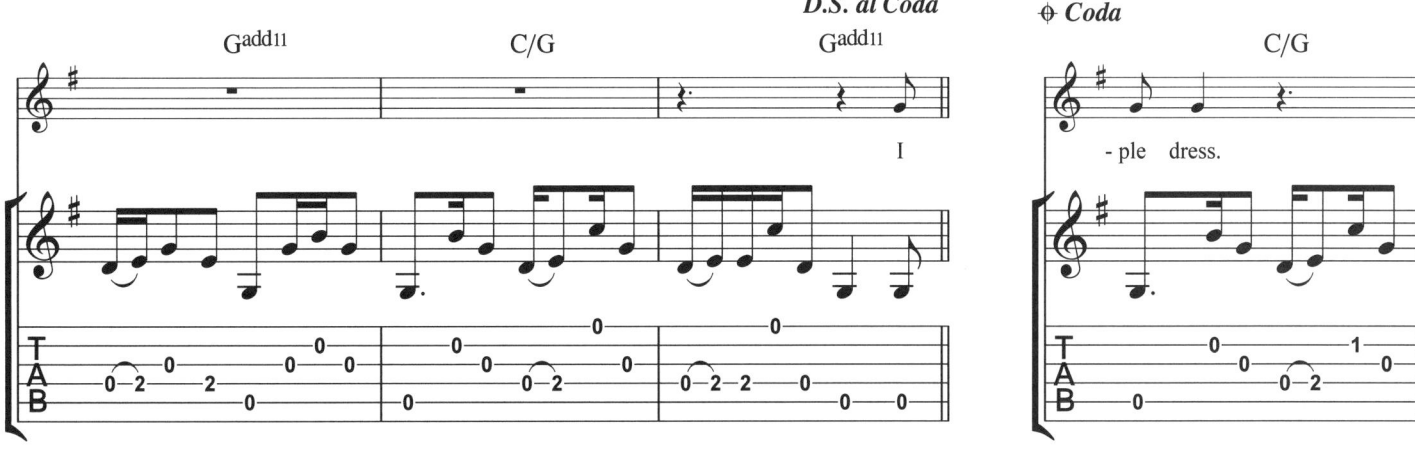

D.S. al Coda   ⊕ *Coda*

I   - ple dress.

MIKE POST THEME

Words & Music by
Pete Townshend

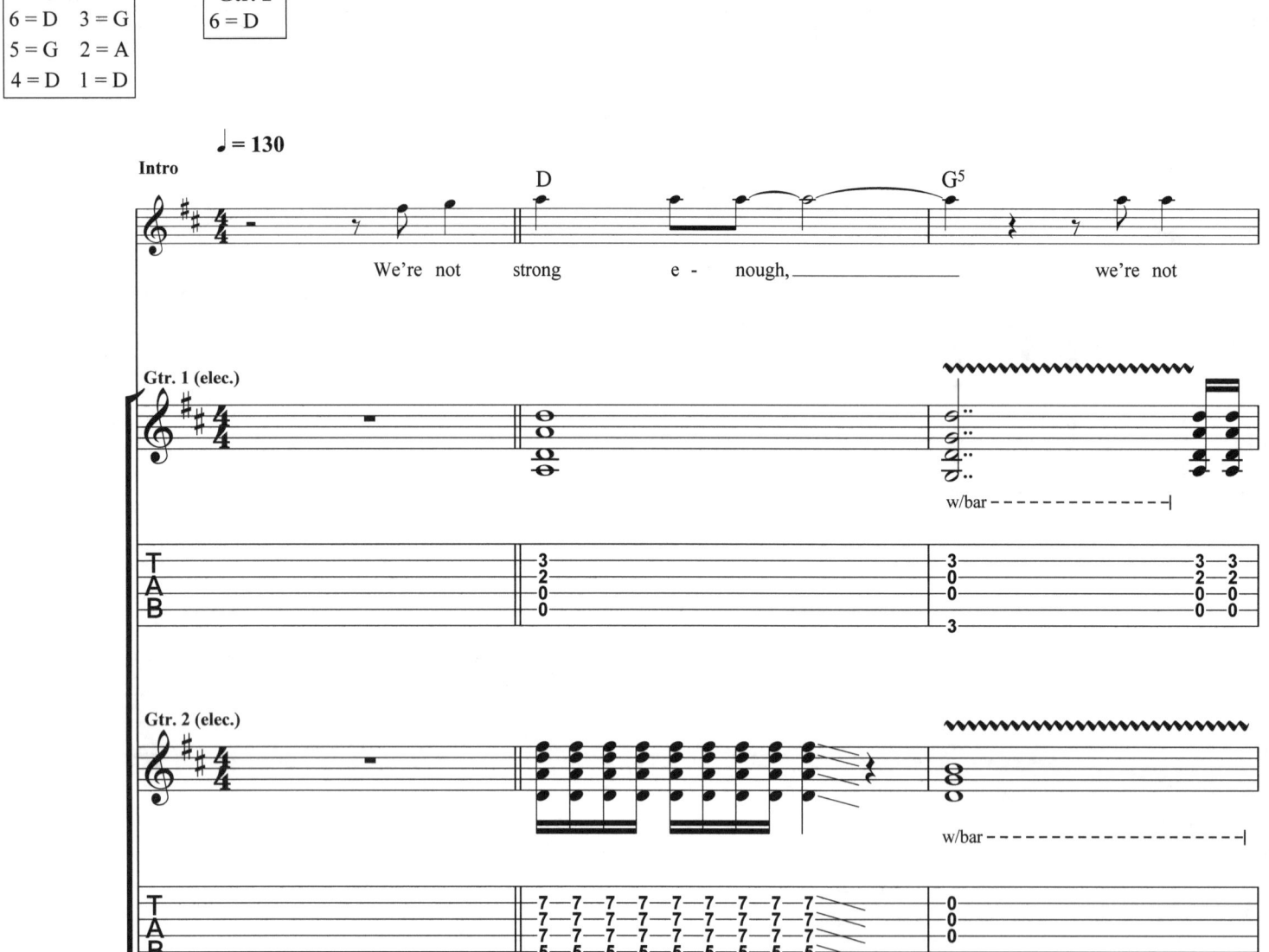

© Copyright 2006 Eel Pie Publishing Limited.
BMG Music Publishing Limited.
All Rights Reserved. International Copyright Secured.

D
G5
D
young e - nough.
We're not a - lone e - nough or
Gtr. 3 w/fig. 1 (x3)
w/bar
G5
D
(G5)
cold e - nough, E - mo - tion - ally we're not ev - en old e - nough. Late at
w/bar

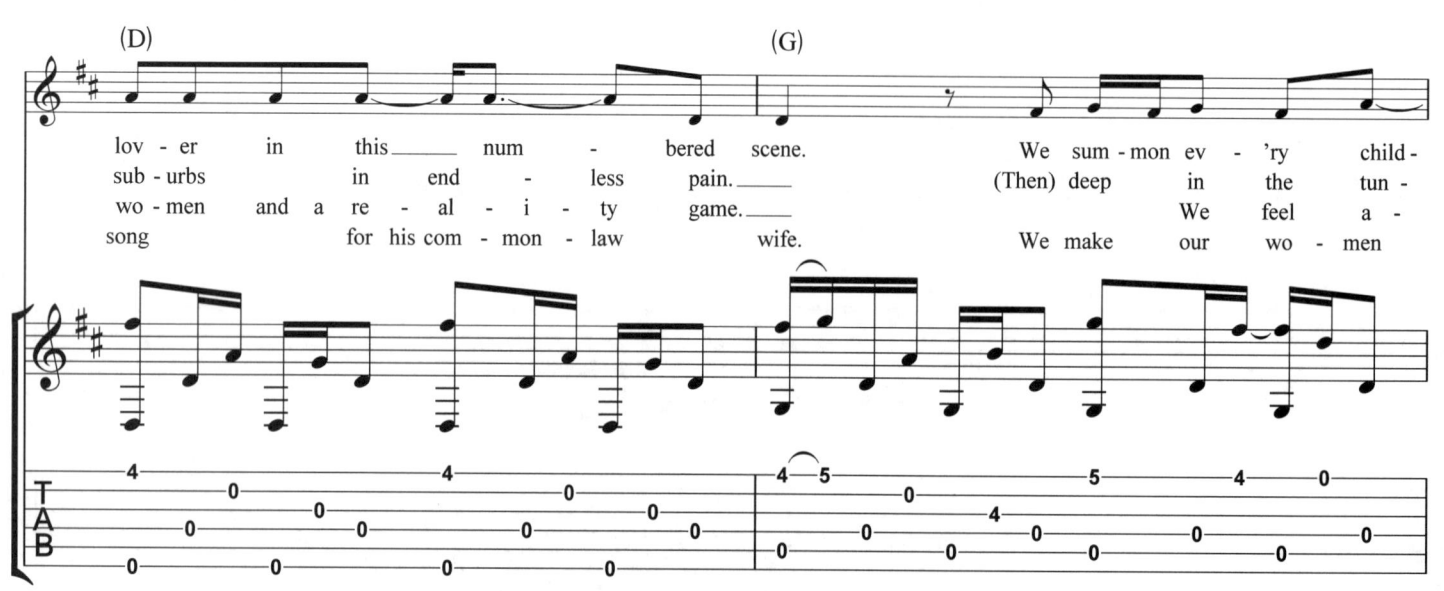

Verse

(D)

night, _____ we're in a vi - de - o - game dream, there is no
night on the un - der - ground _____ train, _____ through end - less
(%) night we find the ra - cing tame, _____ we're faced with
(%) time in ev -'ry lit - tle punk's life, when he has to write a

omit 1°
mp

(G)

(D)

lov - er in this _____ num - bered scene. We sum - mon ev - 'ry child -
sub - urbs in end - less pain. _____ (Then) deep in the tun -
wo - men and a re - al - i - ty game. _____ We feel a -
song for his com - mon - law wife. We make our wo - men

(G)

2° To Coda ✛

Bridge

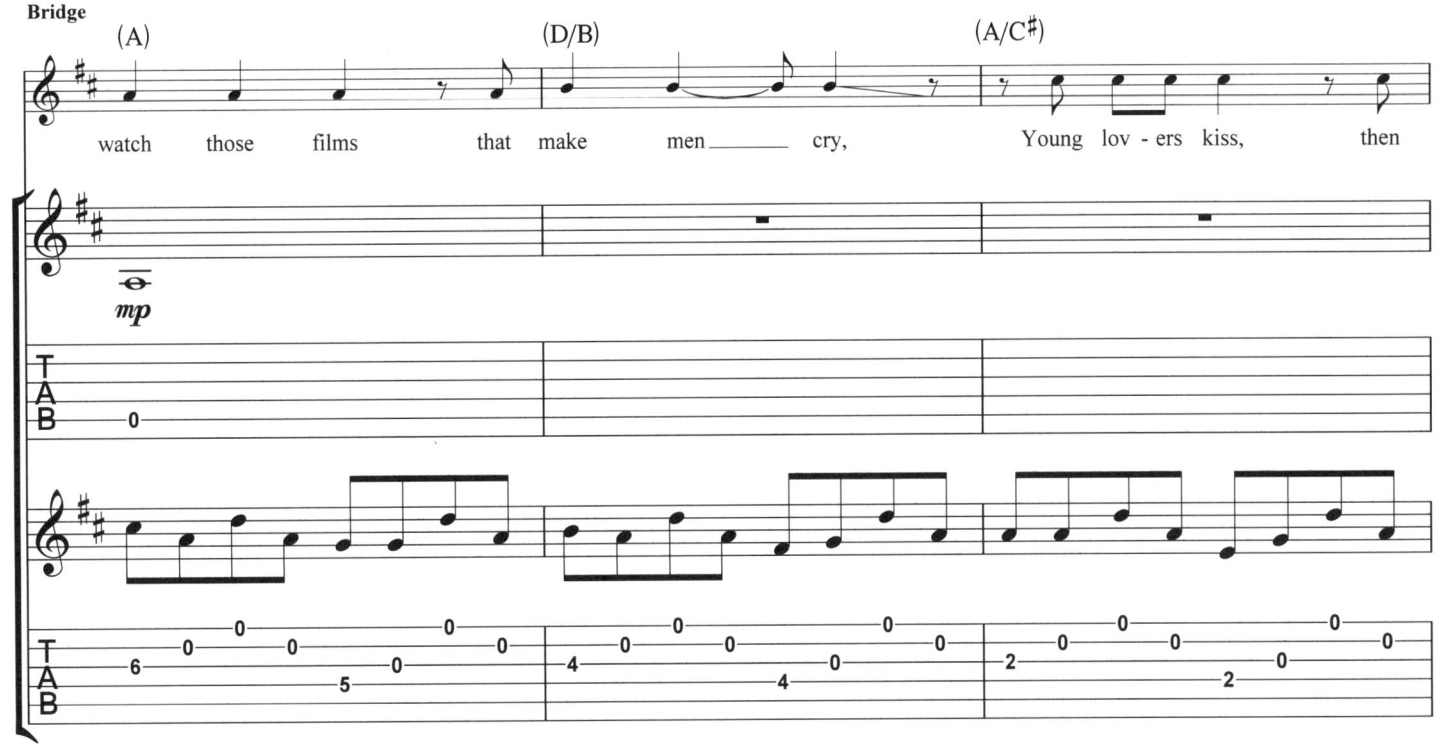

watch those films that make men ___ cry, Young lov - ers kiss, then

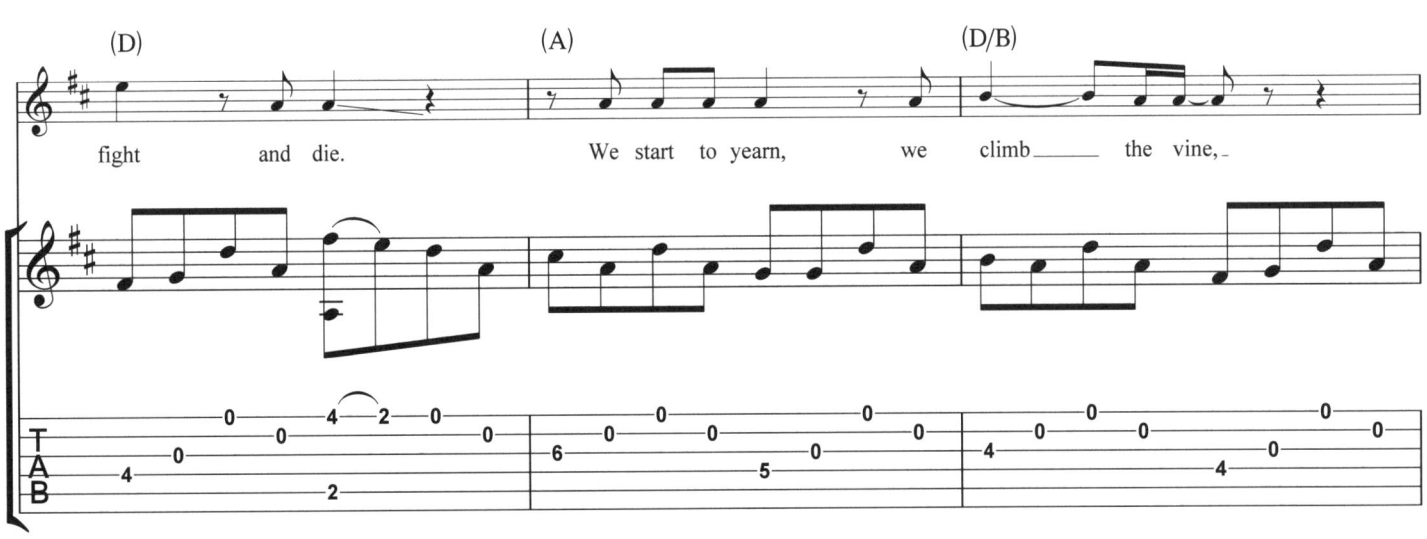

fight and die. We start to yearn, we climb ___ the vine, ___

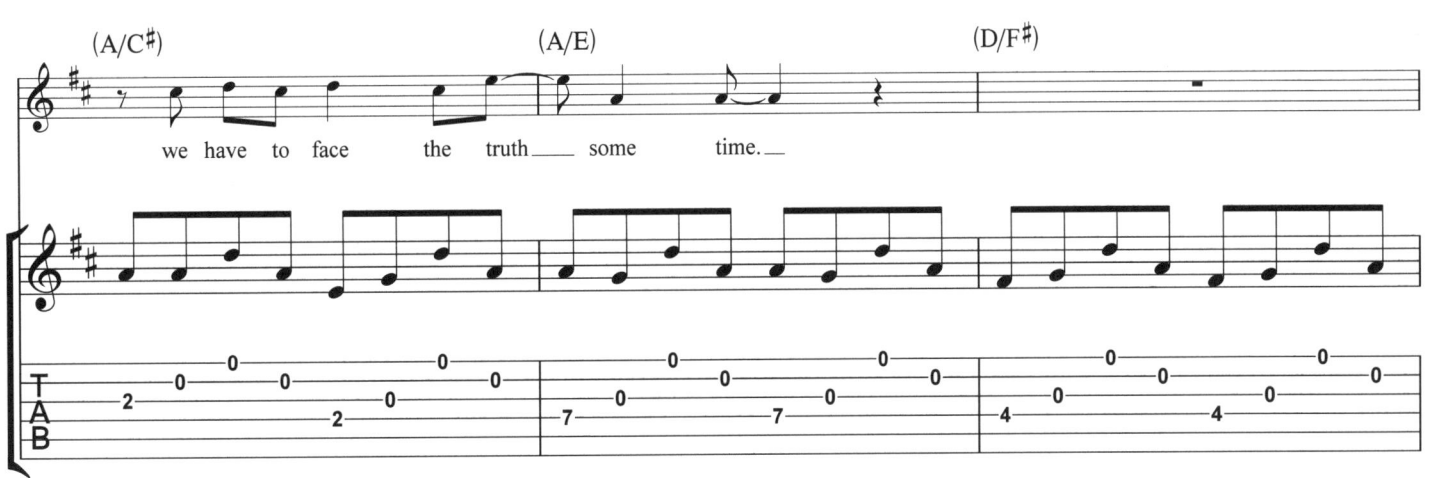

we have to face the truth ___ some time. ___

23

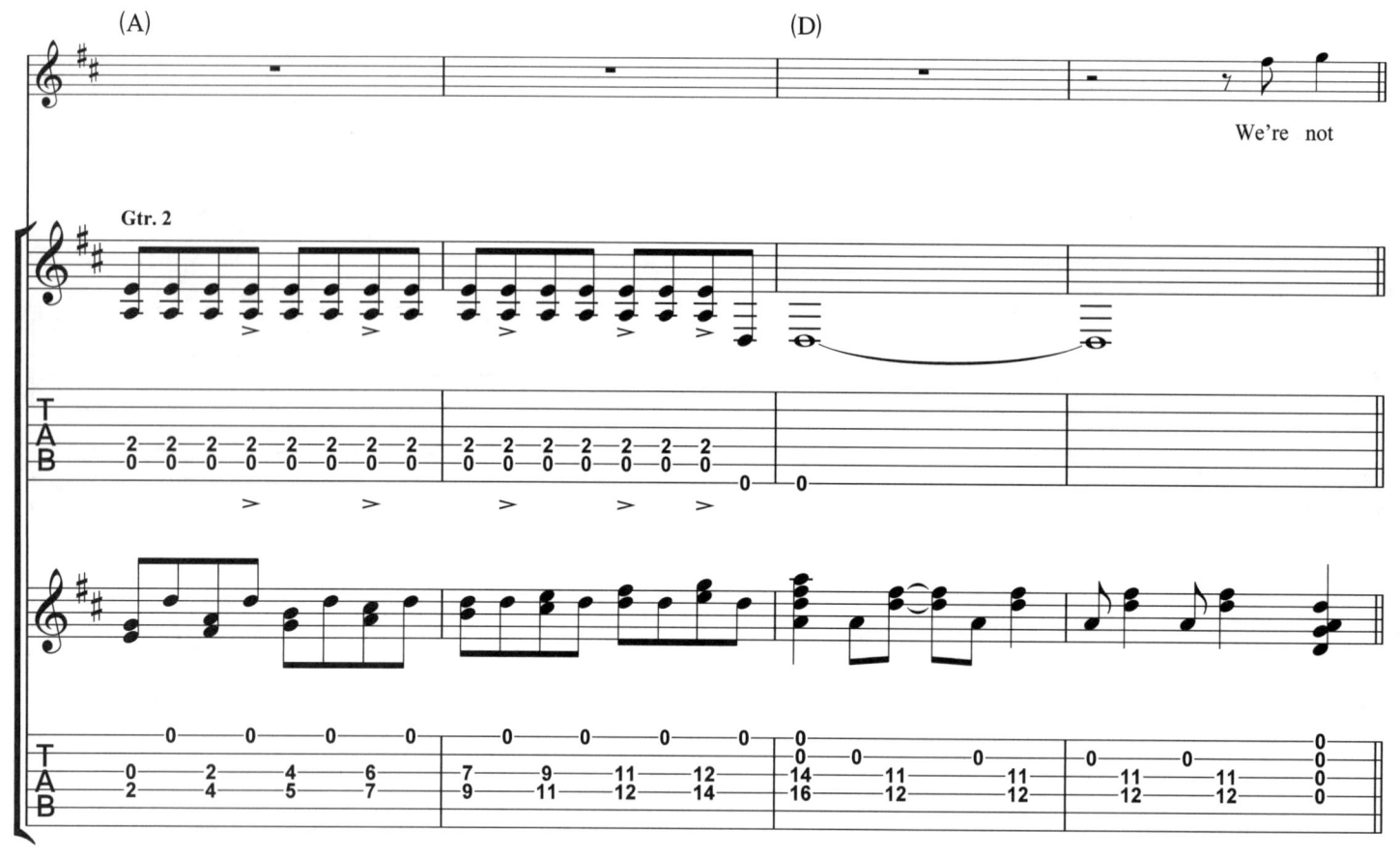

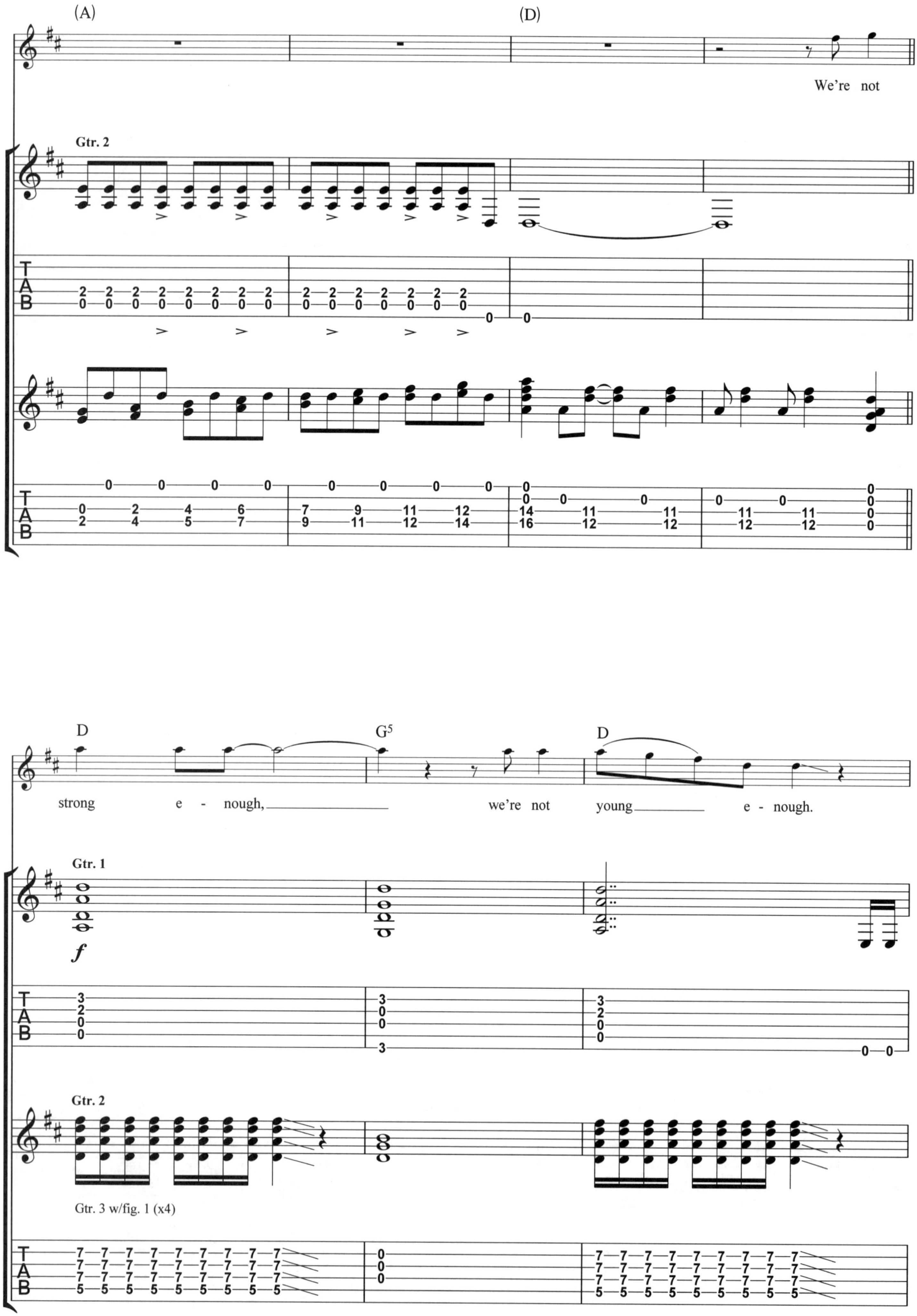

We're not
strong   e - nough,_____   we're not   young_____ e - nough.

Gtr. 1

Gtr. 2

Gtr. 3 w/fig. 1 (x4)

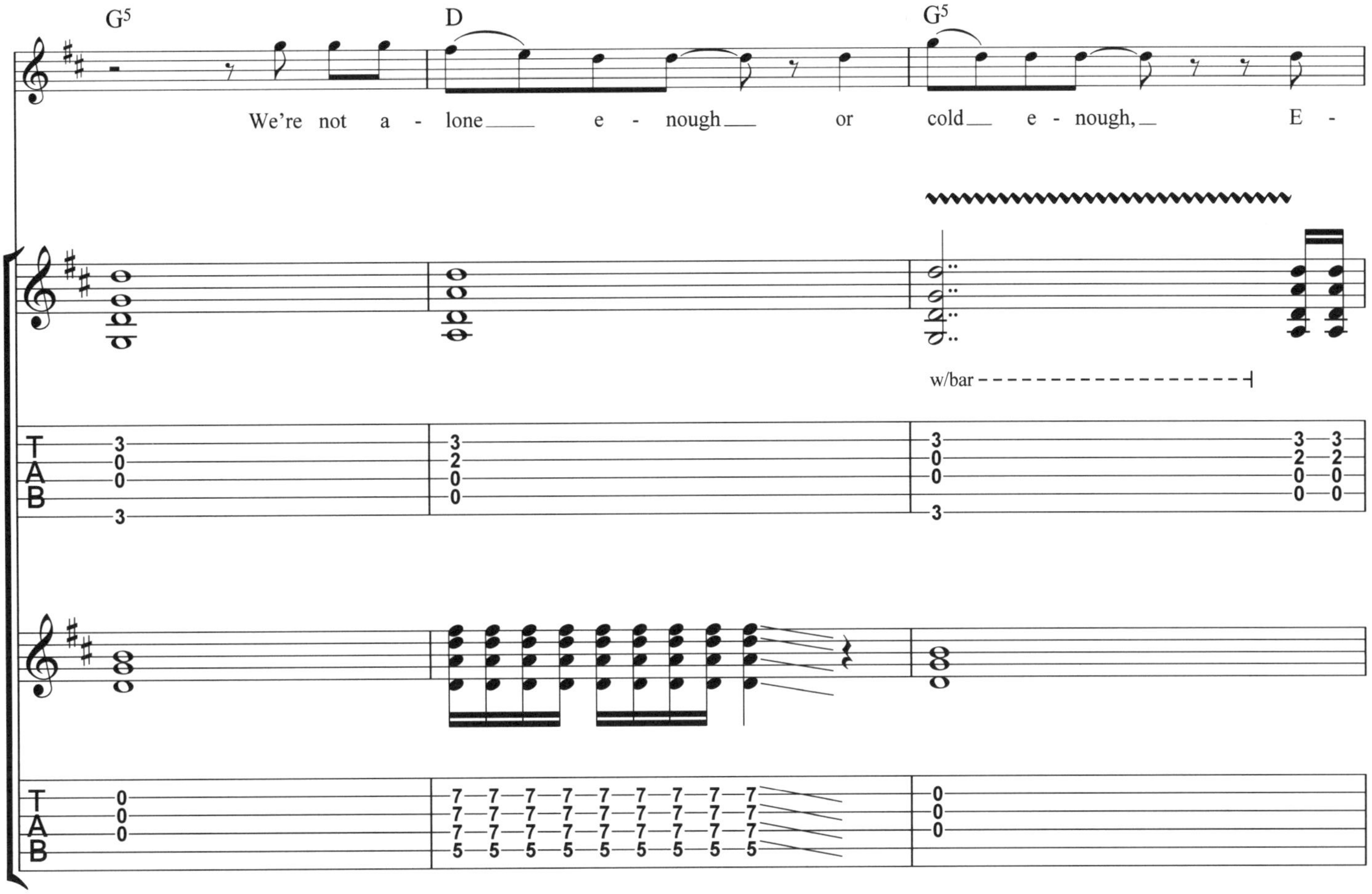
G5
D
G5
We're not a - lone e - nough or cold e - nough, E -
w/bar

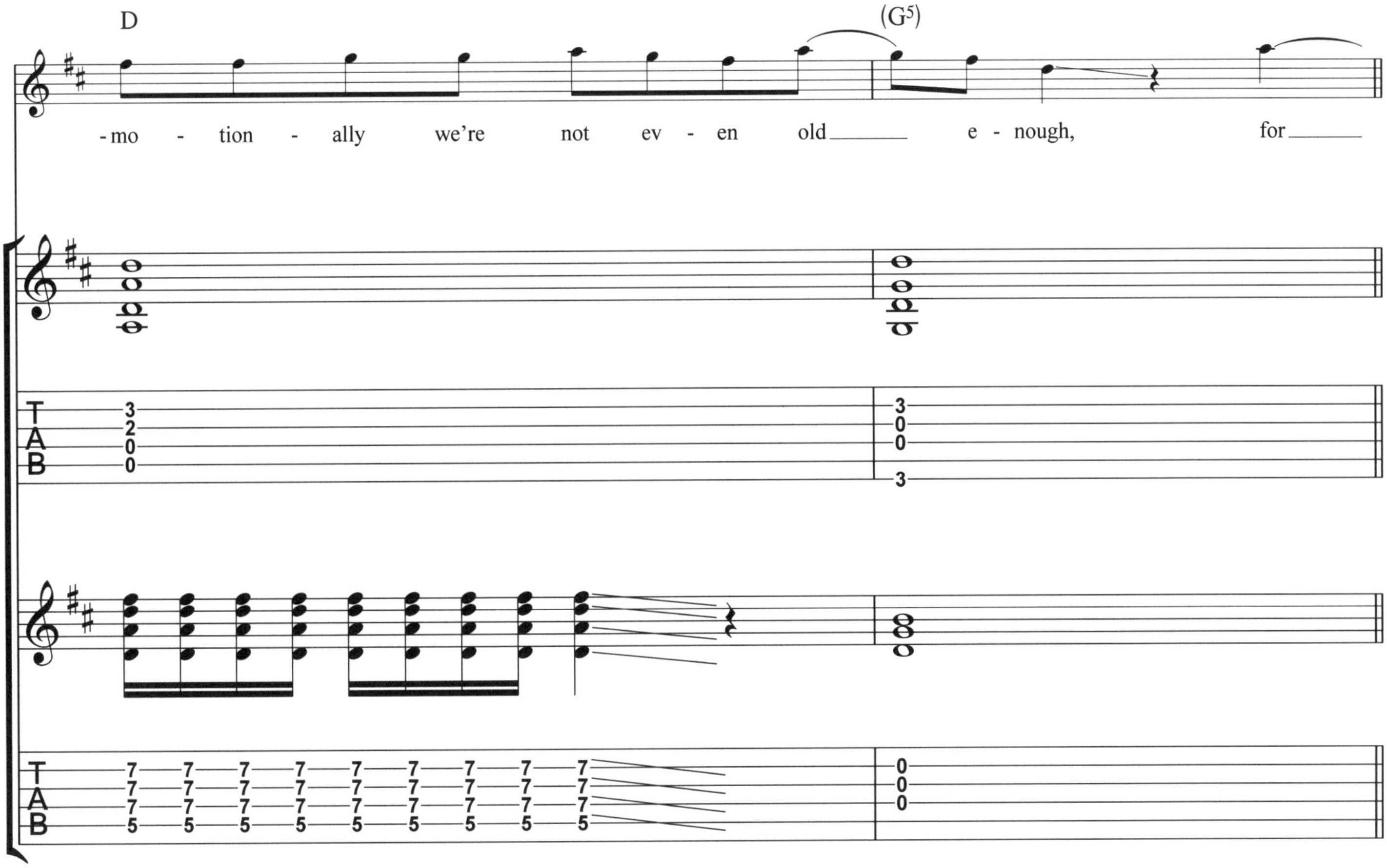
D
(G5)
-mo - tion - ally we're not ev - en old e - nough, for

G6 G5/F♯ G5/D Csus2 G/B G5 G6 G5/F♯ G5/D Dsus2
ya.

D.S. al Coda
G6 G5/F♯ G5/D Csus2 G/B G5 G6 G5/F♯ G5/D Dsus2
But late at

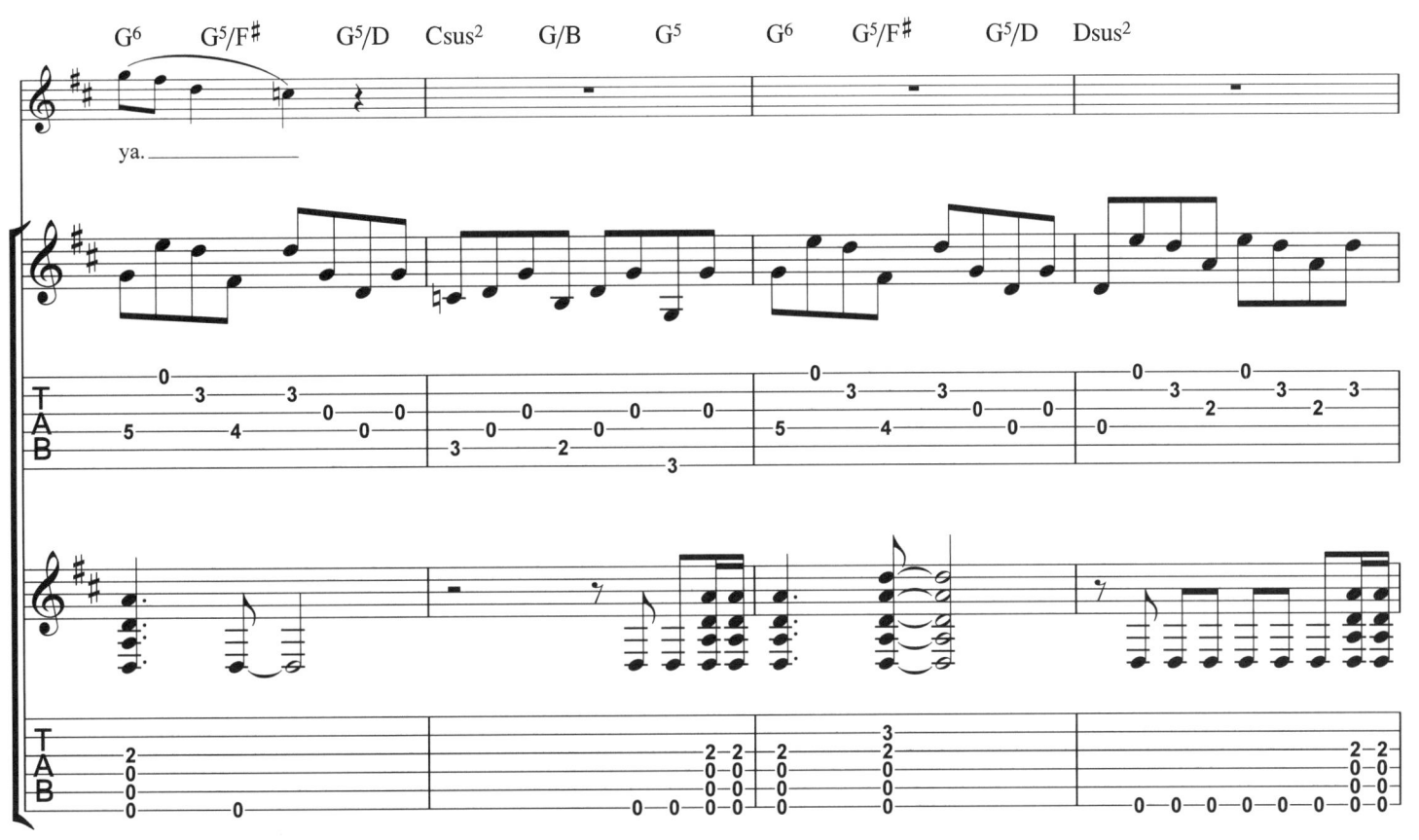

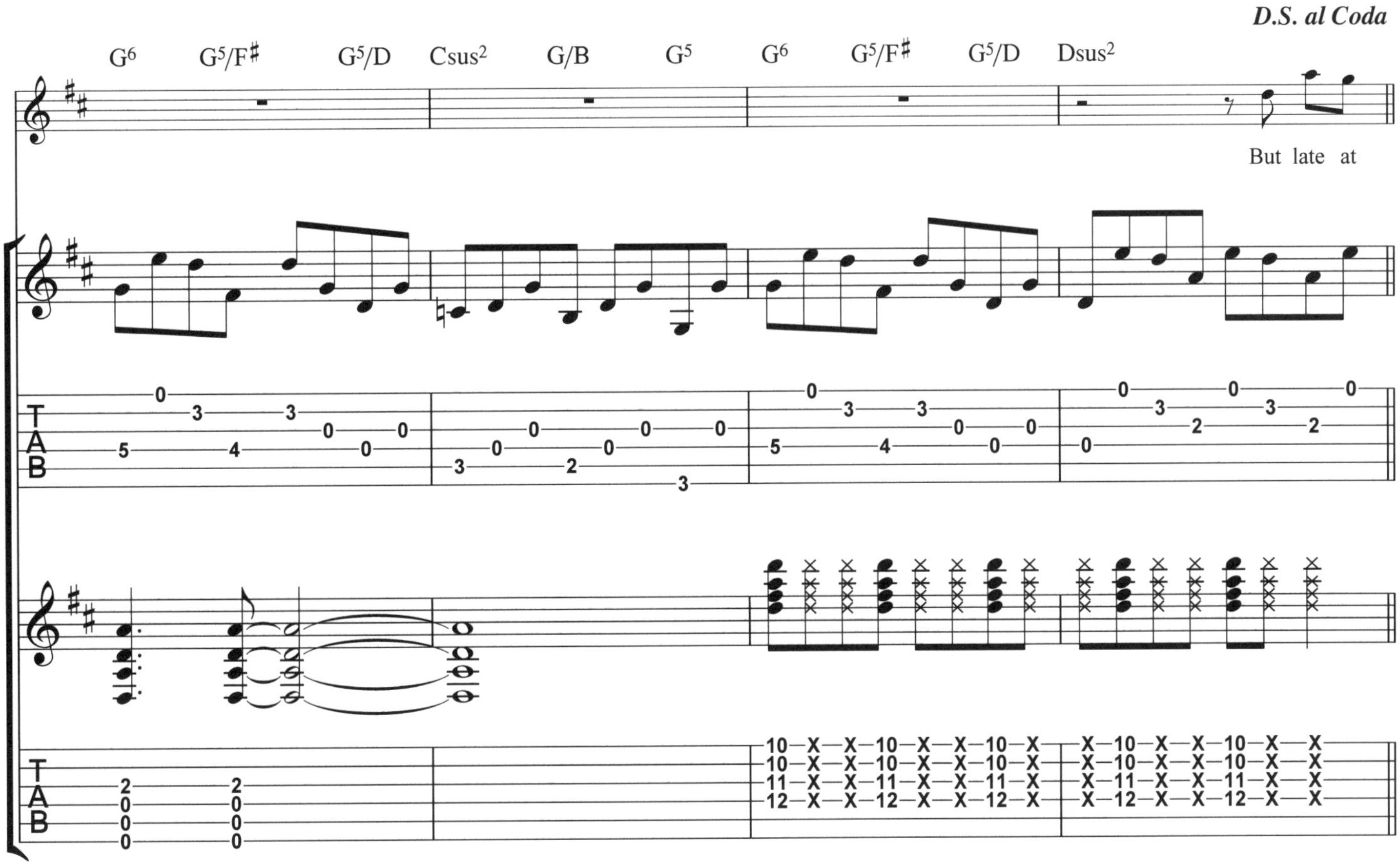

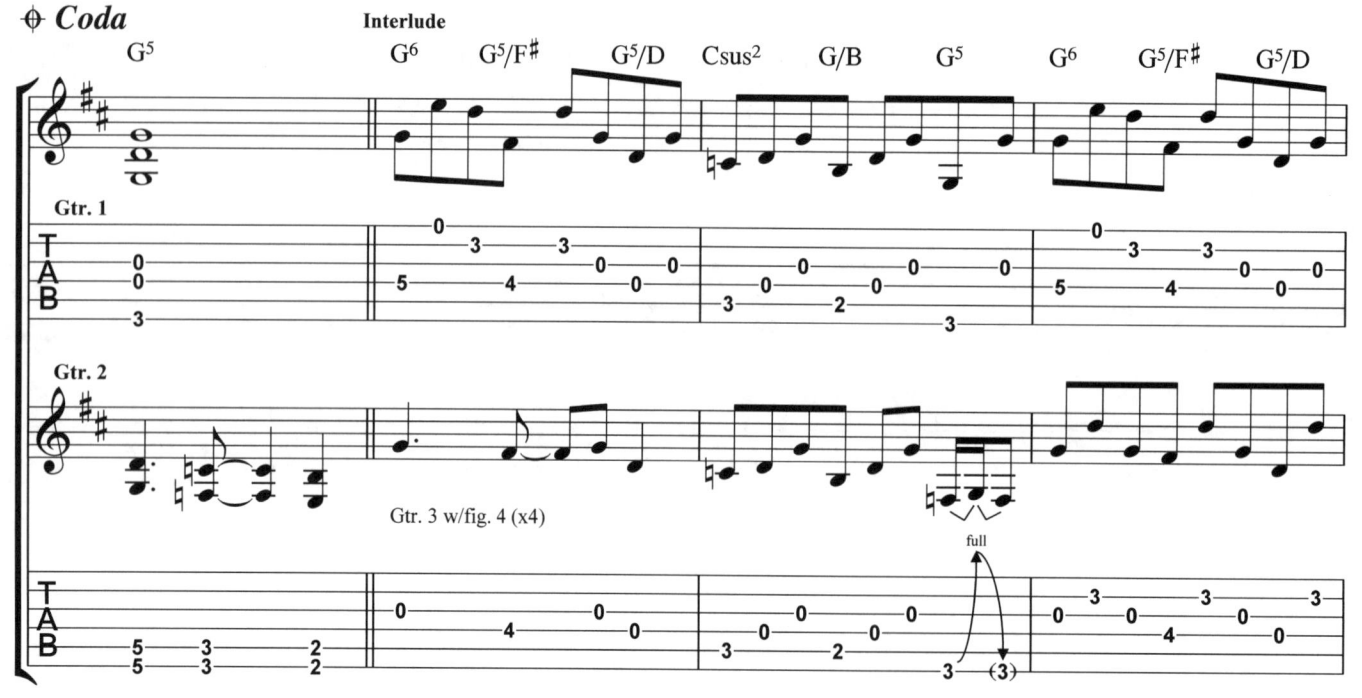

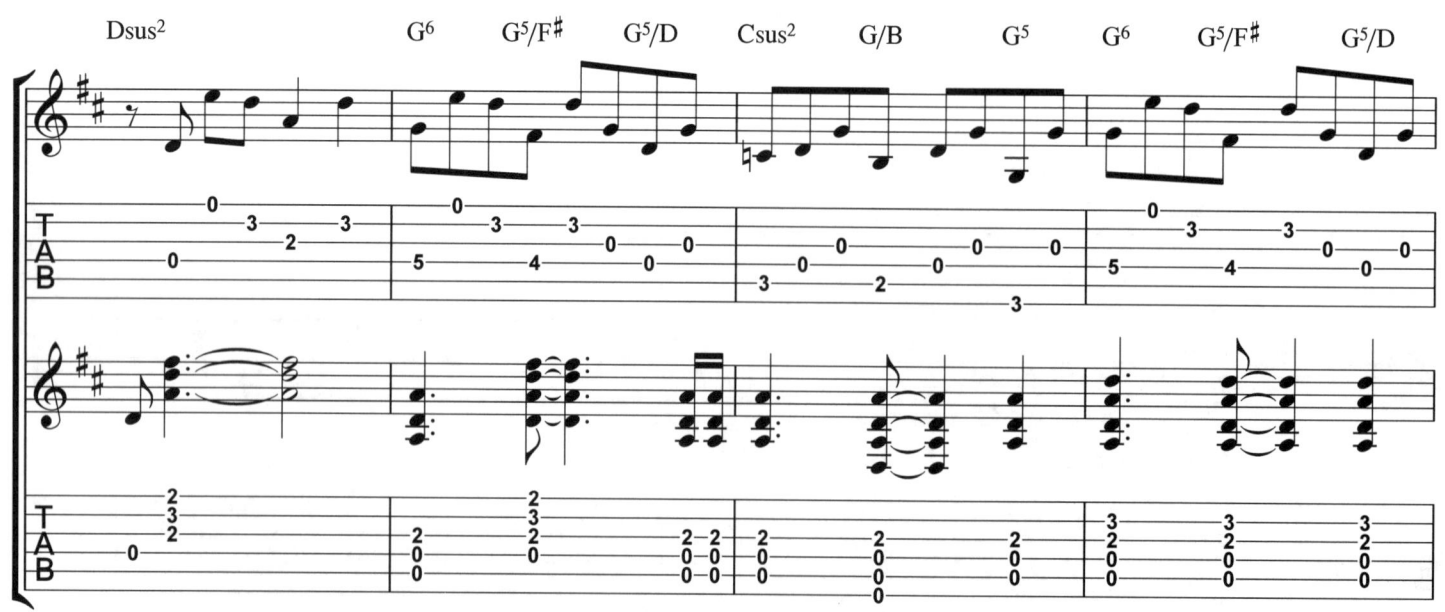

28

(A/E)
(D/F♯)
(A)
some time.
Gtr. 2
A5
Gtr. 1
D
Dsus2
D
Gtr. 2

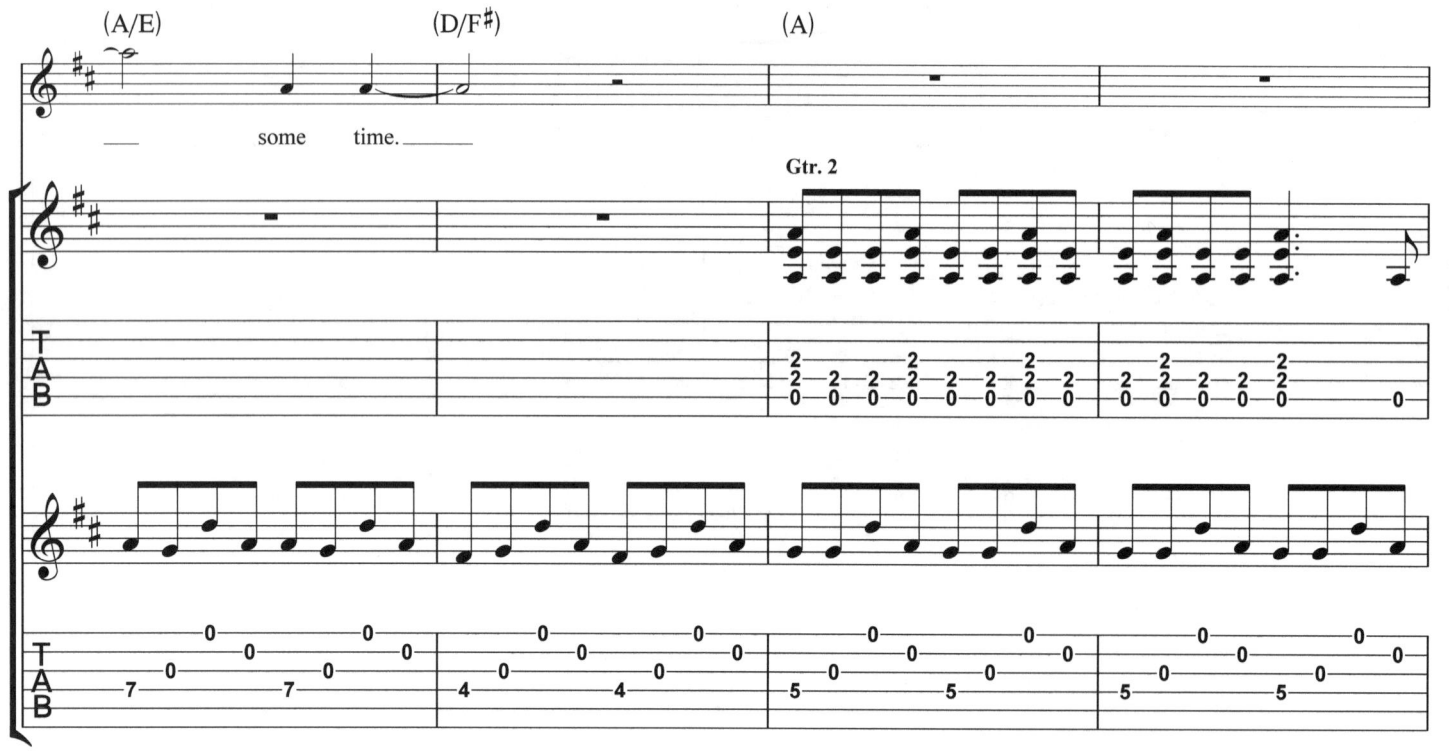

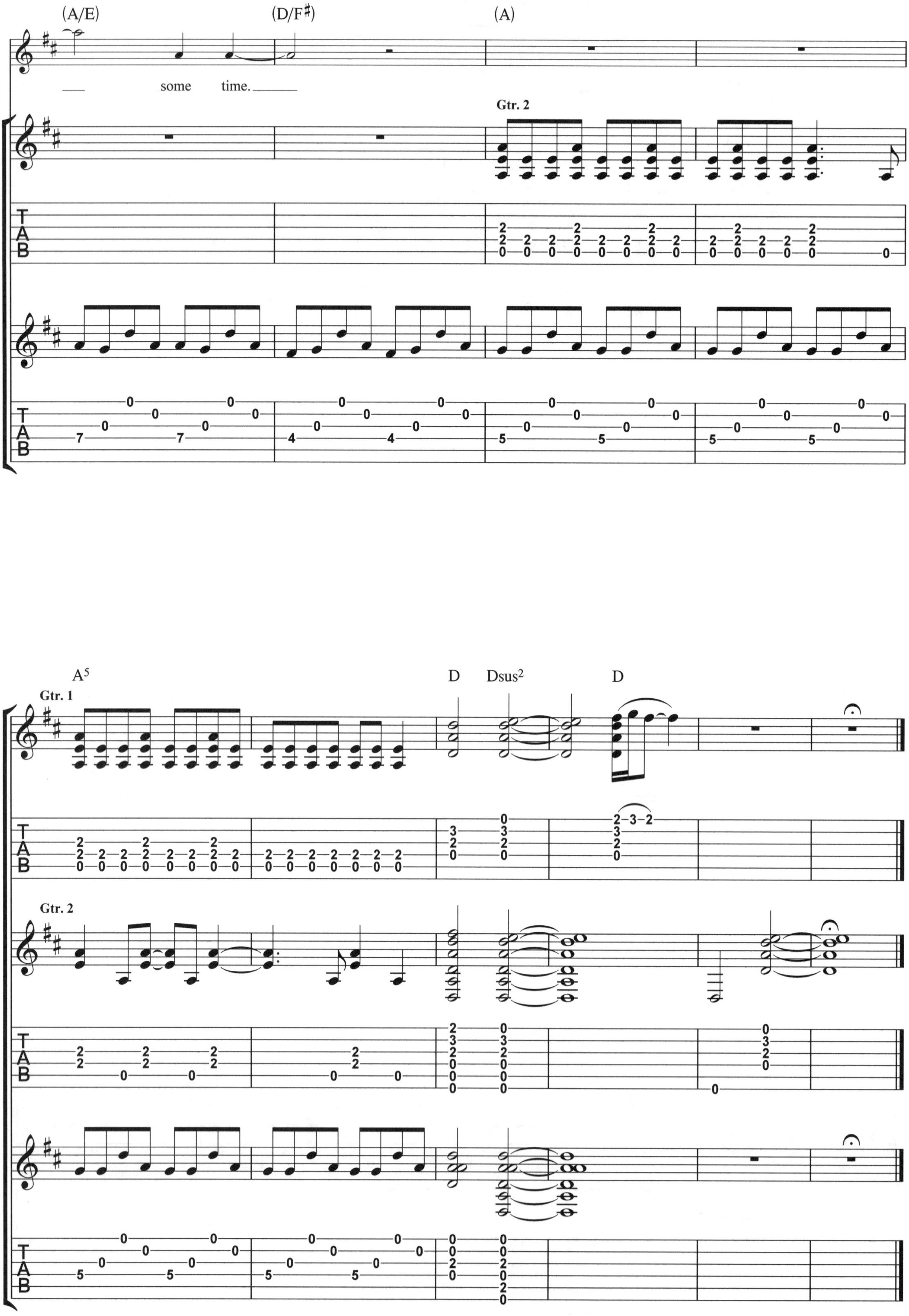

IN THE ETHER

Words & Music by
Pete Townshend

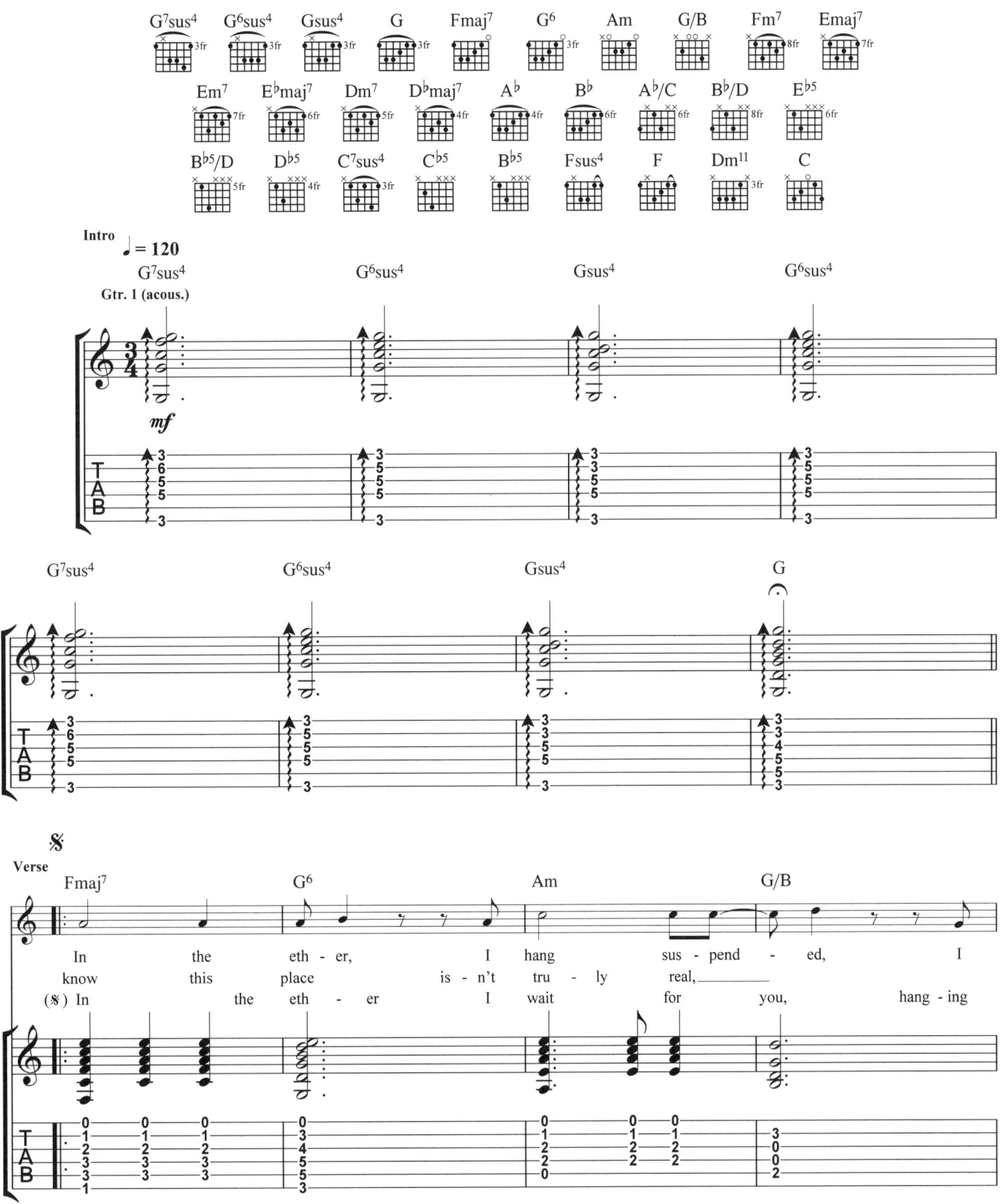

© Copyright 2006 Eel Pie Publishing Limited.
BMG Music Tovnblishing Limited.
All Rights Reserved. International Copyright Secured.

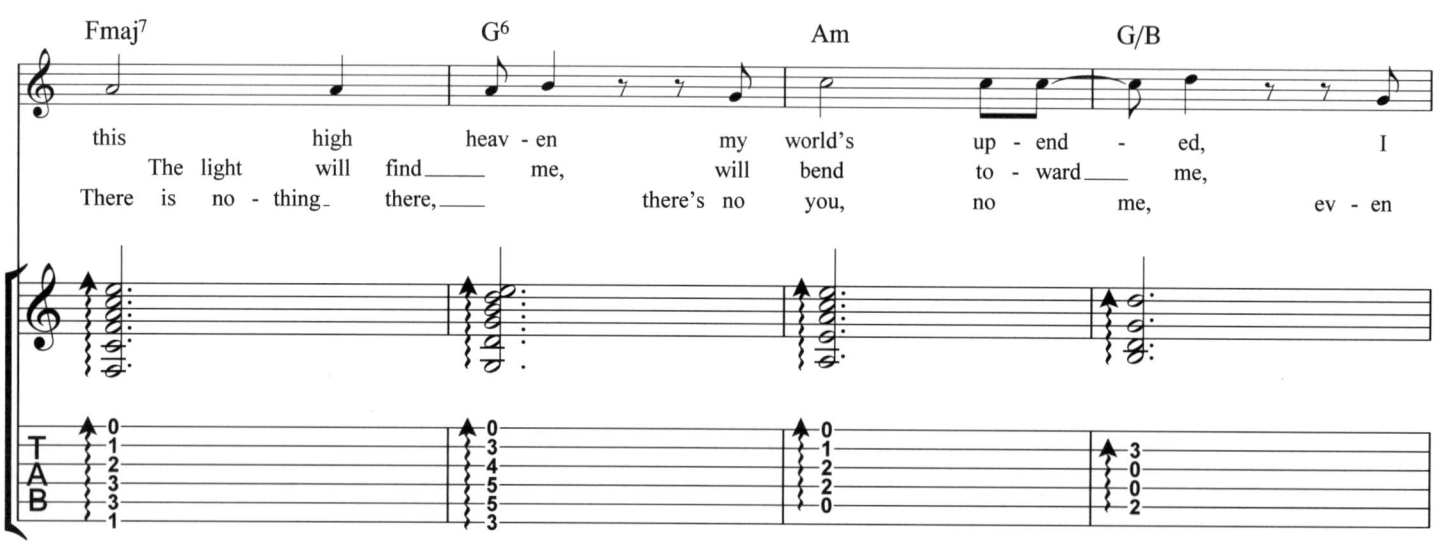

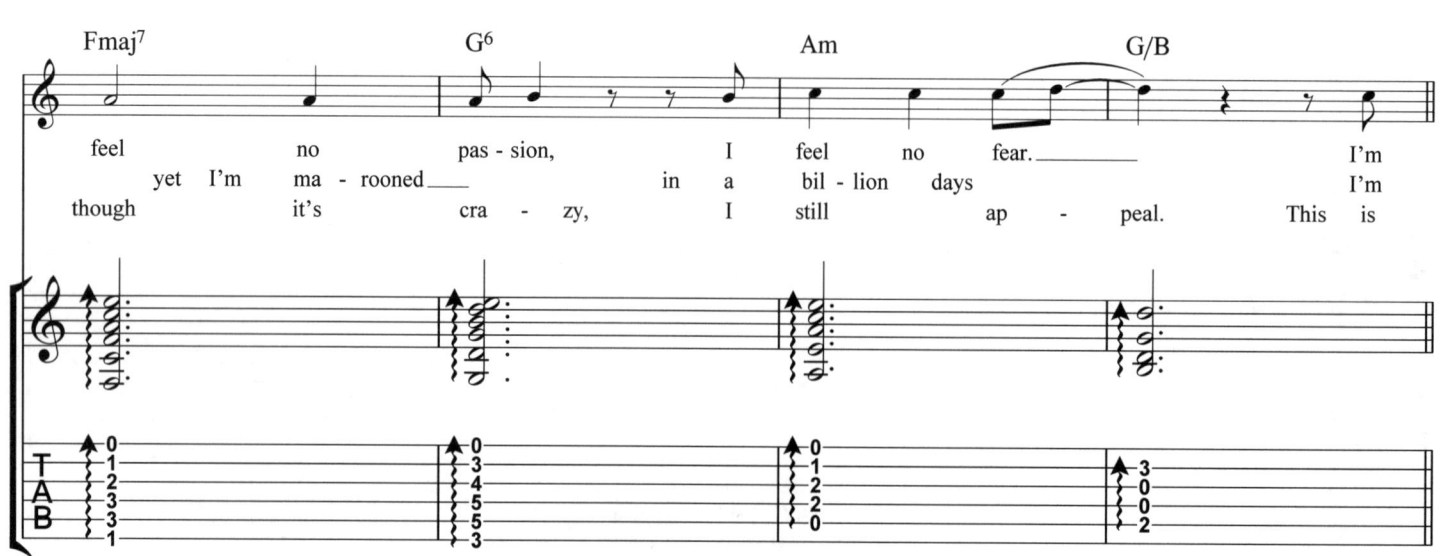

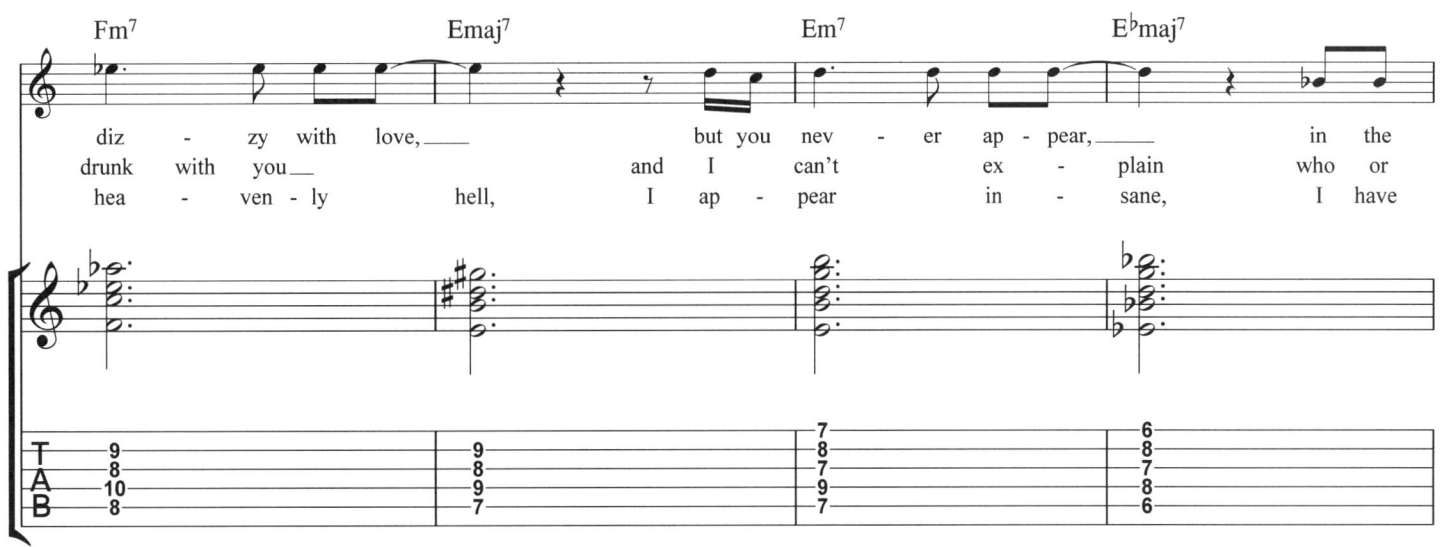

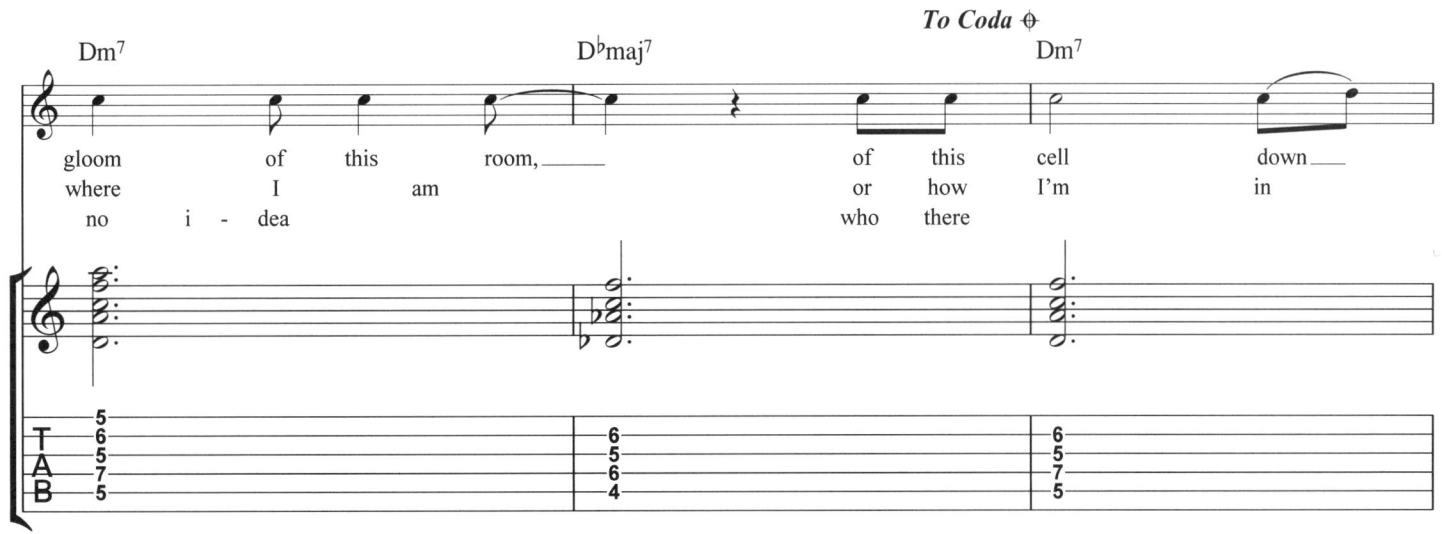

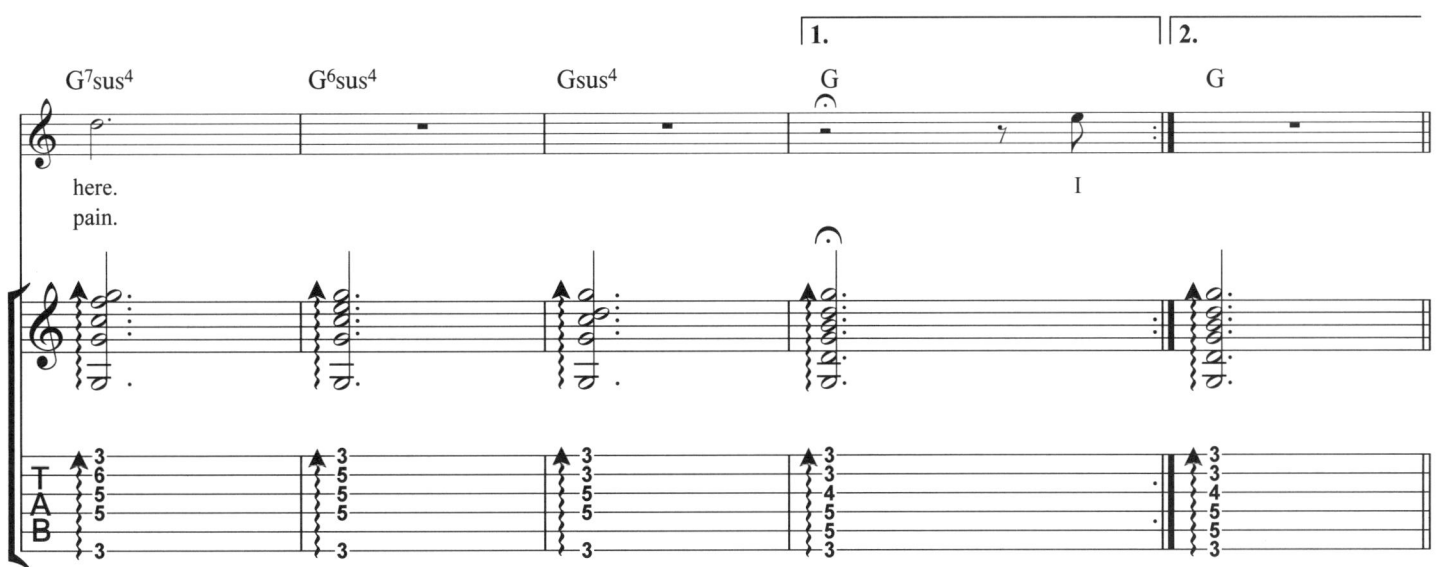

33

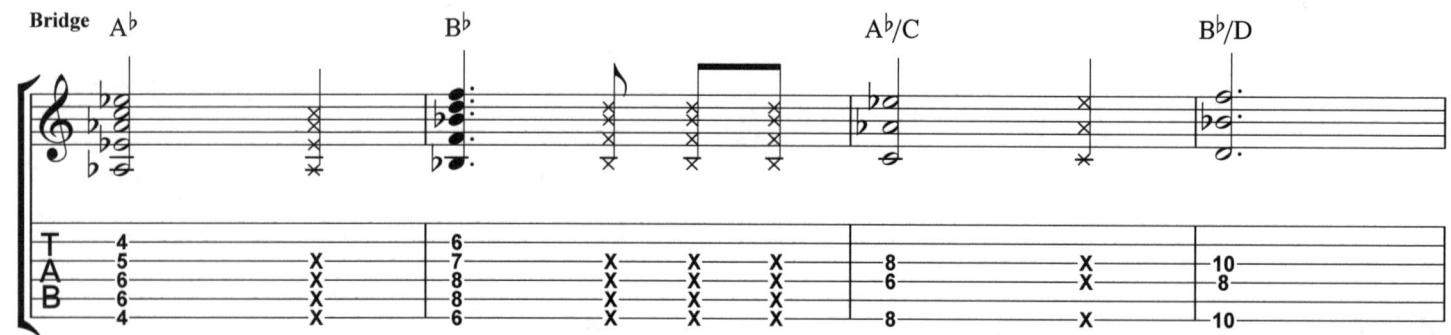

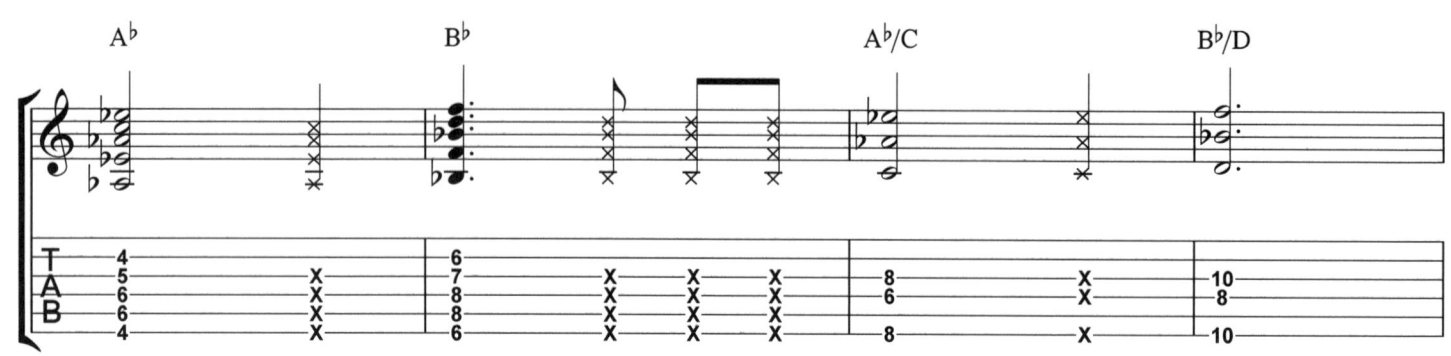

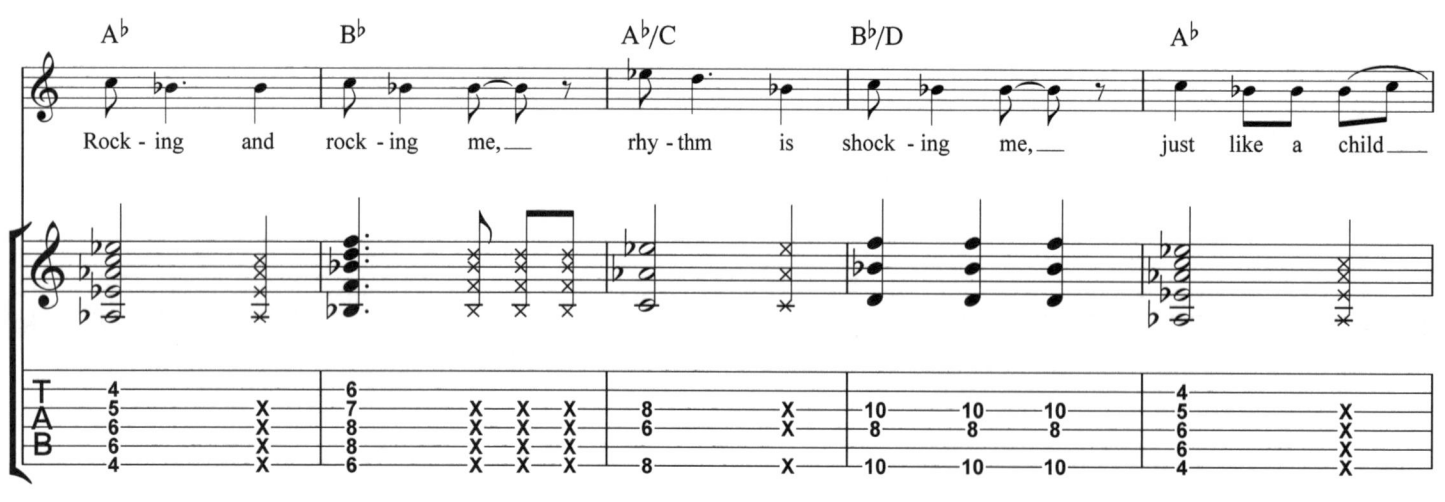

Rock - ing and rock - ing me, ___ rhy - thm is shock - ing me, ___ just like a child ___

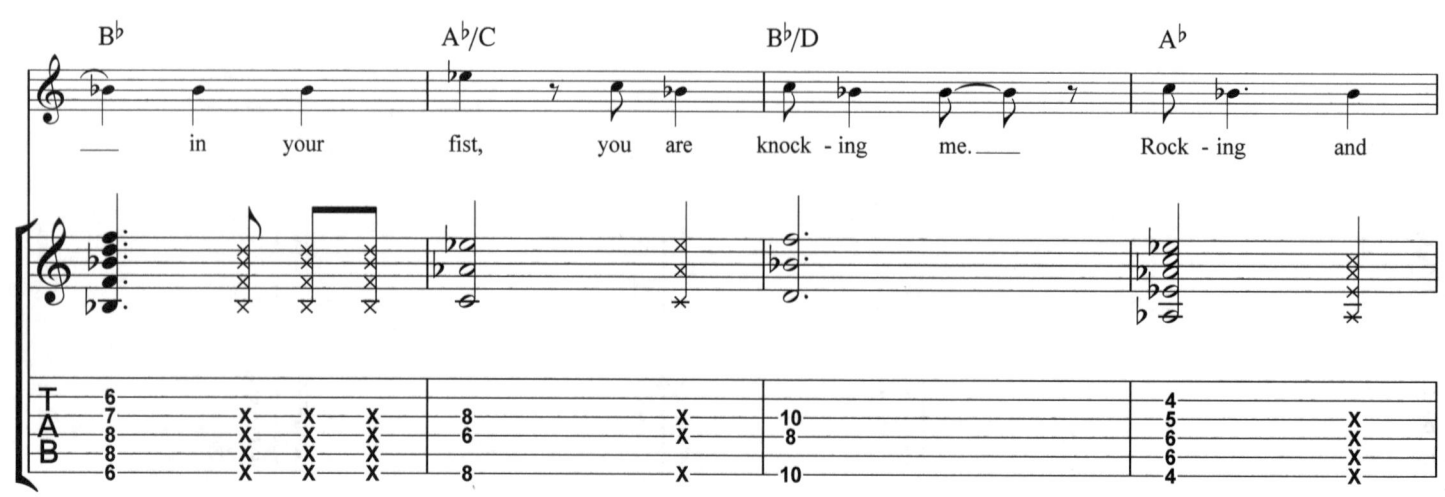

___ in your fist, you are knock - ing me. ___ Rock - ing and

34

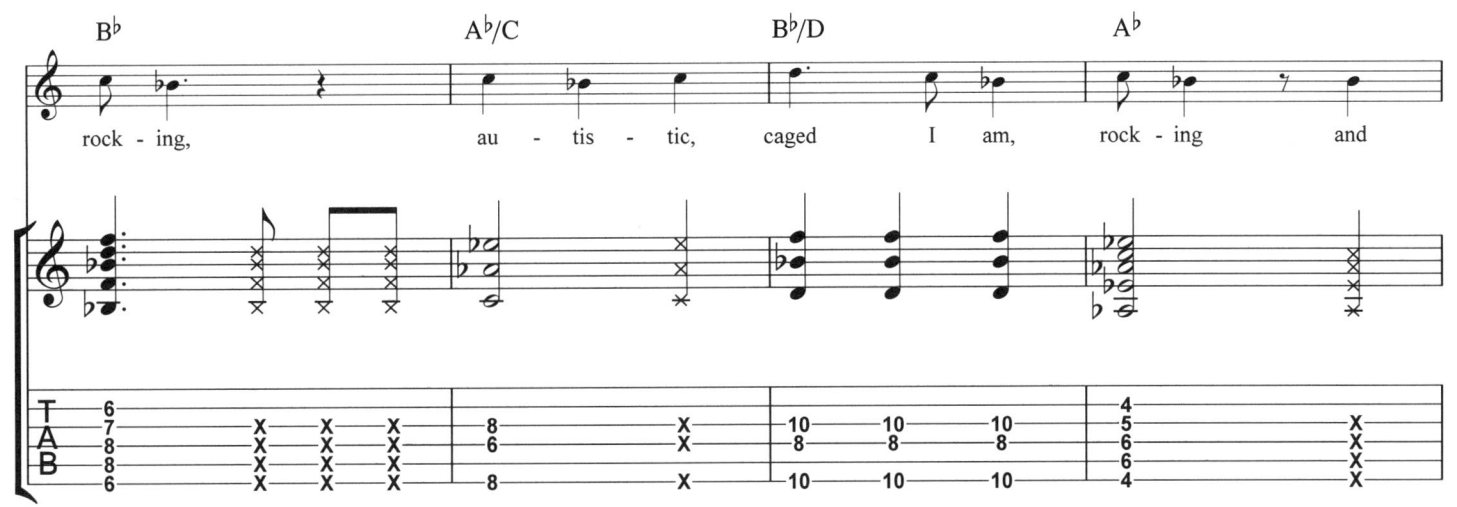

rock - ing,   au - tis - tic, caged   I   am, rock - ing   and

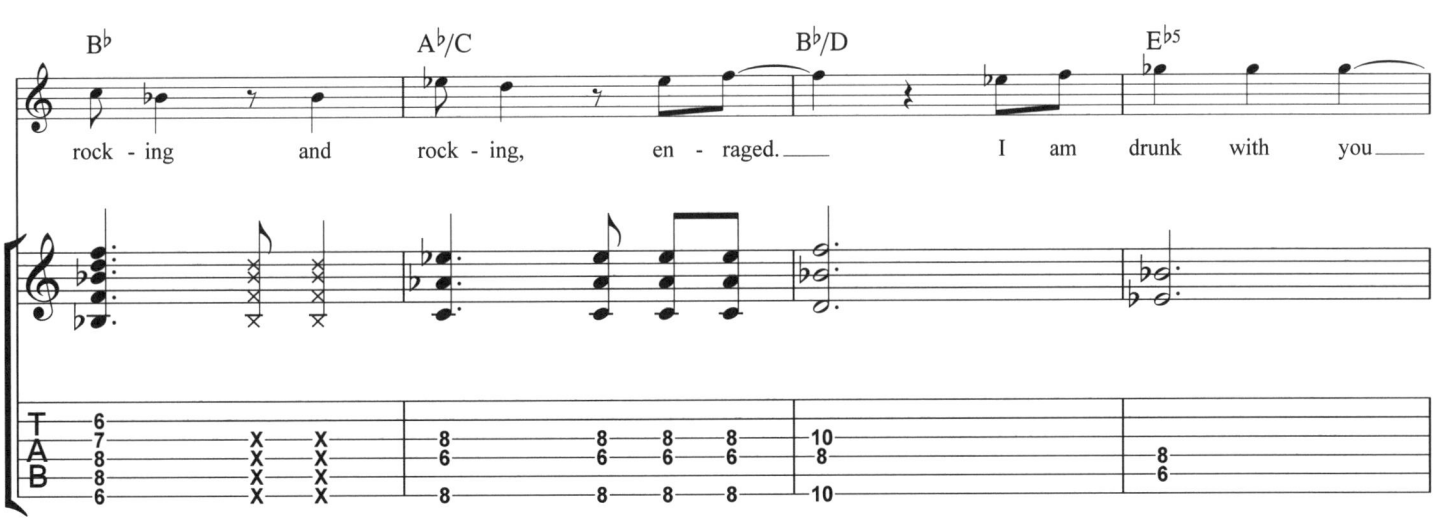

rock - ing   and   rock - ing,   en - raged.____   I   am   drunk   with   you____

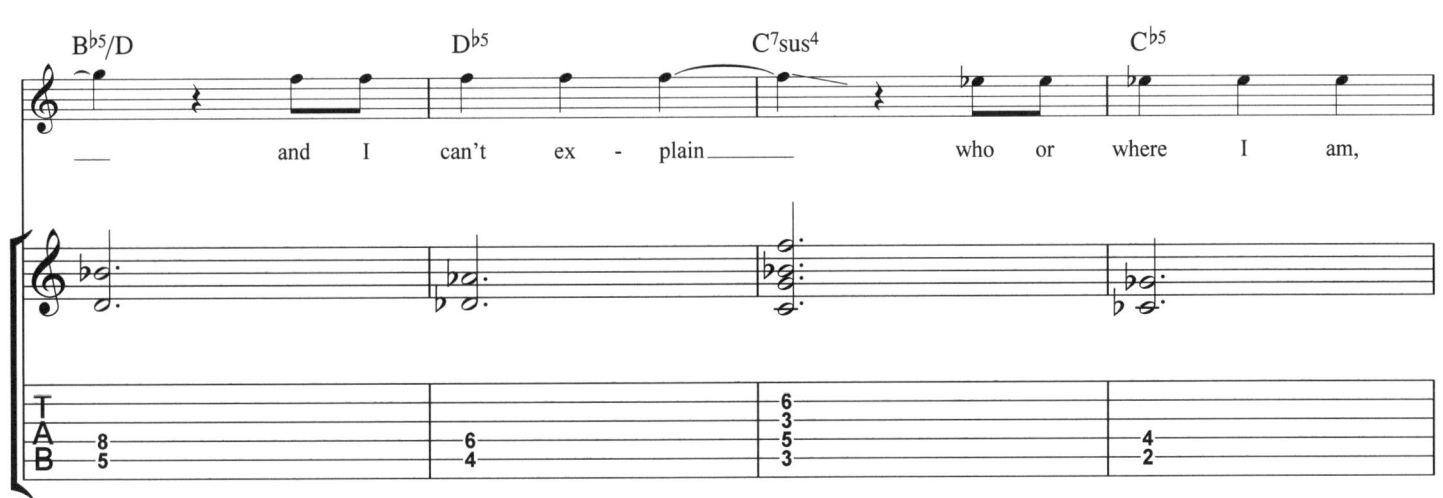

____   and   I   can't   ex - plain_____   who   or   where   I   am,

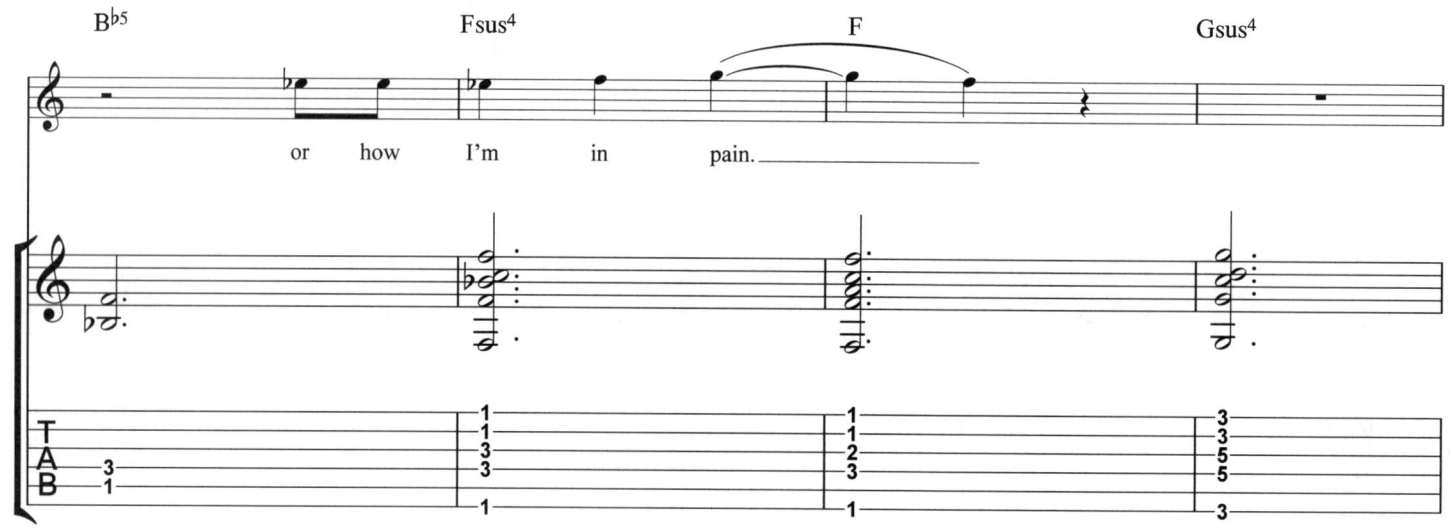

or how I'm in pain.

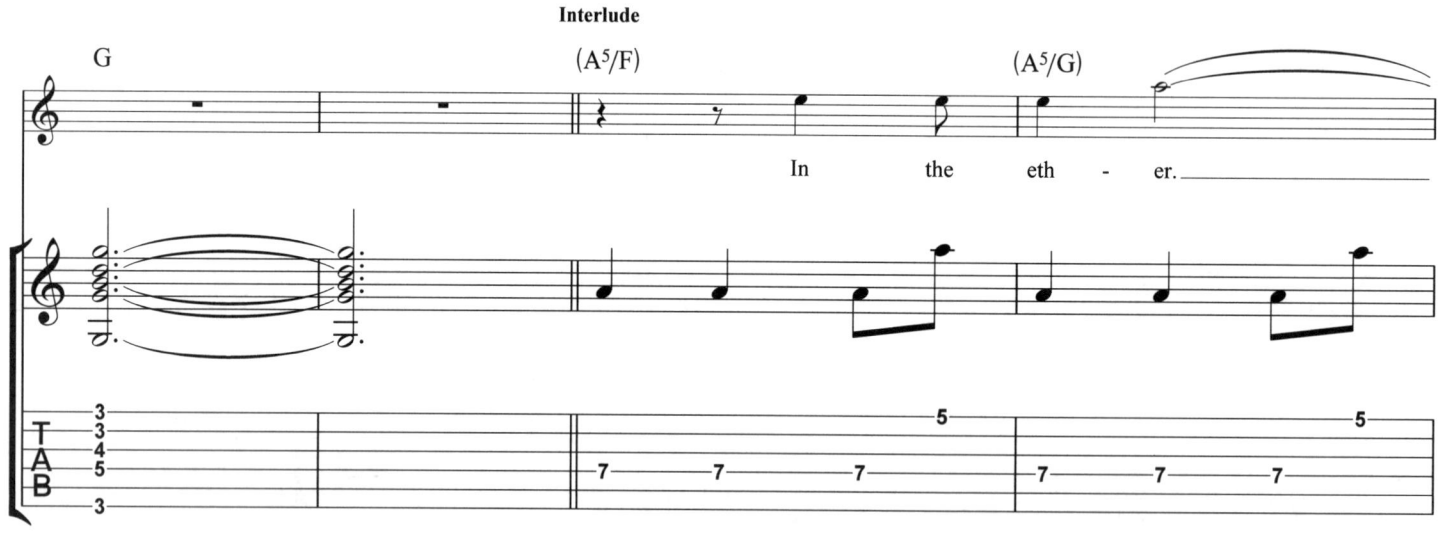

In the eth - er.

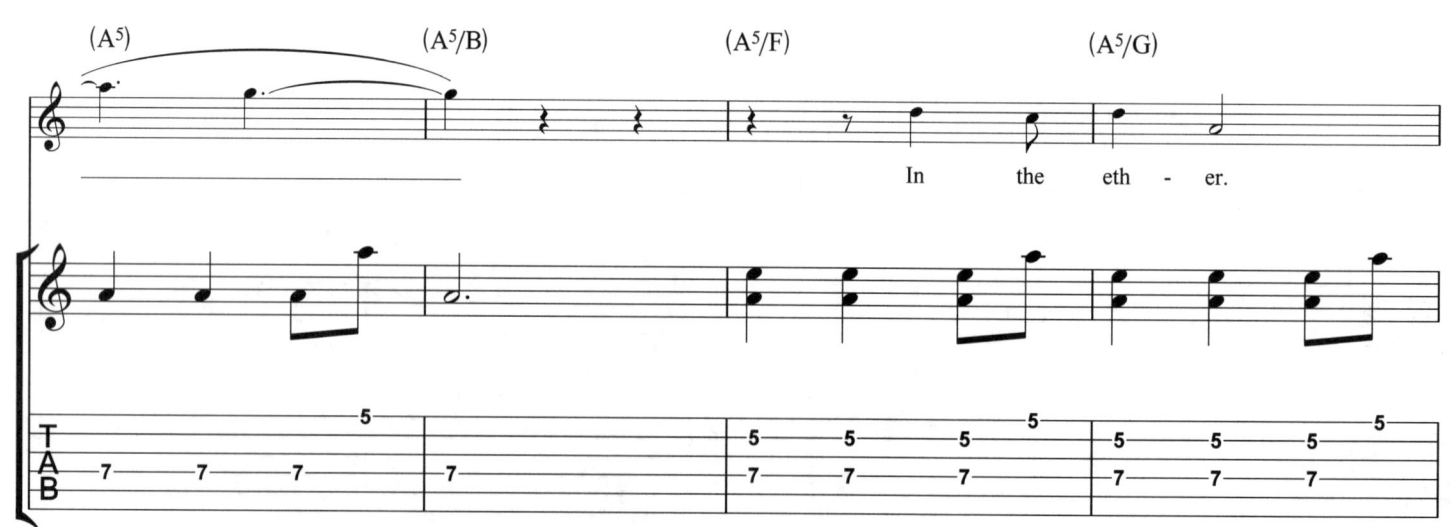

In the eth - er.

36

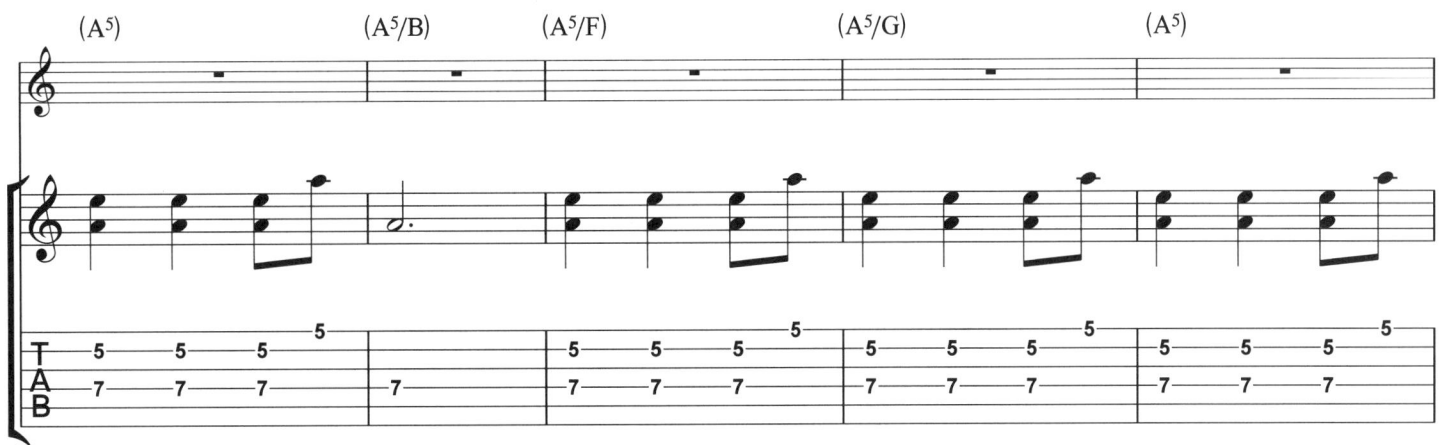

D.S. al Coda

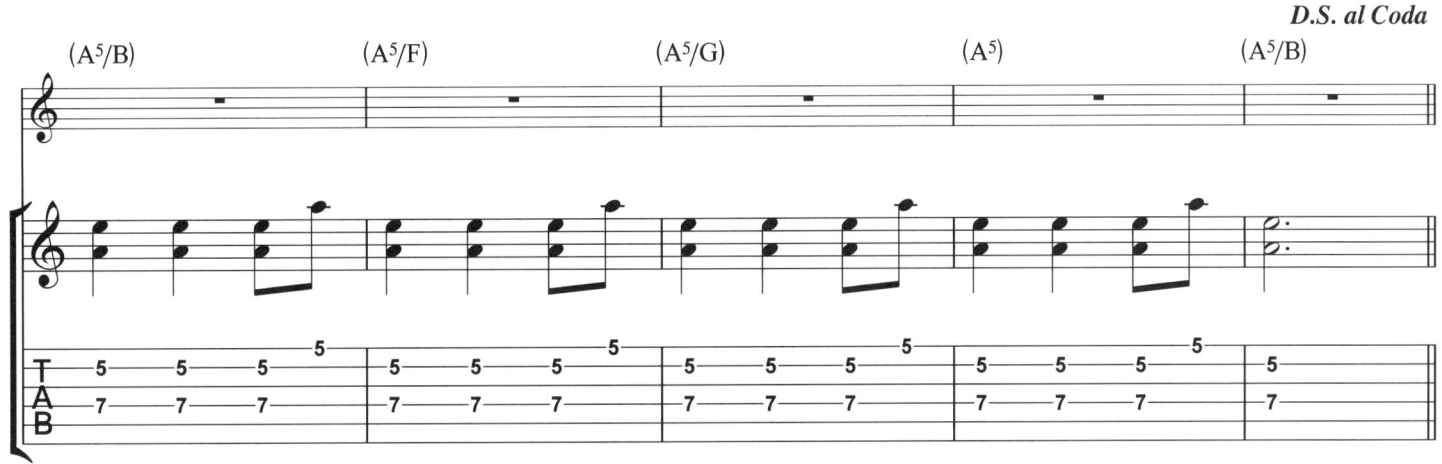

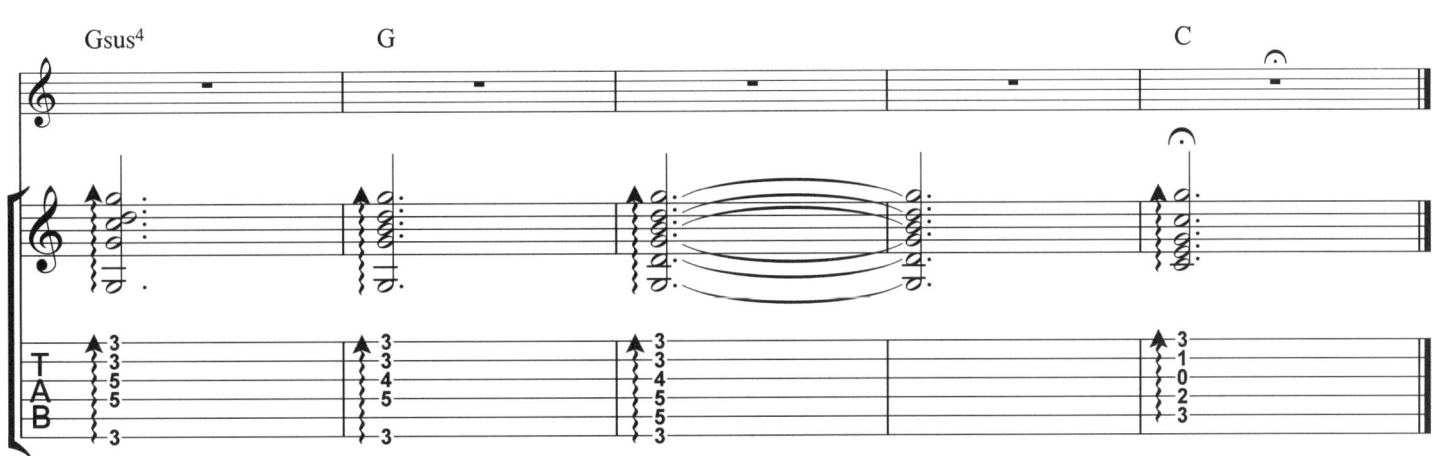

37

BLACK WIDOW'S EYES

Words & Music by
Pete Townshend

Gtr. 1 chords

Gtr. 2 capo 2nd fret	
6 = D	3 = G
5 = A	2 = A
4 = D	1 = D

Gtr. 2 chords - capo 2nd fret

Intro

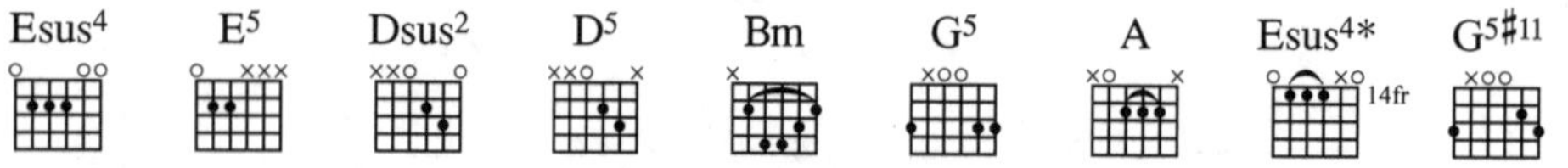

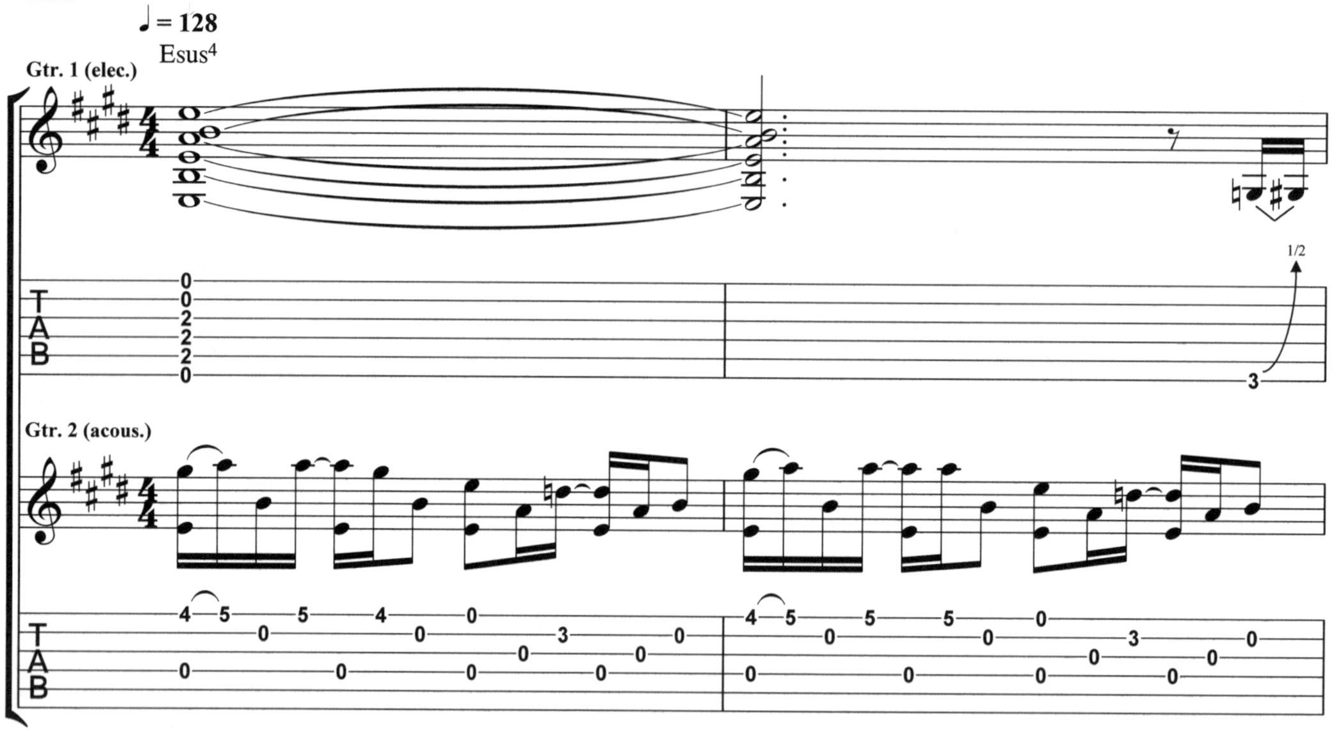

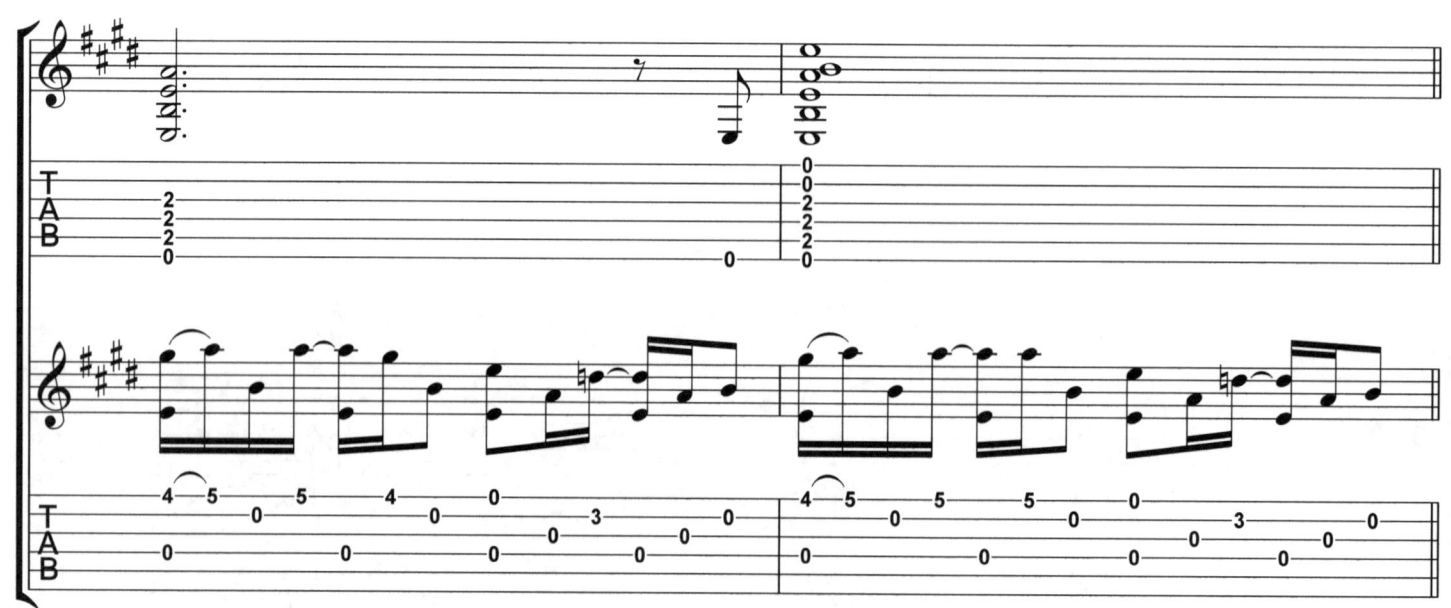

© Copyright 2006 Eel Pie Publishing Limited.
BMG Music Publishing Limited.
All Rights Reserved. International Copyright Secured.

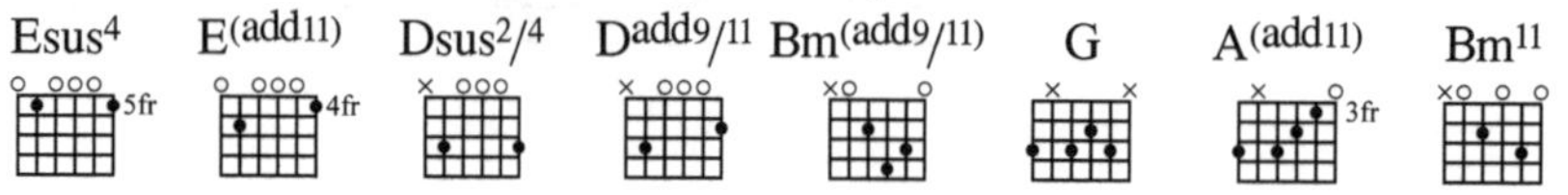

Verse
E5
Dsus2
E5
You jumped out of an al-ley, with sur-prise in your Black Wi-dow's
I rose up to the sta-tion, Smelt your scent by the
1/2
D5
E5
D5
eyes.
I was pre-pared to be un-pre-pared,
door.
You'd stood wait-ing so pa tient, just one
1/2

E5
D5
Chorus
Bm
been pre - par - ing for lies.
wave, then no more.
I fell
I fell
G5
A
Bm
G5
A
right in love with you,
in - to a thou - sand parts I
right in love with you,
there'd been no - thing I could

41

44

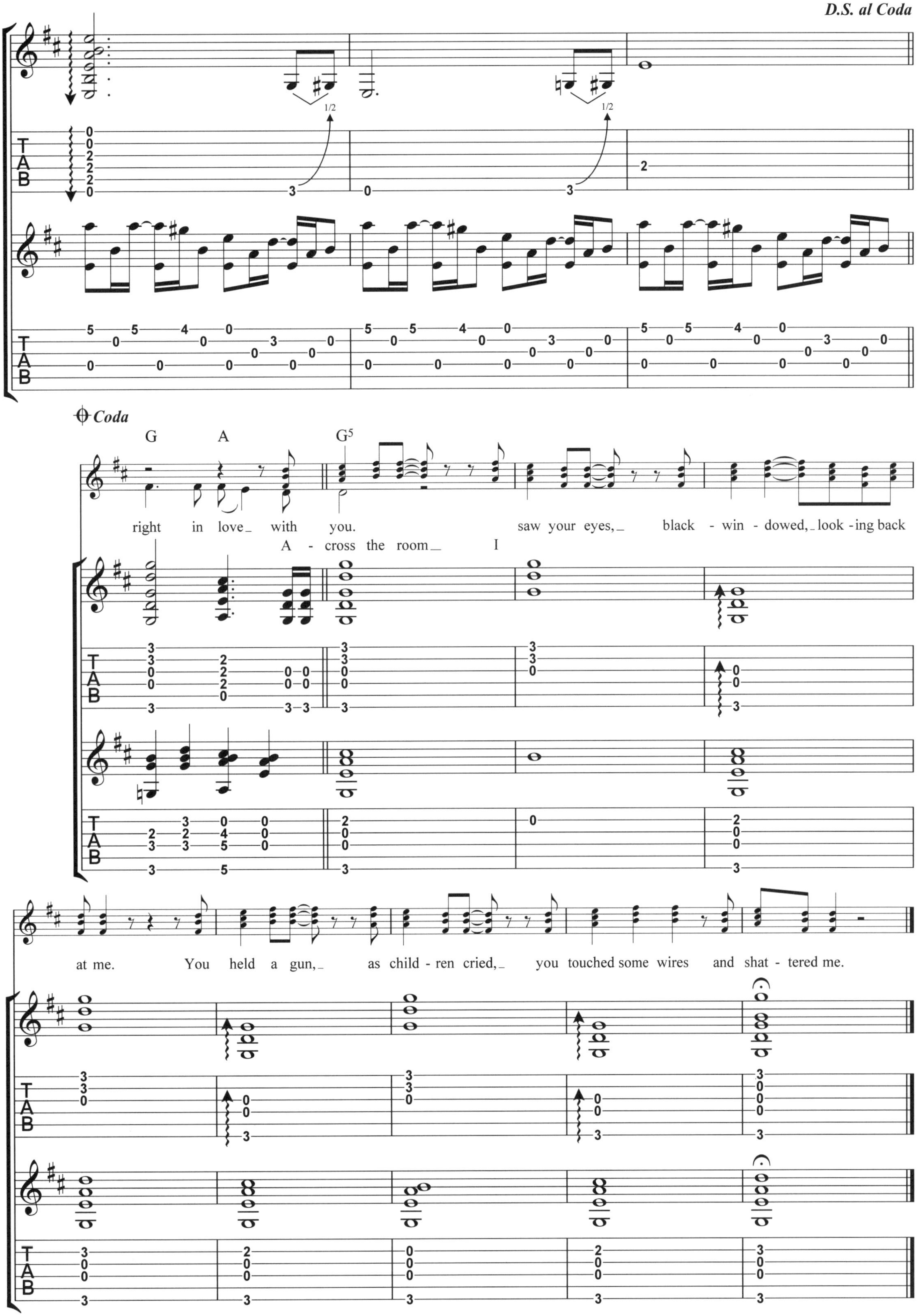

Coda

right in love with you. saw your eyes, black - win - dowed, look - ing back

A - cross the room I

at me. You held a gun, as child - ren cried, you touched some wires and shat - tered me.

TWO THOUSAND YEARS

Words & Music by
Pete Townshend

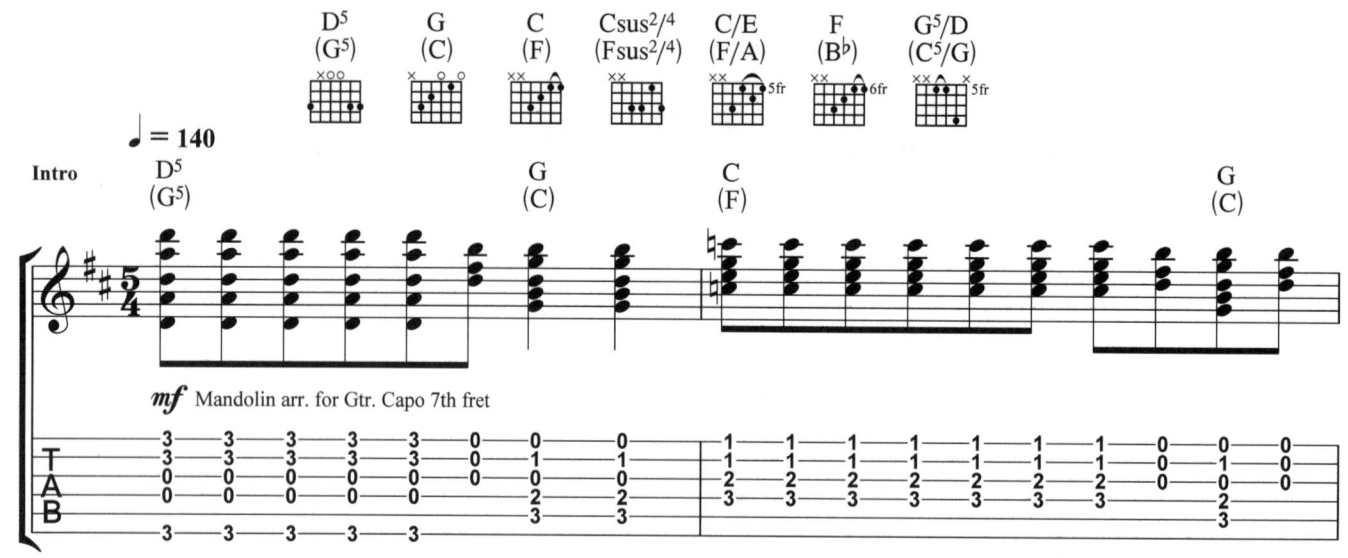

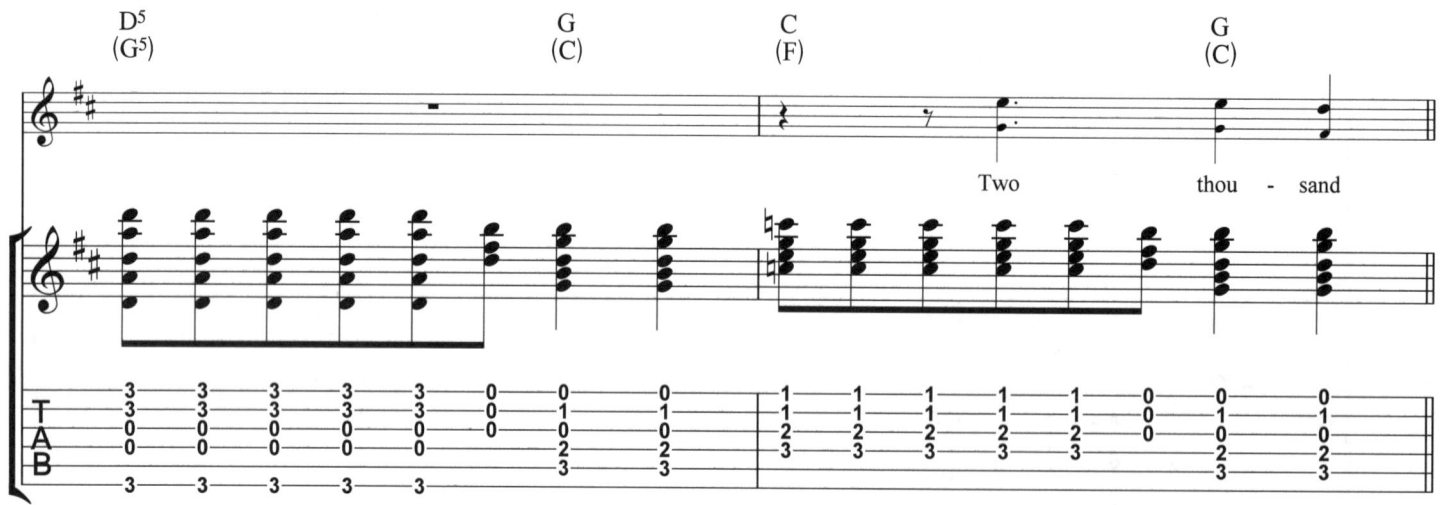

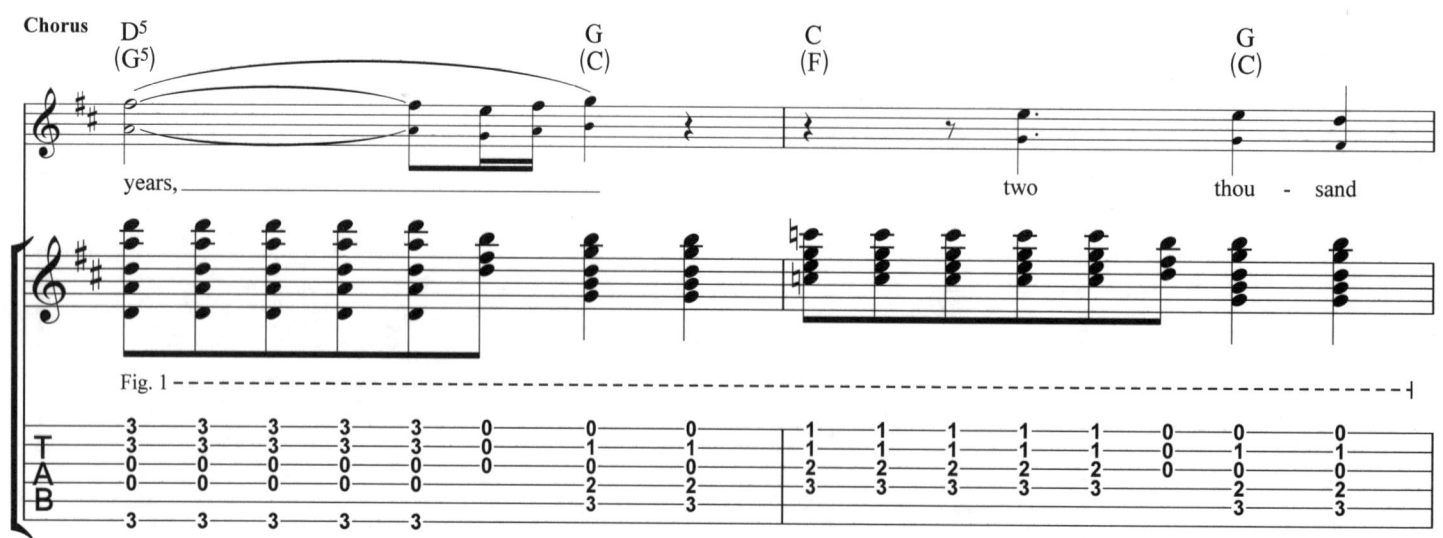

© Copyright 2006 Eel Pie Publishing Limited.
BMG Music Publishing Limited.
All Rights Reserved. International Copyright Secured.

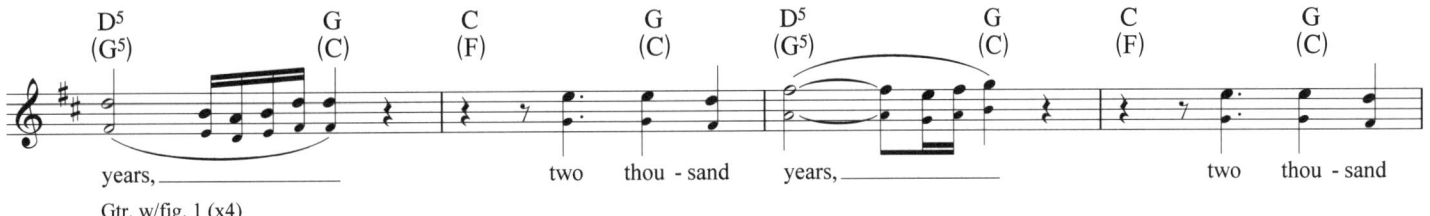

years, _____ two thou-sand years, _____ two thou-sand

Gtr. w/fig. 1 (x4)

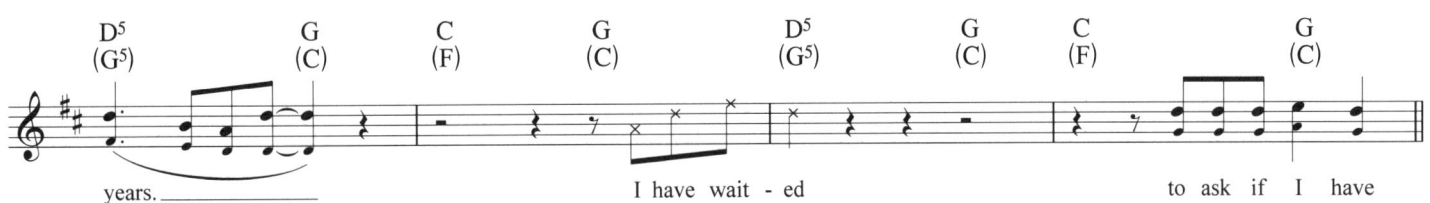

years. _____ I have wait-ed to ask if I have

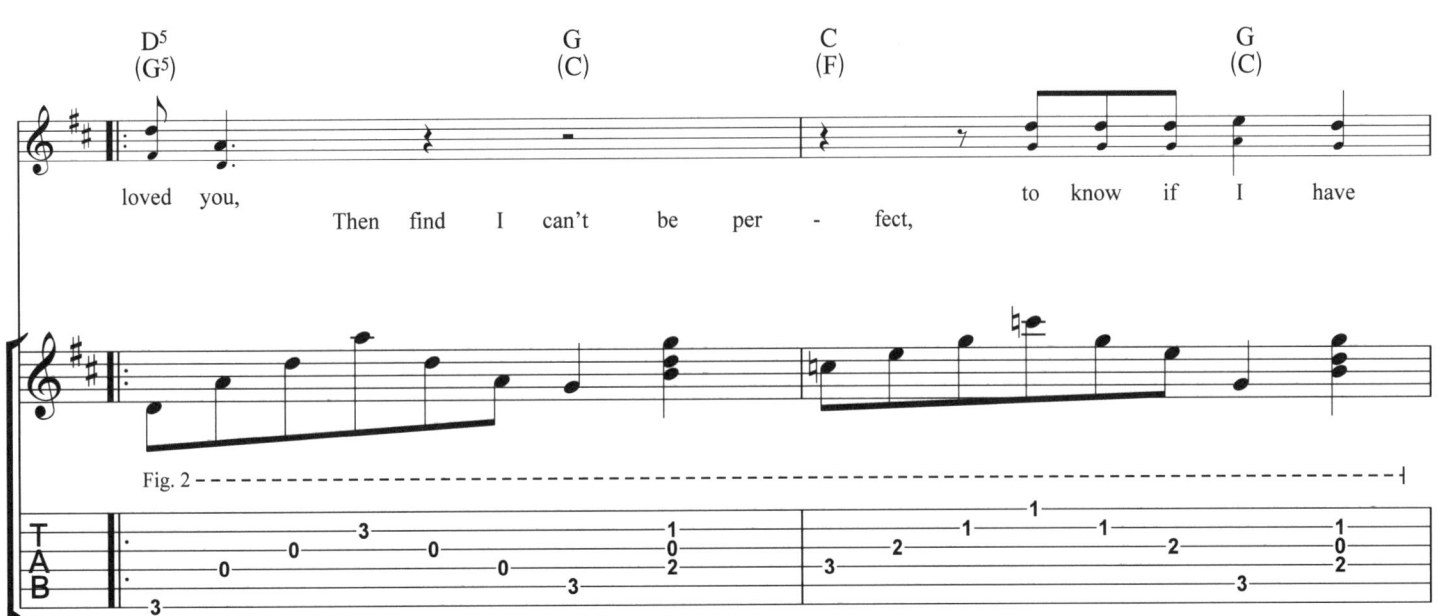

loved you, Then find I can't be per - fect, to know if I have

Fig. 2

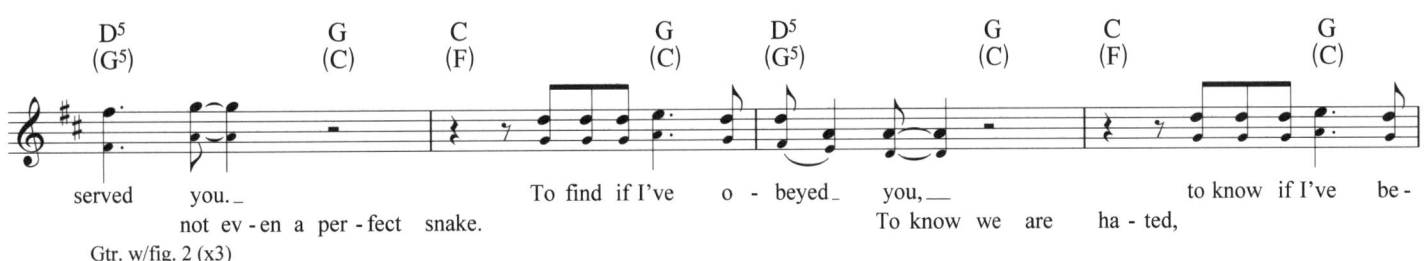

served you. _ To find if I've o - beyed _ you, _ to know if I've be-
not ev-en a per-fect snake. To know we are ha-ted,

Gtr. w/fig. 2 (x3)

Chorus

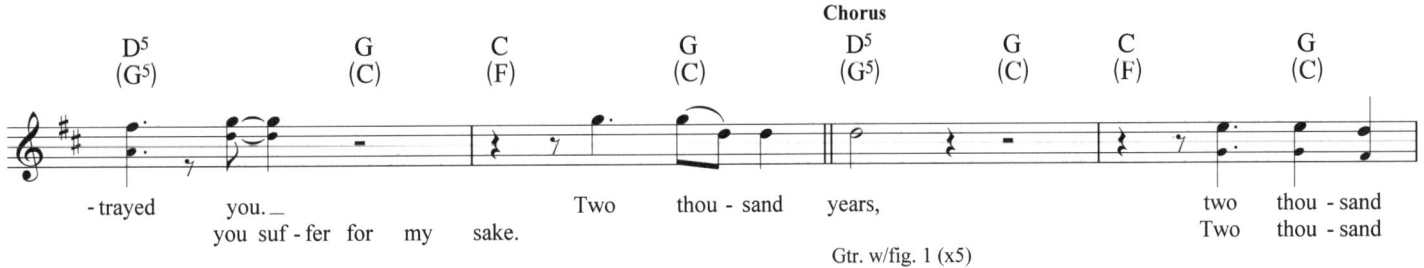

-trayed you. Two thou-sand years, two thou-sand
you suf-fer for my sake. Two thou-sand

Gtr. w/fig. 1 (x5)

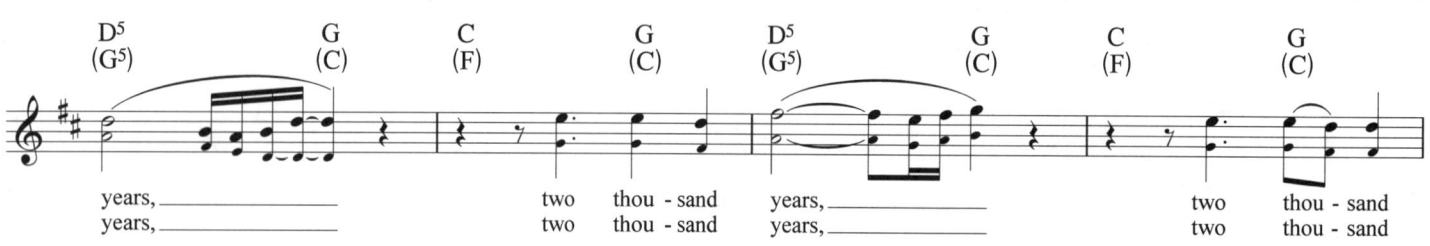

years,_____ two thou-sand years,_____ two thou-sand
years,_____ two thou-sand years,_____ two thou-sand

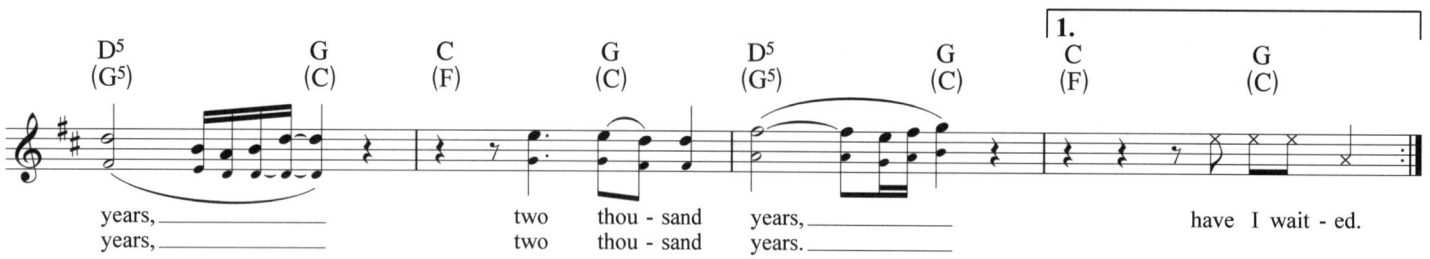

1.

years,_____ two thou-sand years,_____ have I wait-ed.
years,_____ two thou-sand years._____

2.

Bridge

And so I have a chance____ to love

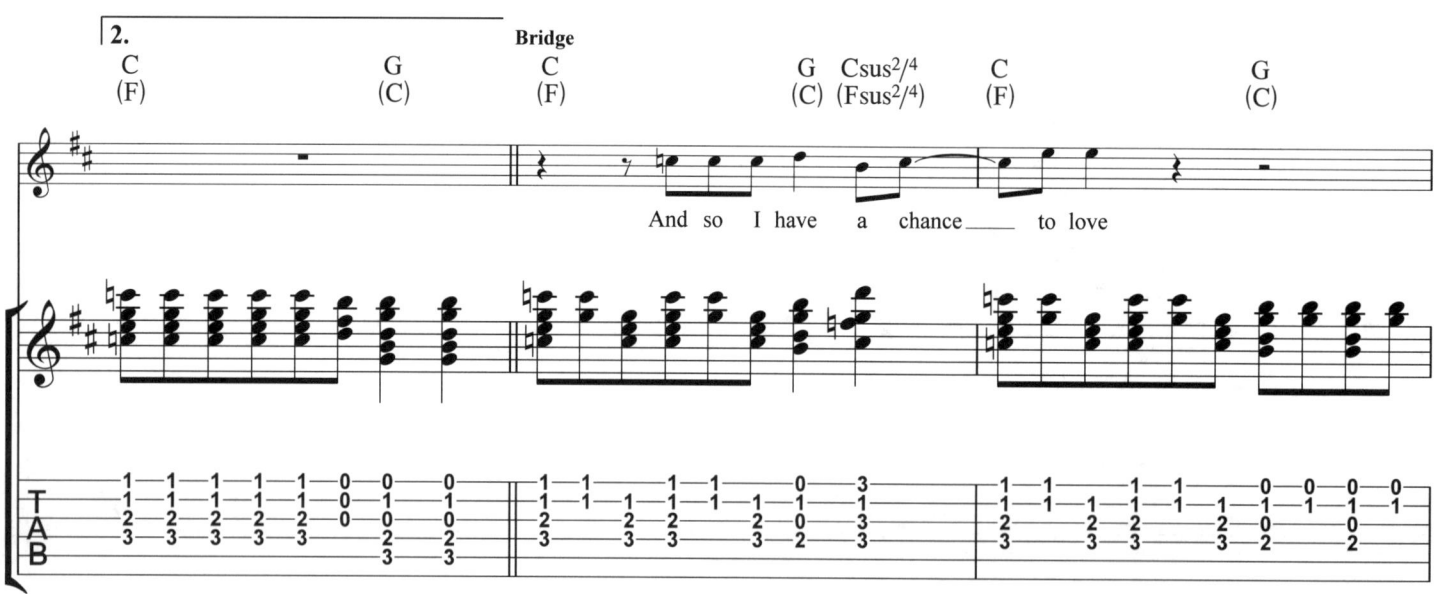

as you in-tend-ed. You real-ly lived and died____

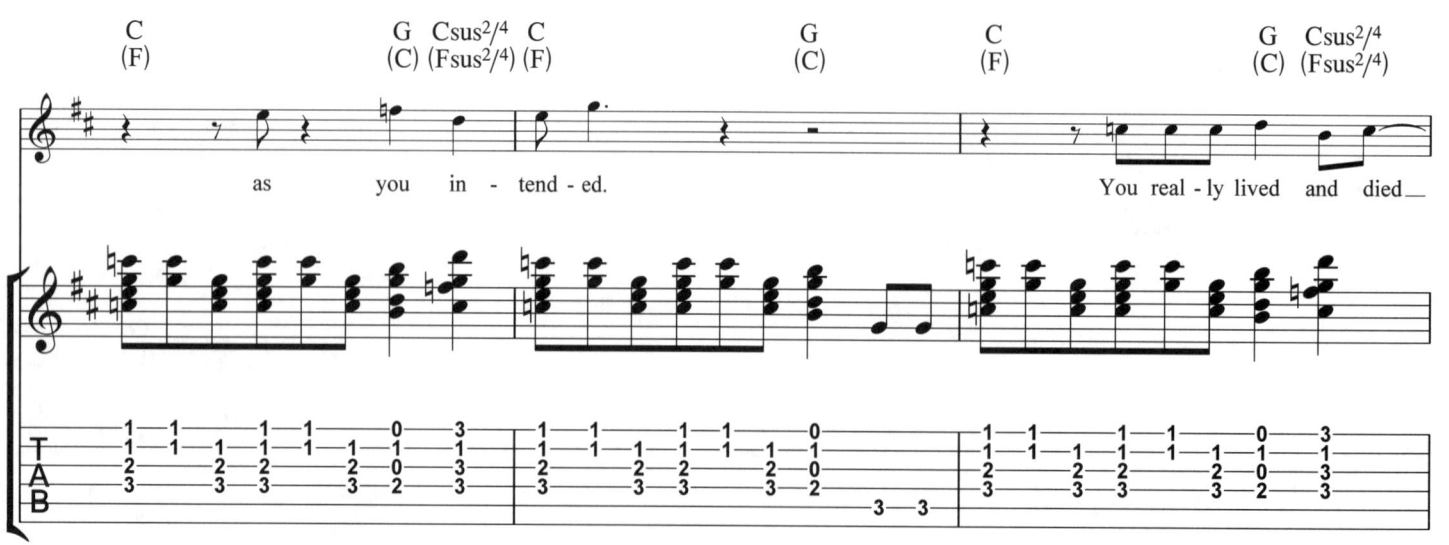

GOD SPEAKS OF MARTY ROBBINS

Words & Music by
Pete Townshend

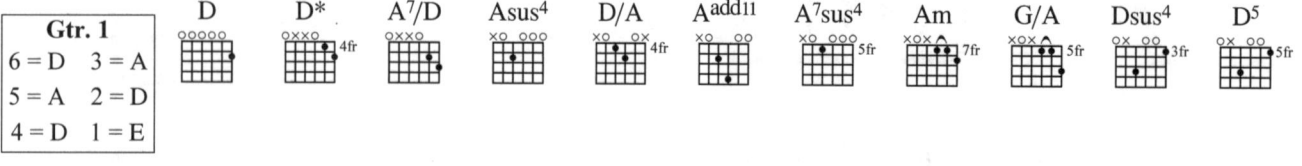

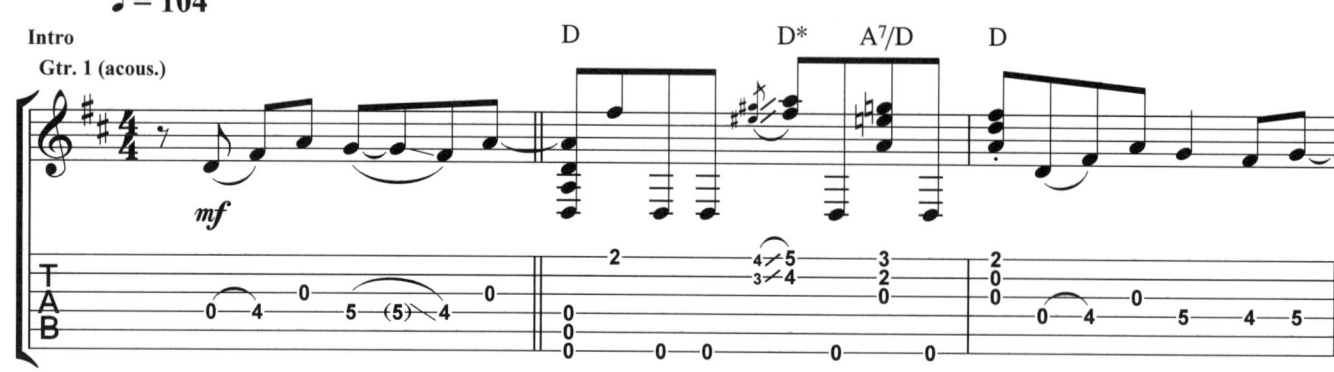

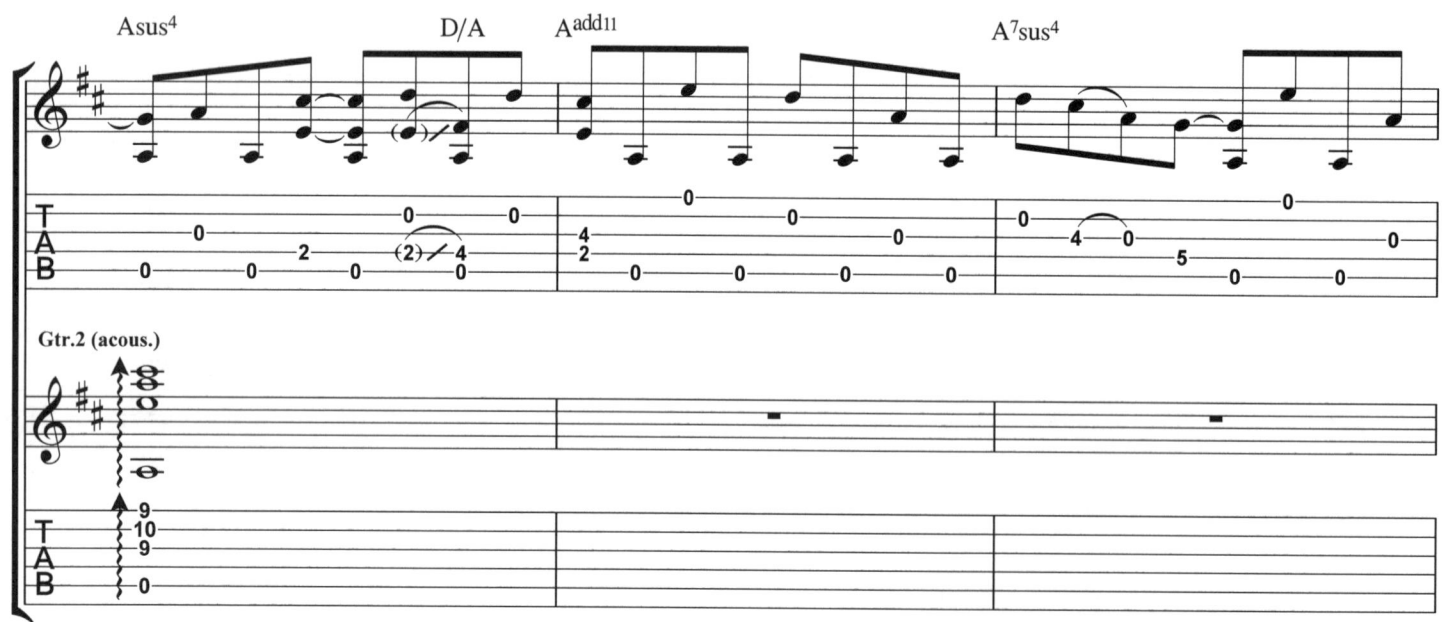

And when the world be - gan,

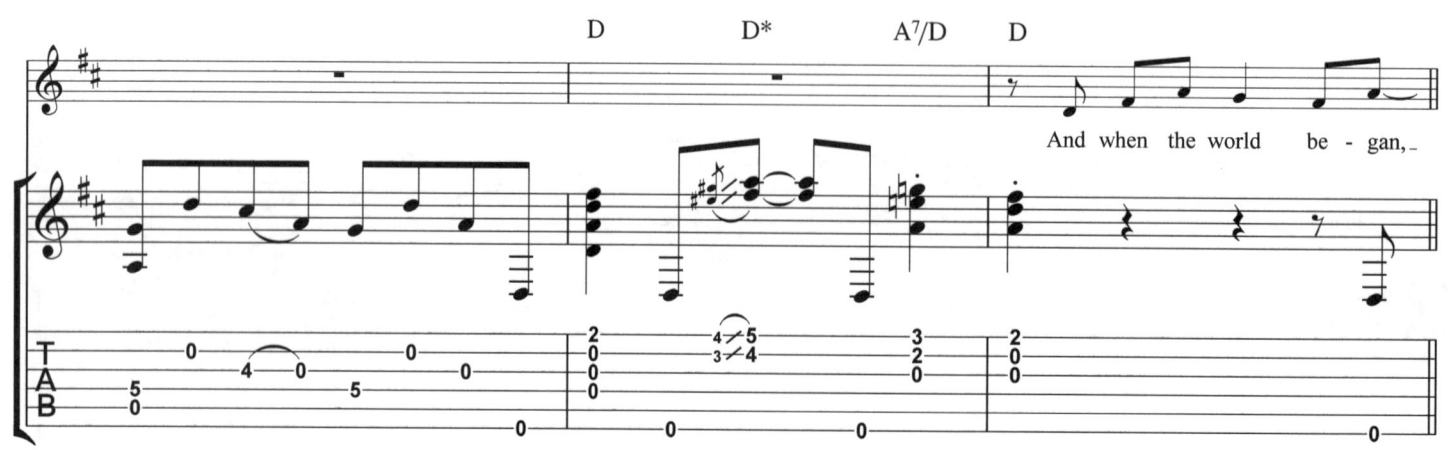

© Copyright 2006 Eel Pie Publishing Limited.
BMG Music Publishing Limited.
All Rights Reserved. International Copyright Secured.

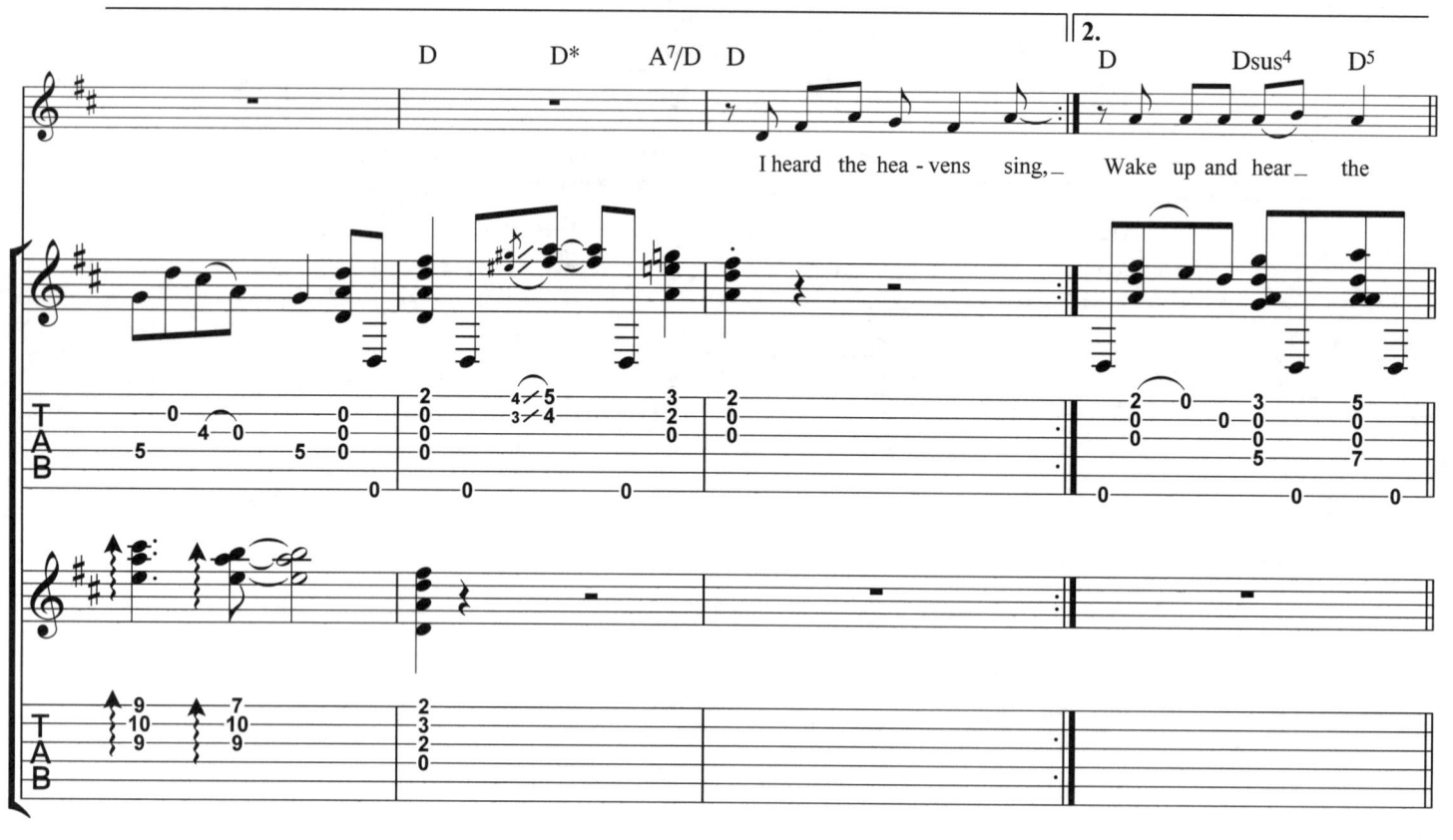

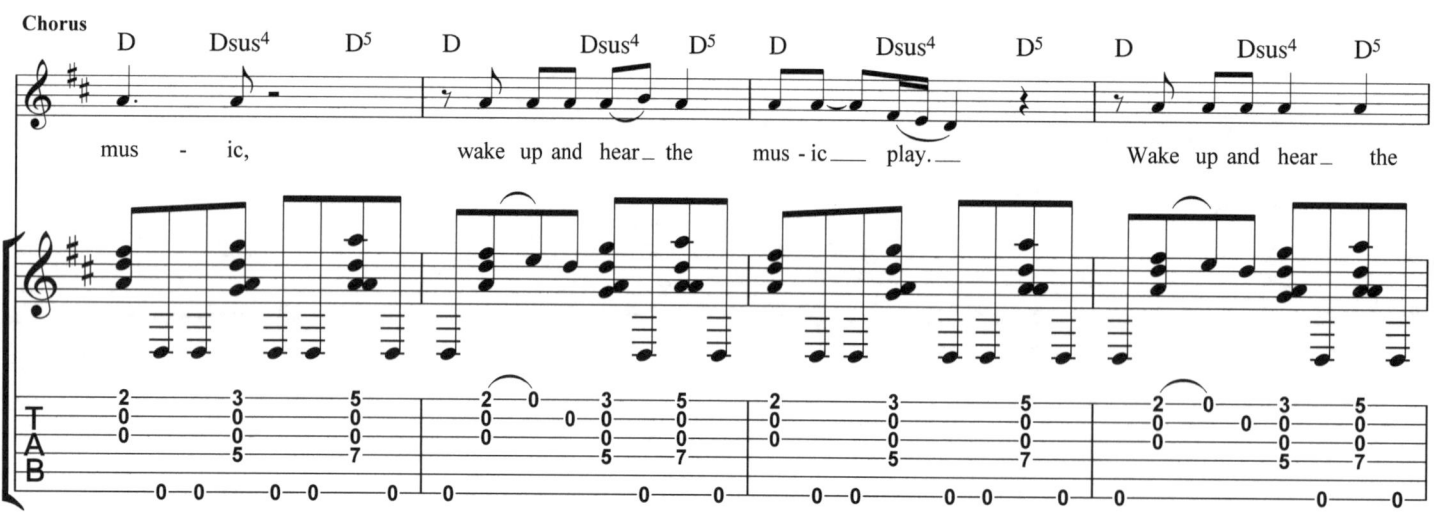

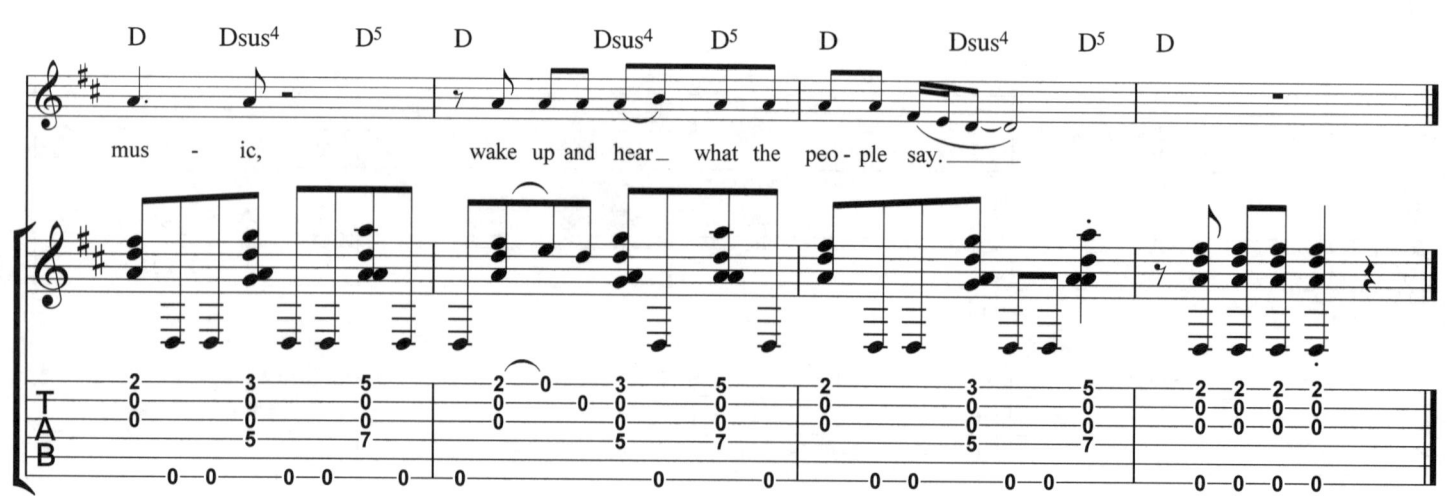

IT'S NOT ENOUGH

Words & Music by
Pete Townshend & Rachel Fuller

© Copyright 2006 Eel Pie Publishing Limited.
BMG Music Publishing Limited.
All Rights Reserved. International Copyright Secured.

Asus²   G⁵   D   Asus²

a lit-tle more man, a lit-tle more seed. It's not e-nough, it's not e-
what-ev-er I give nev-er feels like e-nough, not e- nough.
I'll al-ways need a lit-tle more ink. It's not e- nough.
lift's go-ing down, and I start act-ing tough. It's not e-nough,

Gtr. 3 w/fig. 1 (x3)

w/bar

G⁵   D   Asus²   G⁵   D

-nough, what-ev-er I give. (What-ev-er you give, it's nev-er e-nough.)
Oh, what-ev-er I give. When
No, nev-er e- nough, what-ev-er I give. How
what-ev-er I give, it's not e-nough. I'll

57

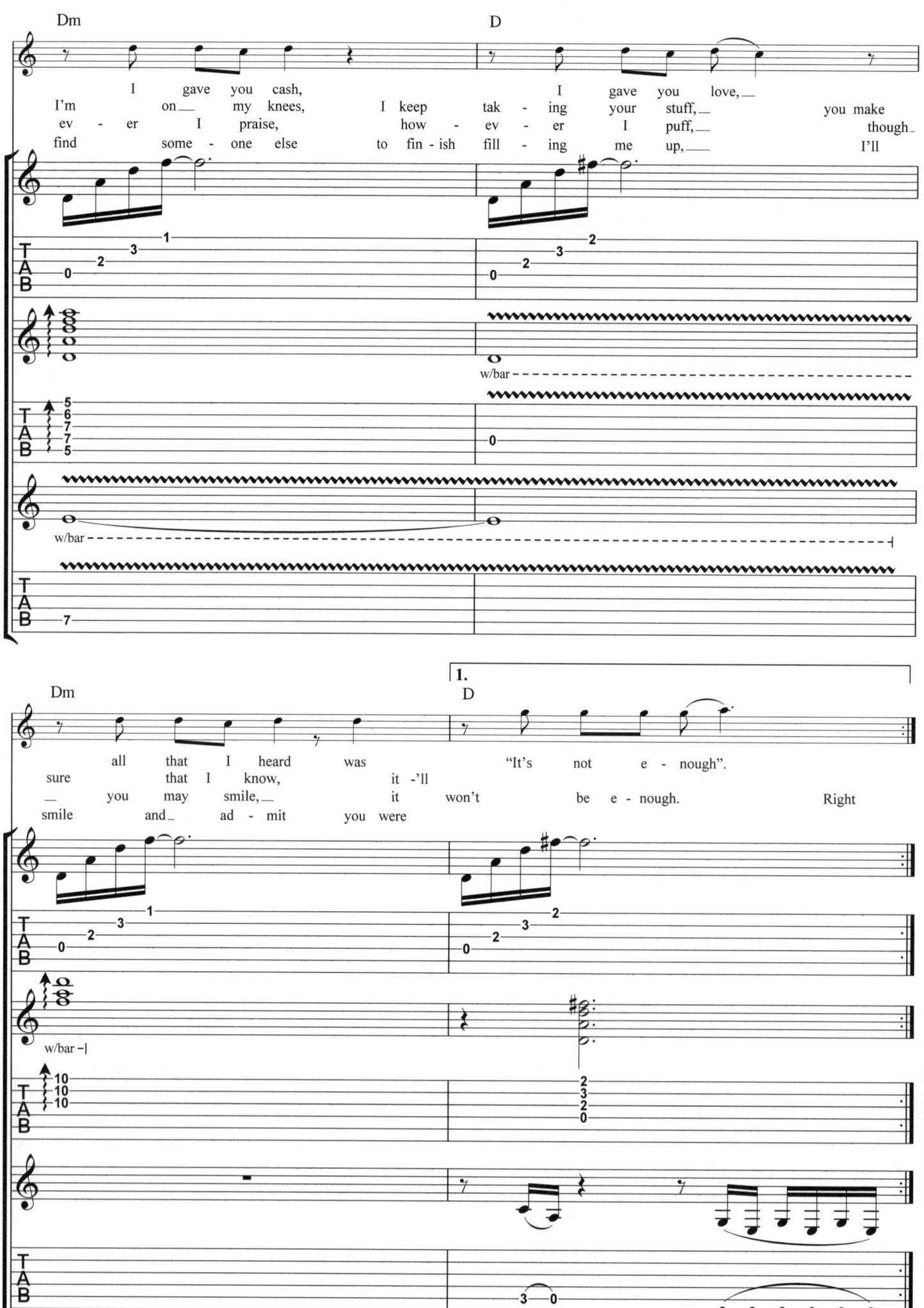

58

Fsus2
C
has - ten my end. He'll choose you ov - er me, be -
make you com - plete. You ap - pear in my dreams with some

Fsus2
C
To Coda
-cause I have lent ev - 'ry ounce of my juice, my
new court - i - er, you need me there to see what you

Fsus2
D.S. al Coda
es - sence is spent.
Coda
Fsus2
3
need to con - vey. It's not e - nough.
w/bar
Asus2
G5
D
Asus2
No, no, it's not e - nough.
Gtr. 3 w/fig. 1 (x8)
w/bar
w/bar

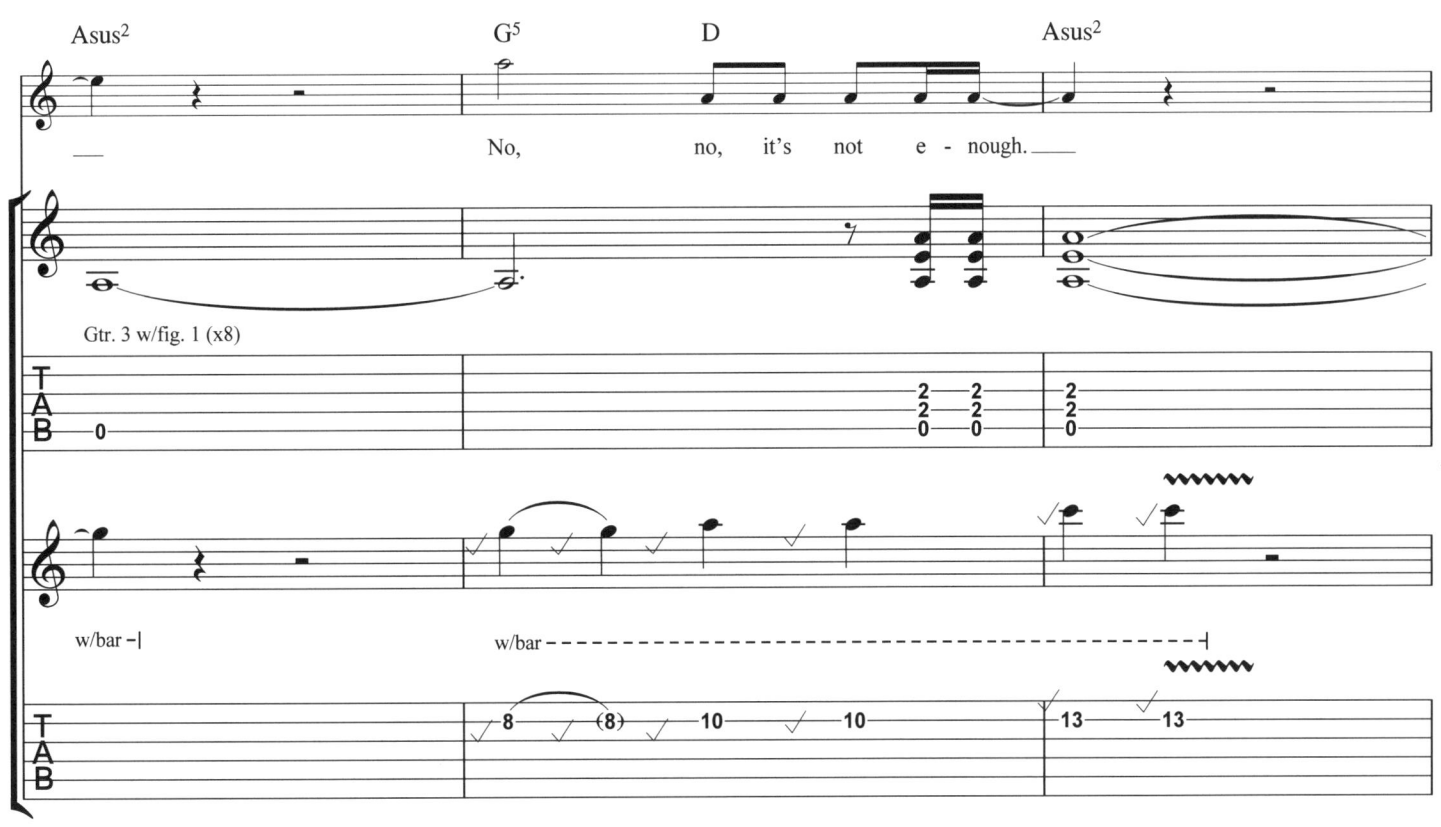

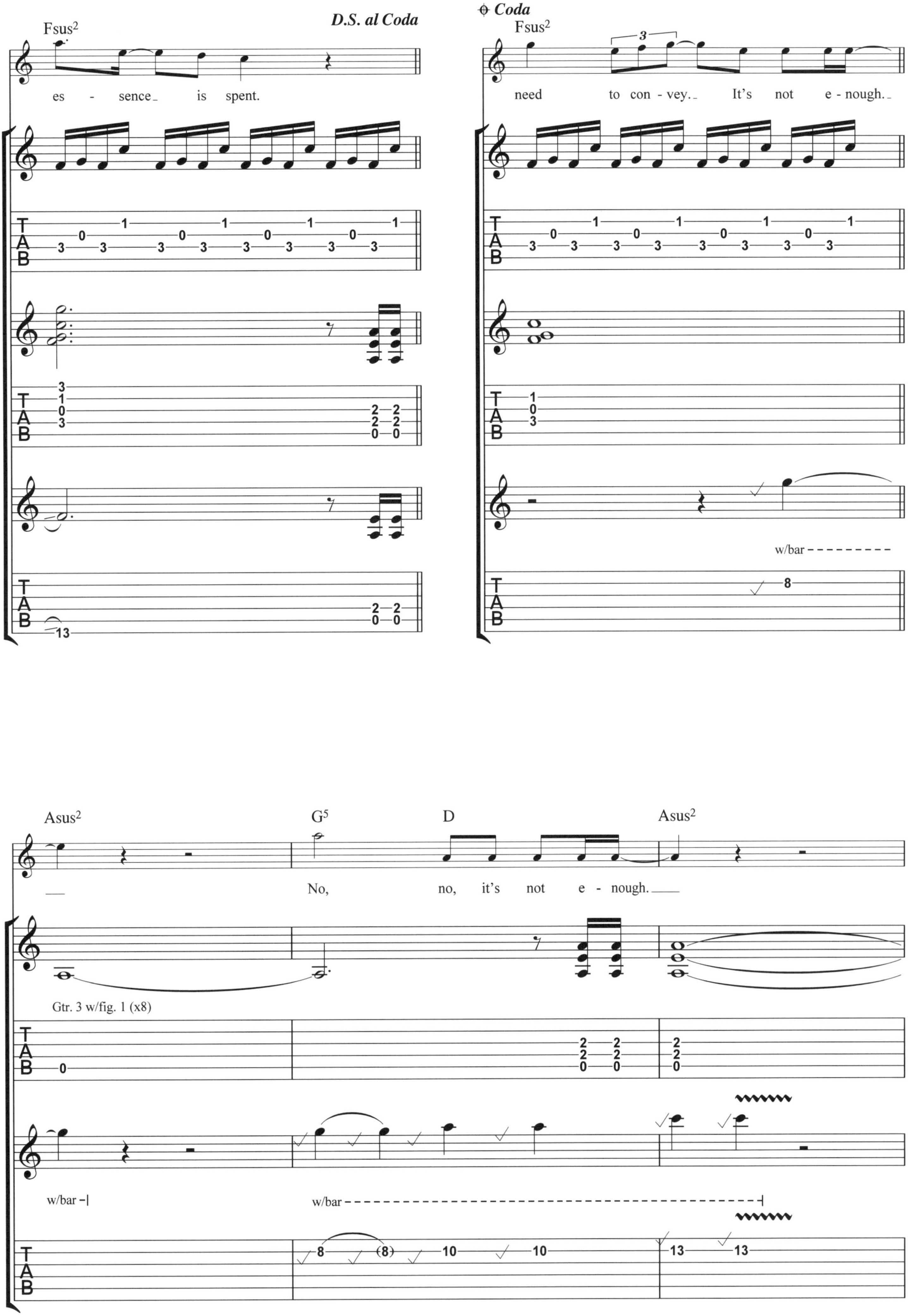

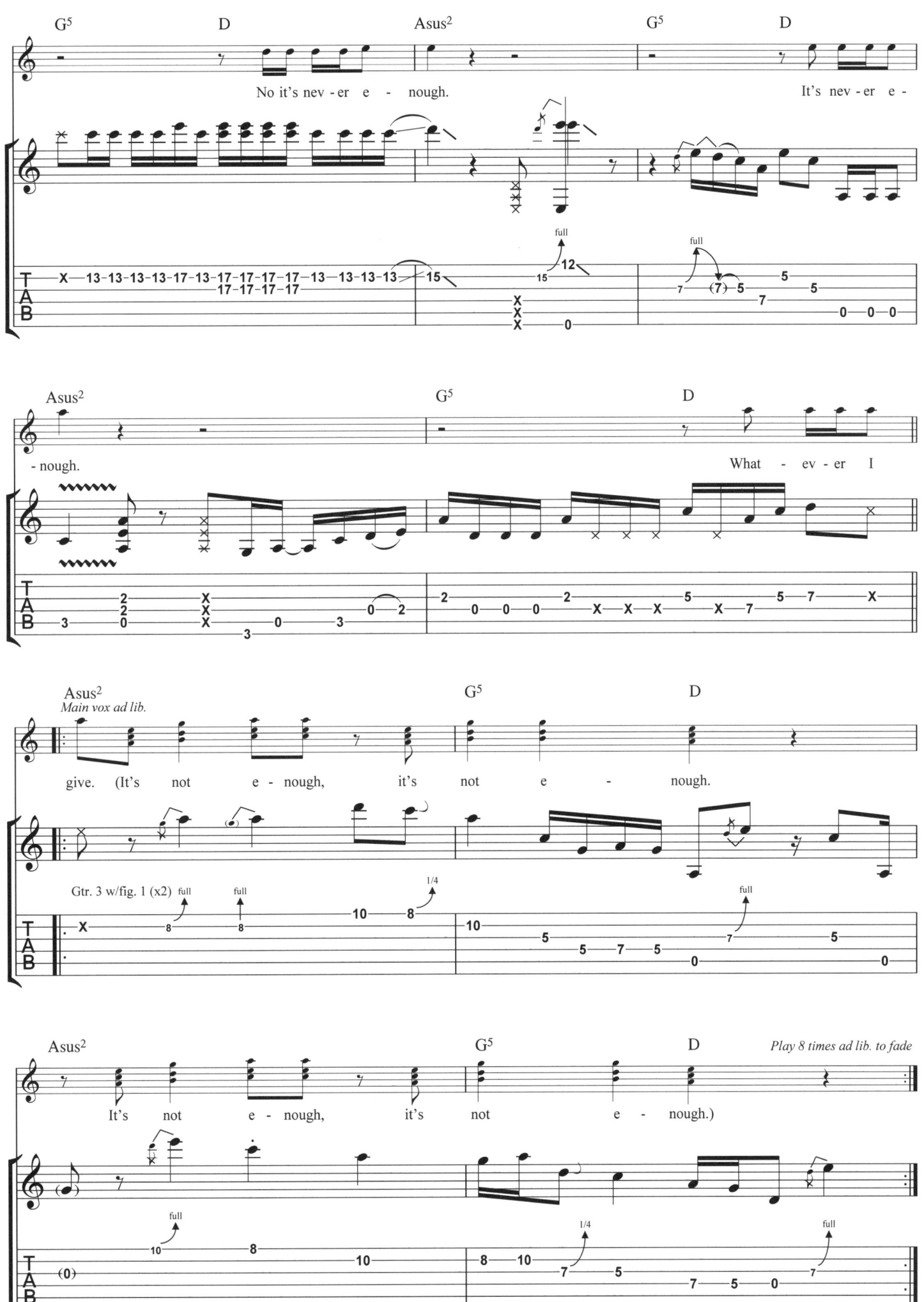

YOU STAND BY ME

Words & Music by
Pete Townshend

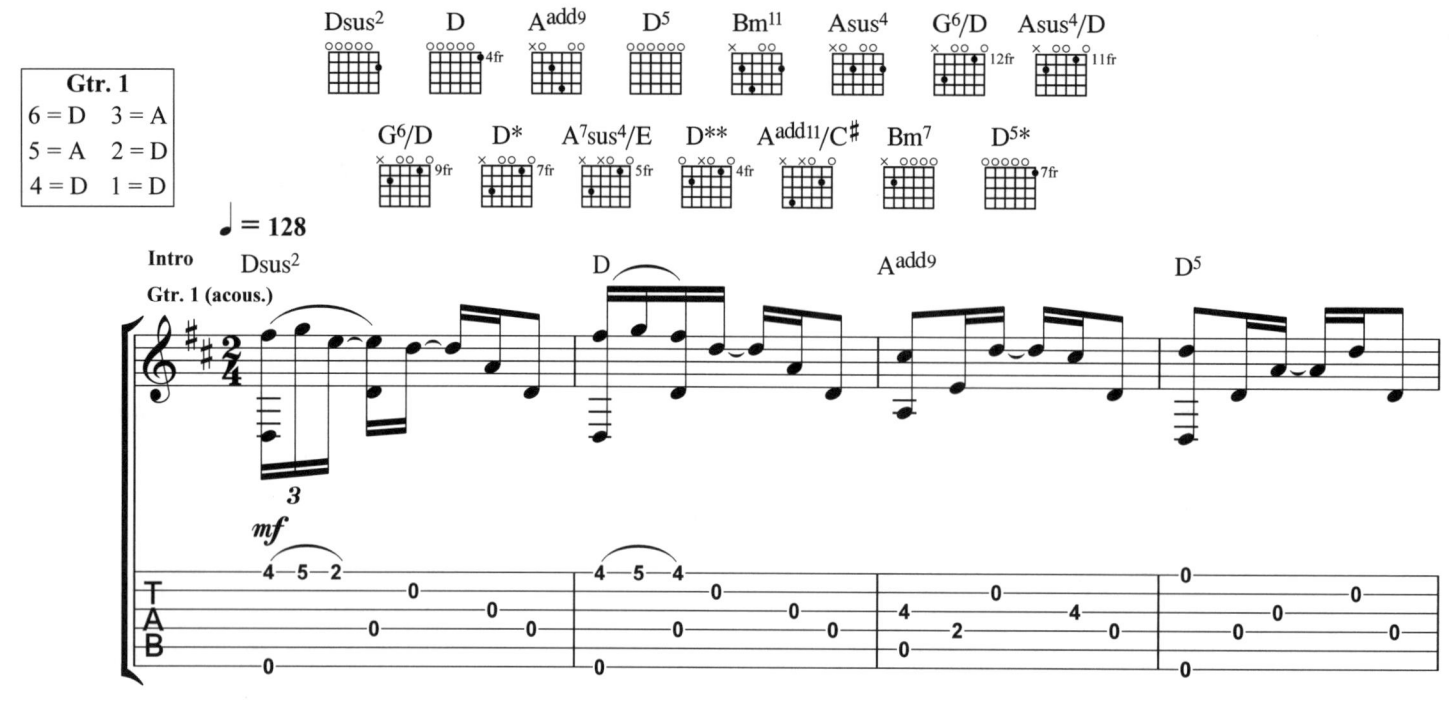

© Copyright 2006 Eel Pie Publishing Limited.
BMG Music Publishing Limited.
All Rights Reserved. International Copyright Secured.

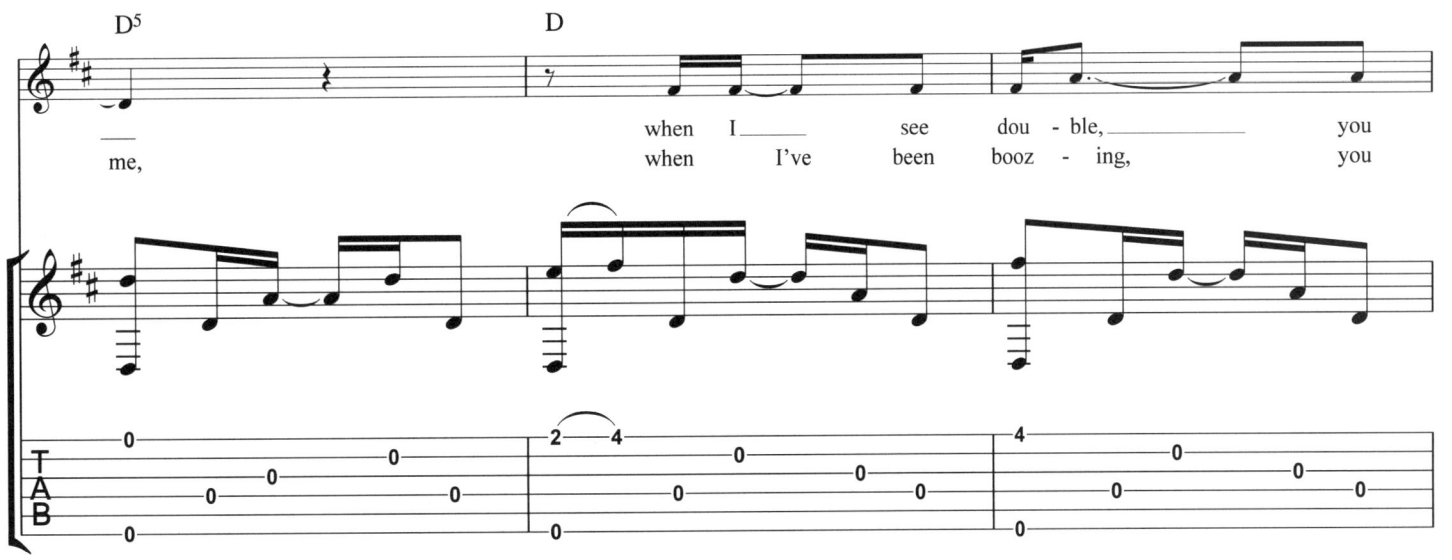

when I _____ see dou - ble, _____ you
me, when I've been booz - ing, you

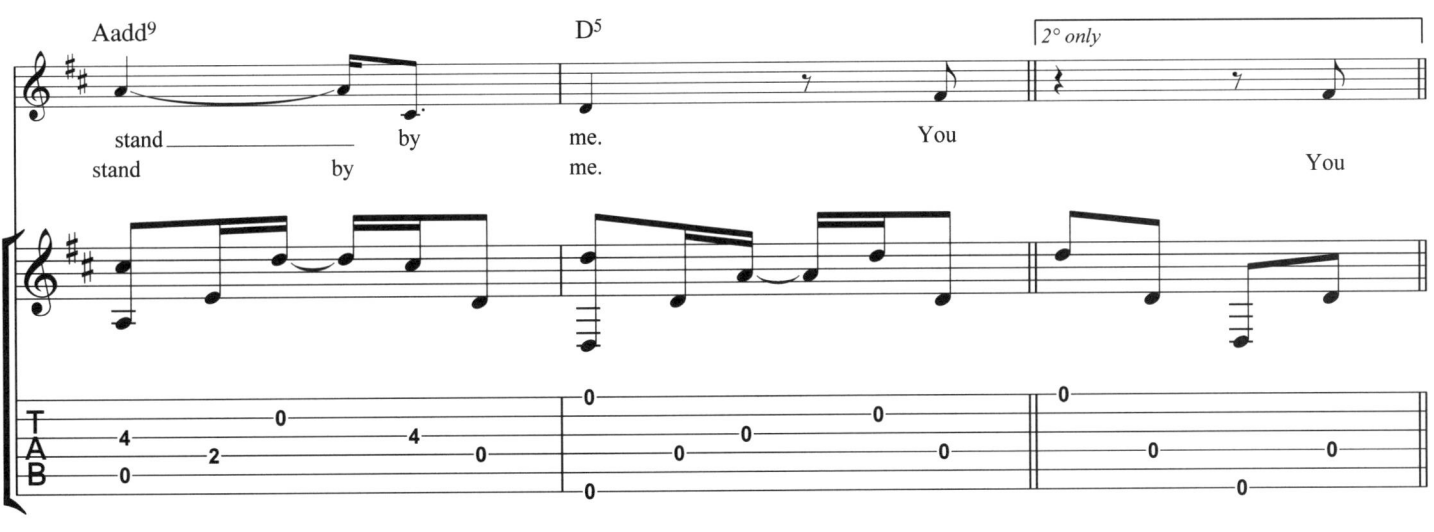

stand _____ by me.
stand by me. You

You

Chorus

take _____ my side a - gainst
take _____ my side a - gainst

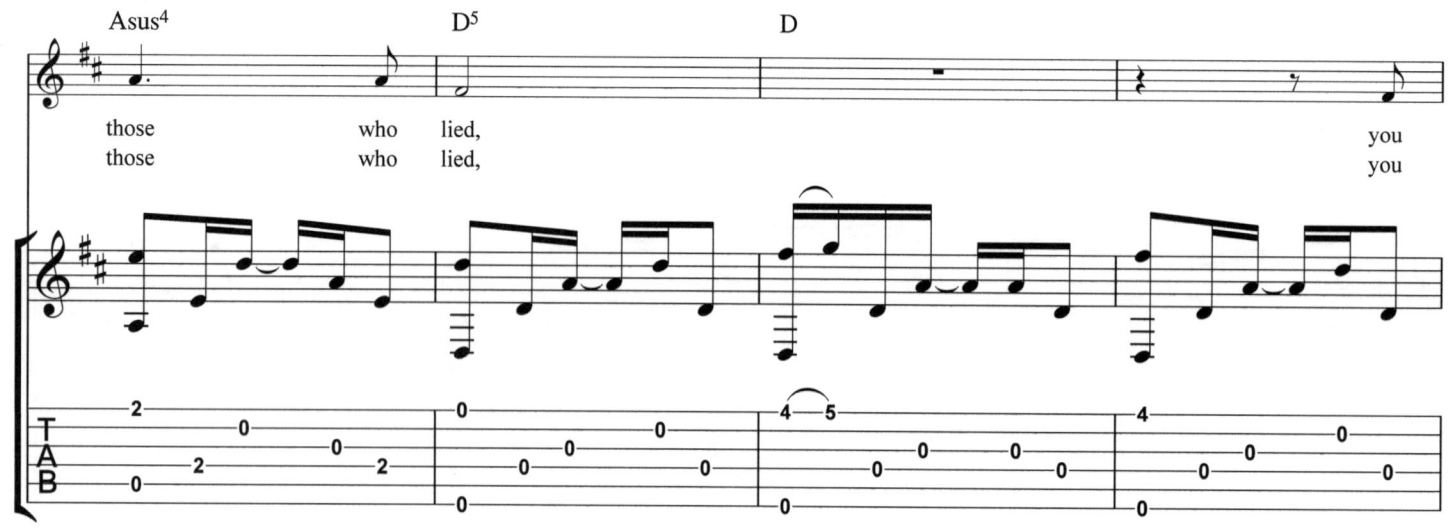

those   who   lied,   you
those   who   lied,   you

take _____ my   side,
take _____ my   side,

gim - me   back   my   pride. _____
gim - me   back   my   pride. _____

Bridge

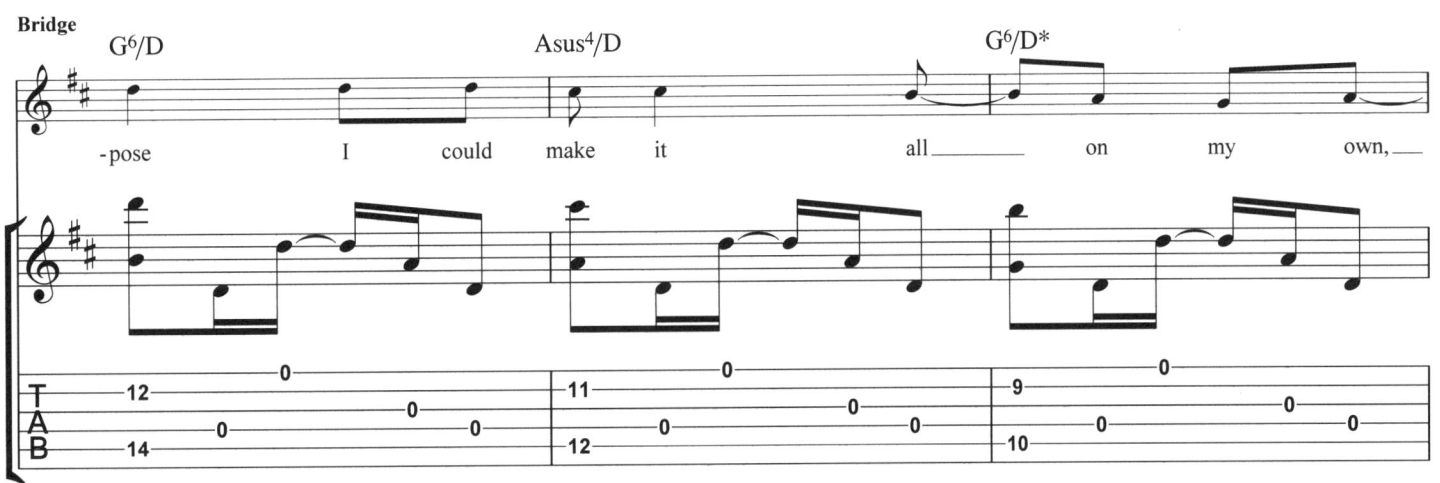

-pose I could make it all on my own,

I know I'd ar - rive all

skin and all bone. You are the strong -

67

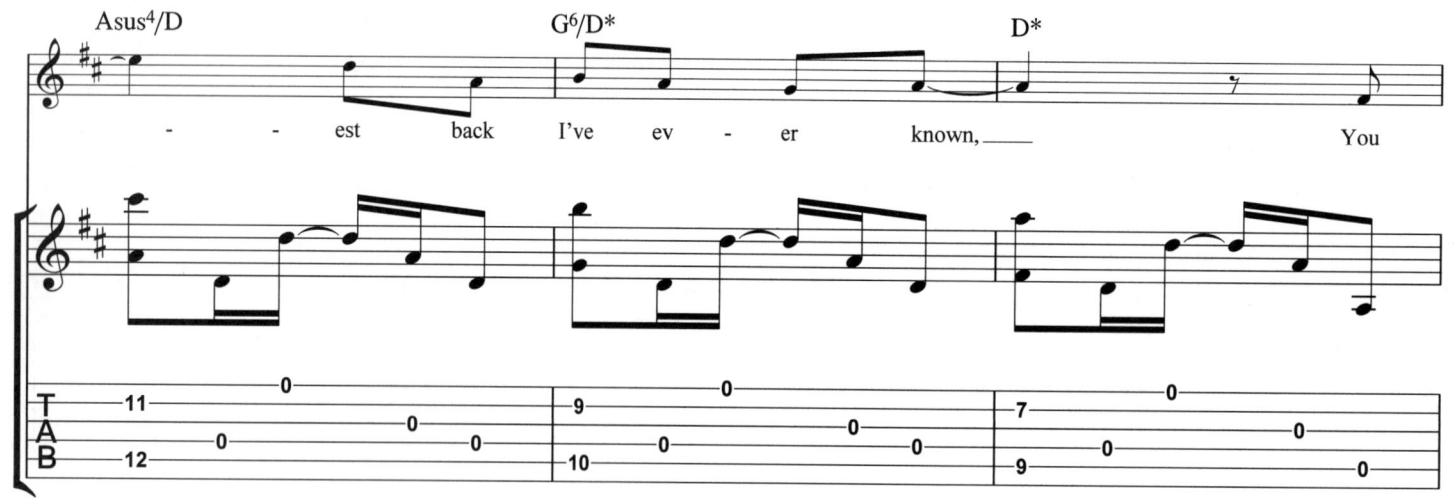

-est back I've ev - er known,_____ You

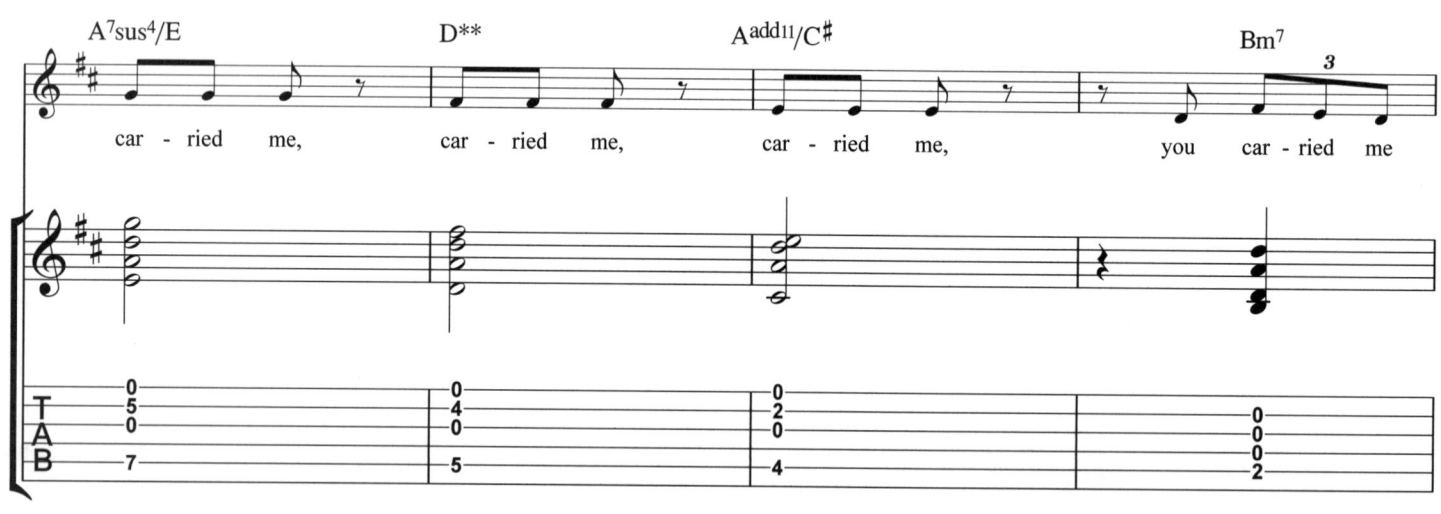

car - ried me, car - ried me, car - ried me, you car - ried me

home.

Outro

When I'm cry - ing, you stand by me,

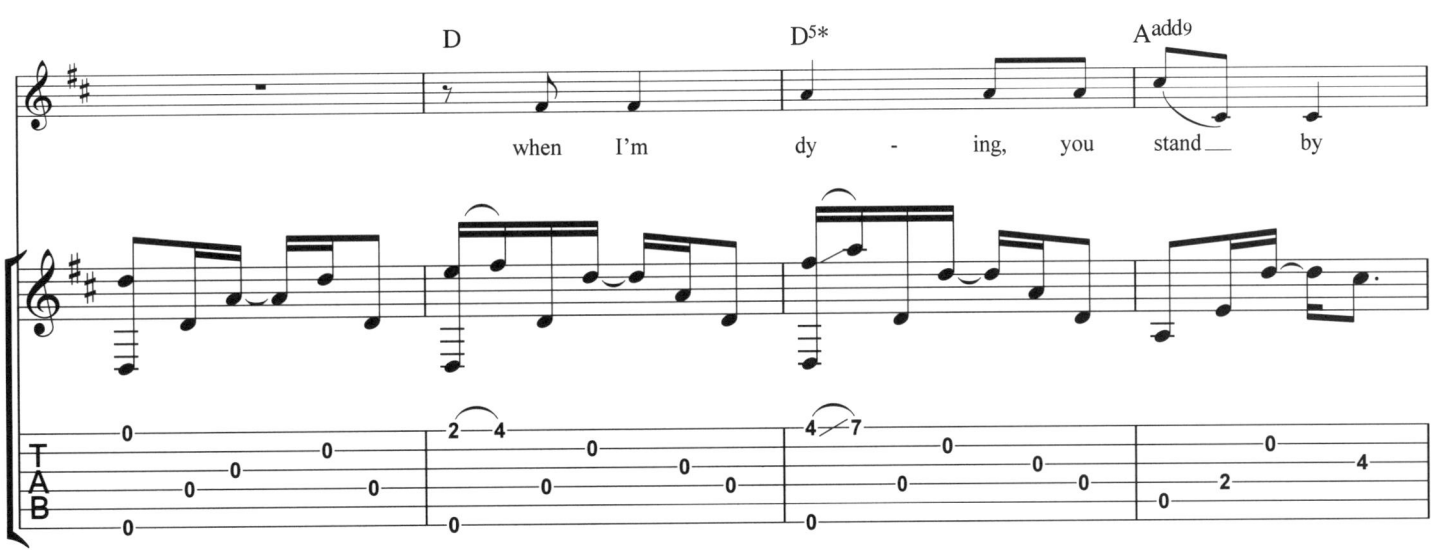

when I'm dy - ing, you stand by

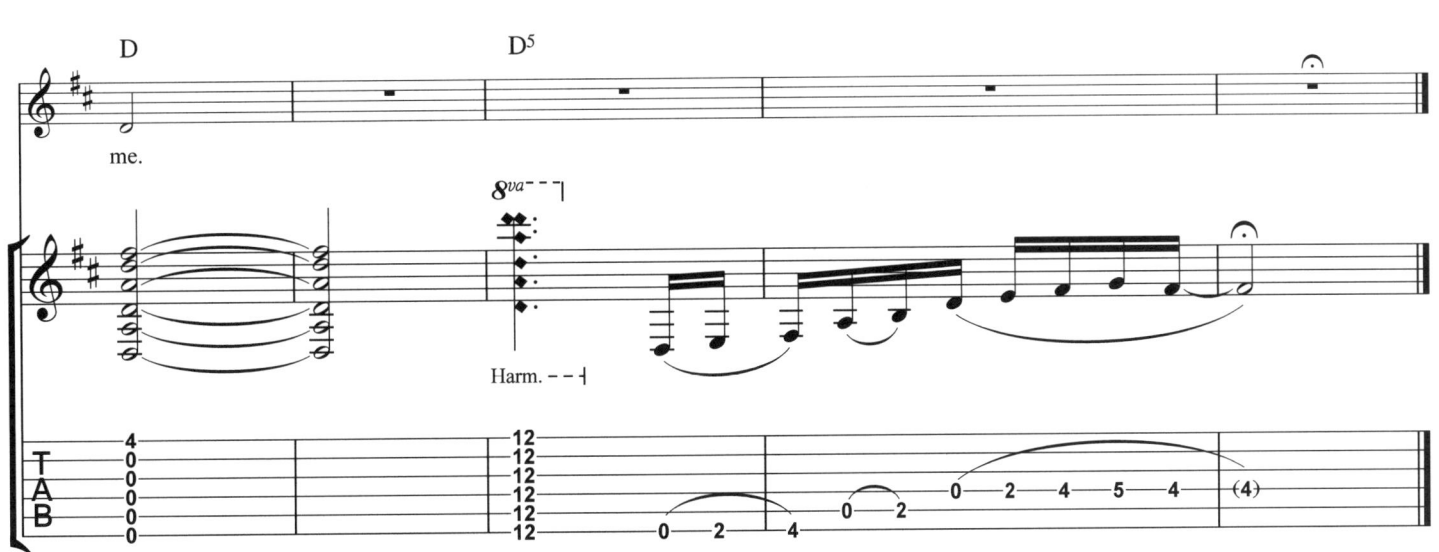

me.

WIRE&GLASS
A MINI-OPERA
SOUND ROUND

Words & Music by
Pete Townshend

© Copyright 2006 Eel Pie Publishing Limited.
BMG Music Publishing Limited.
All Rights Reserved. International Copyright Secured.

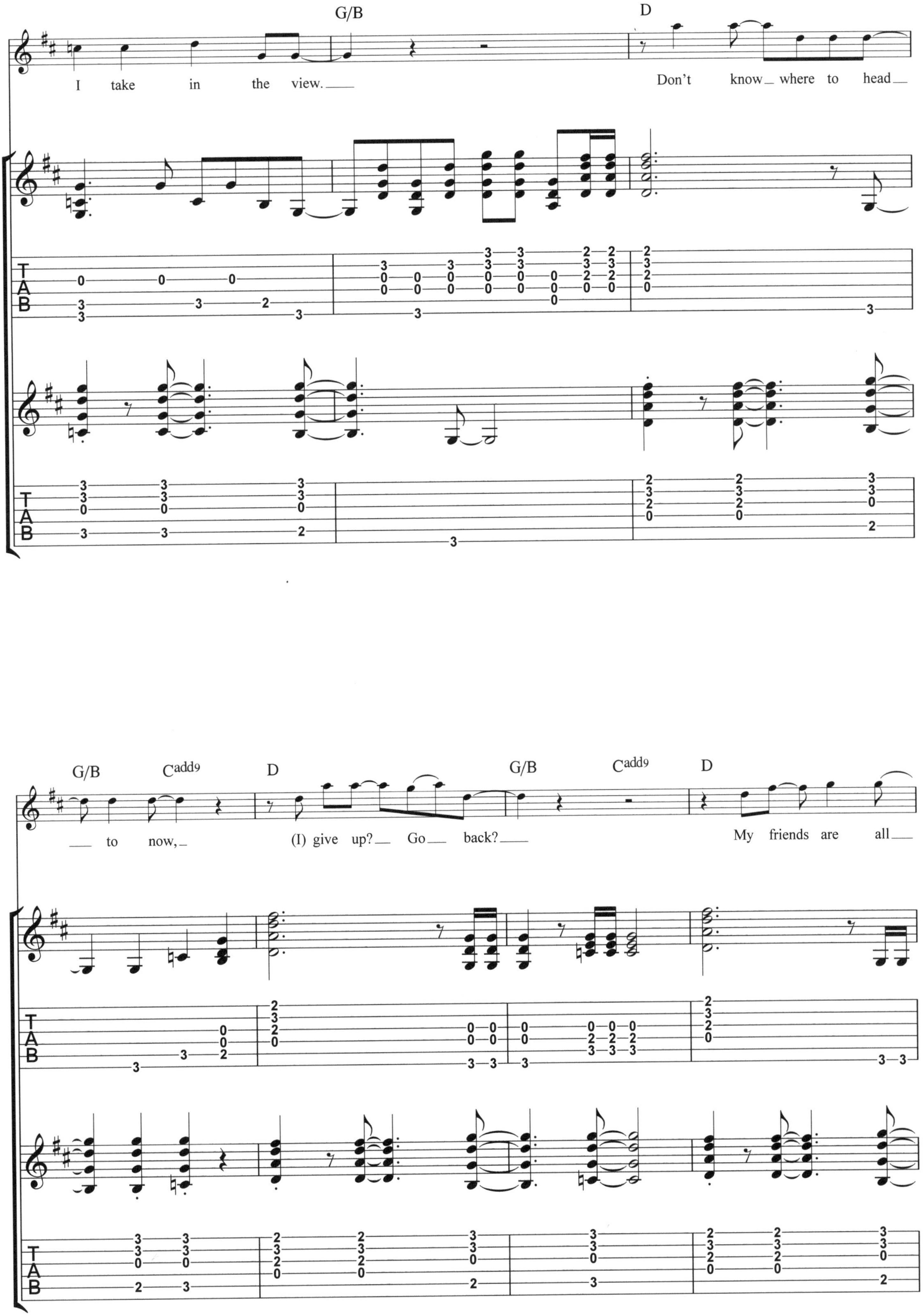

I take in the view.___ Don't know___ where to head___

___ to now,___ (I) give up?___ Go___ back?___ My friends are all___

G/B   Cadd9   D   G/B   Cadd9   D

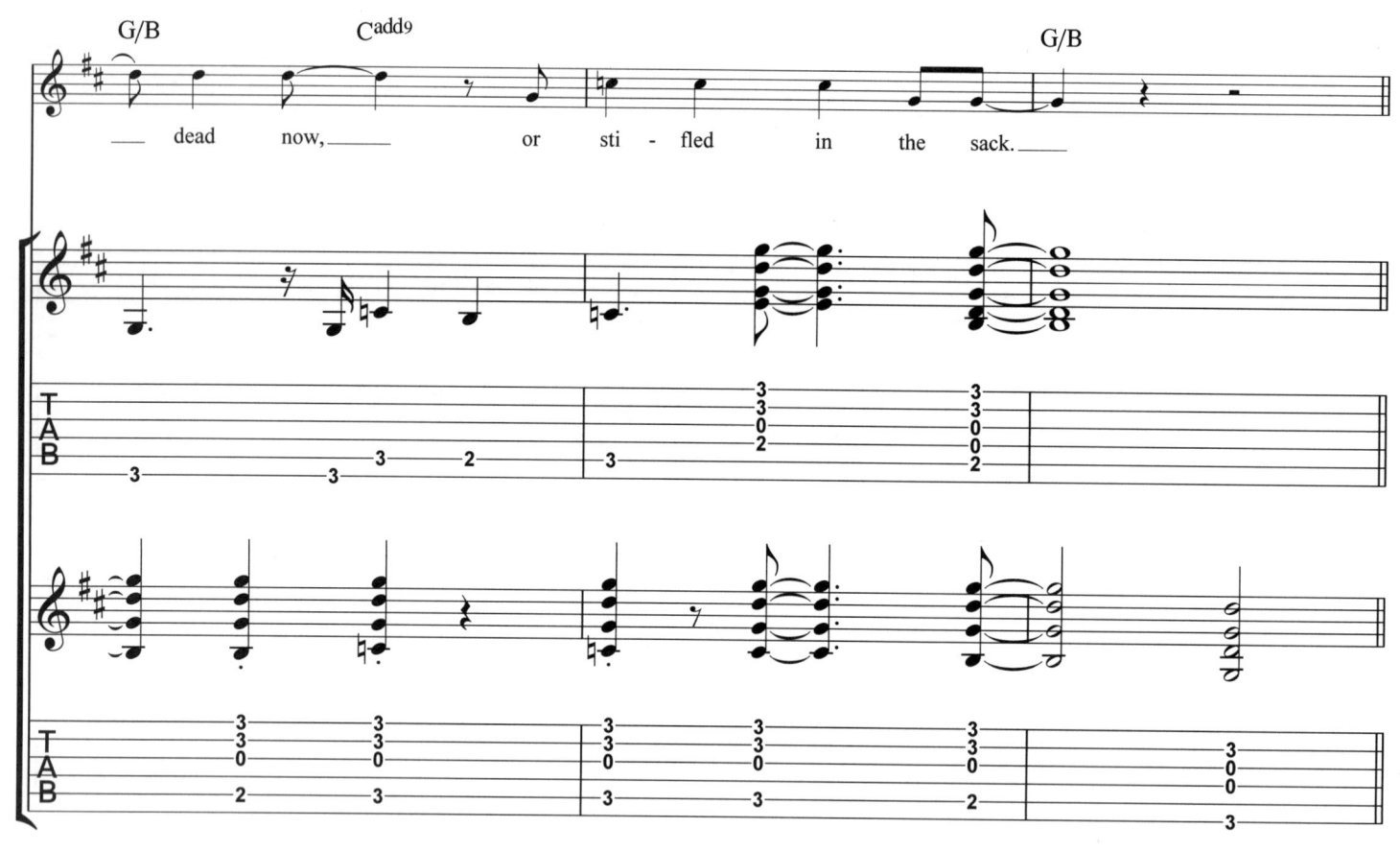

G/B
Cadd9
G/B
dead now, or sti - fled in the sack.

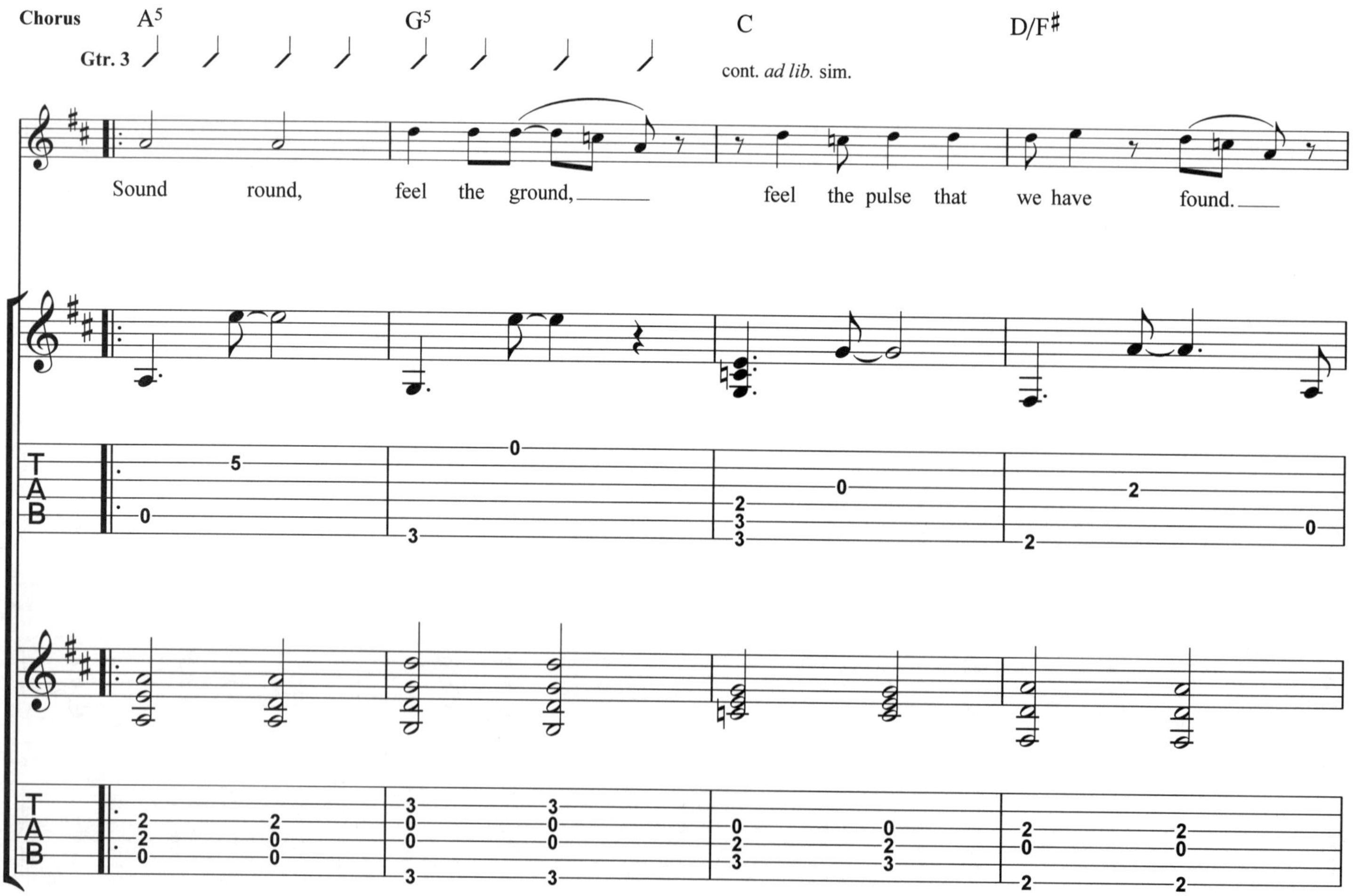
Chorus
A5
G5
C
D/F♯
Gtr. 3
cont. ad lib. sim.
Sound round, feel the ground, feel the pulse that we have found.

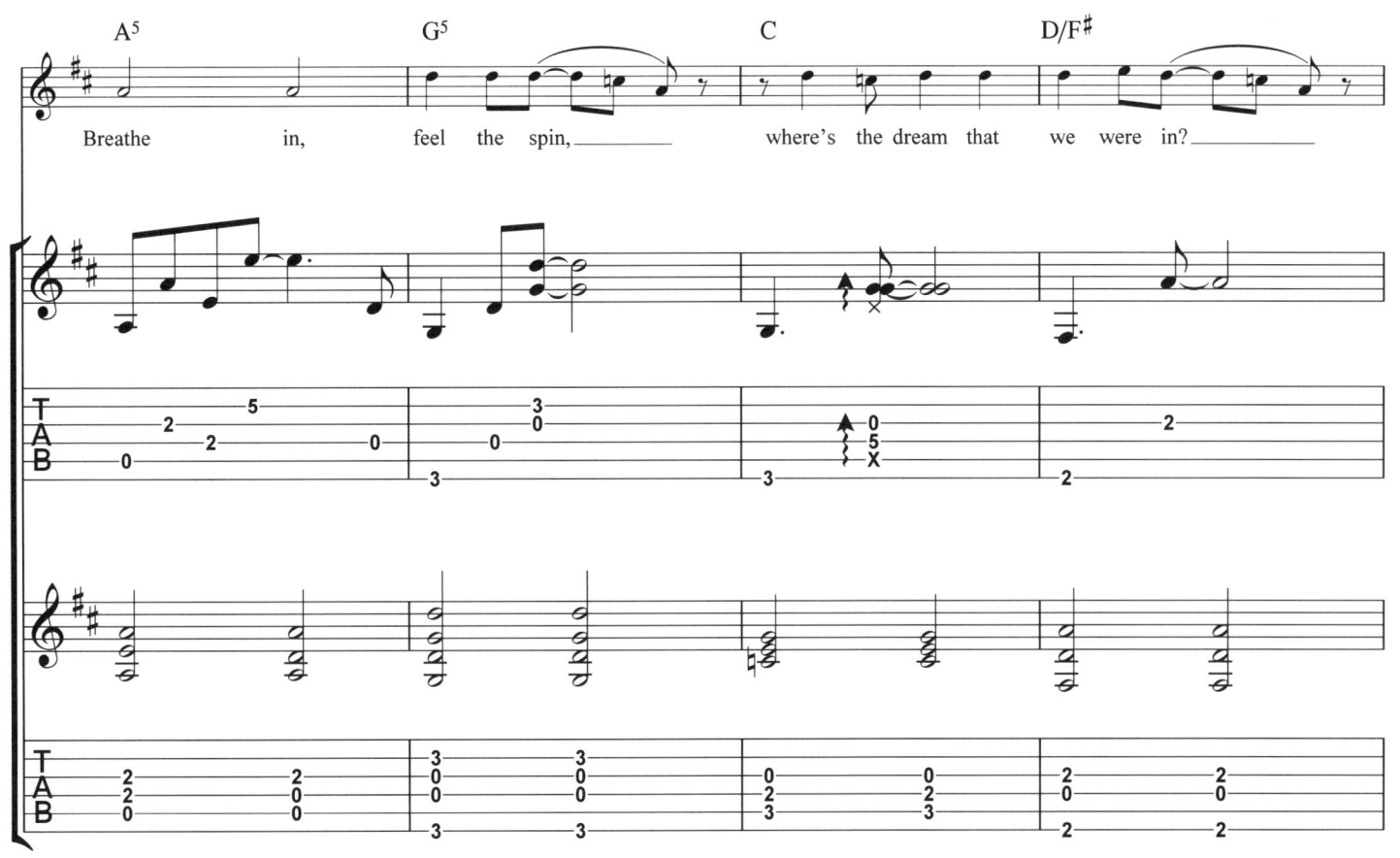

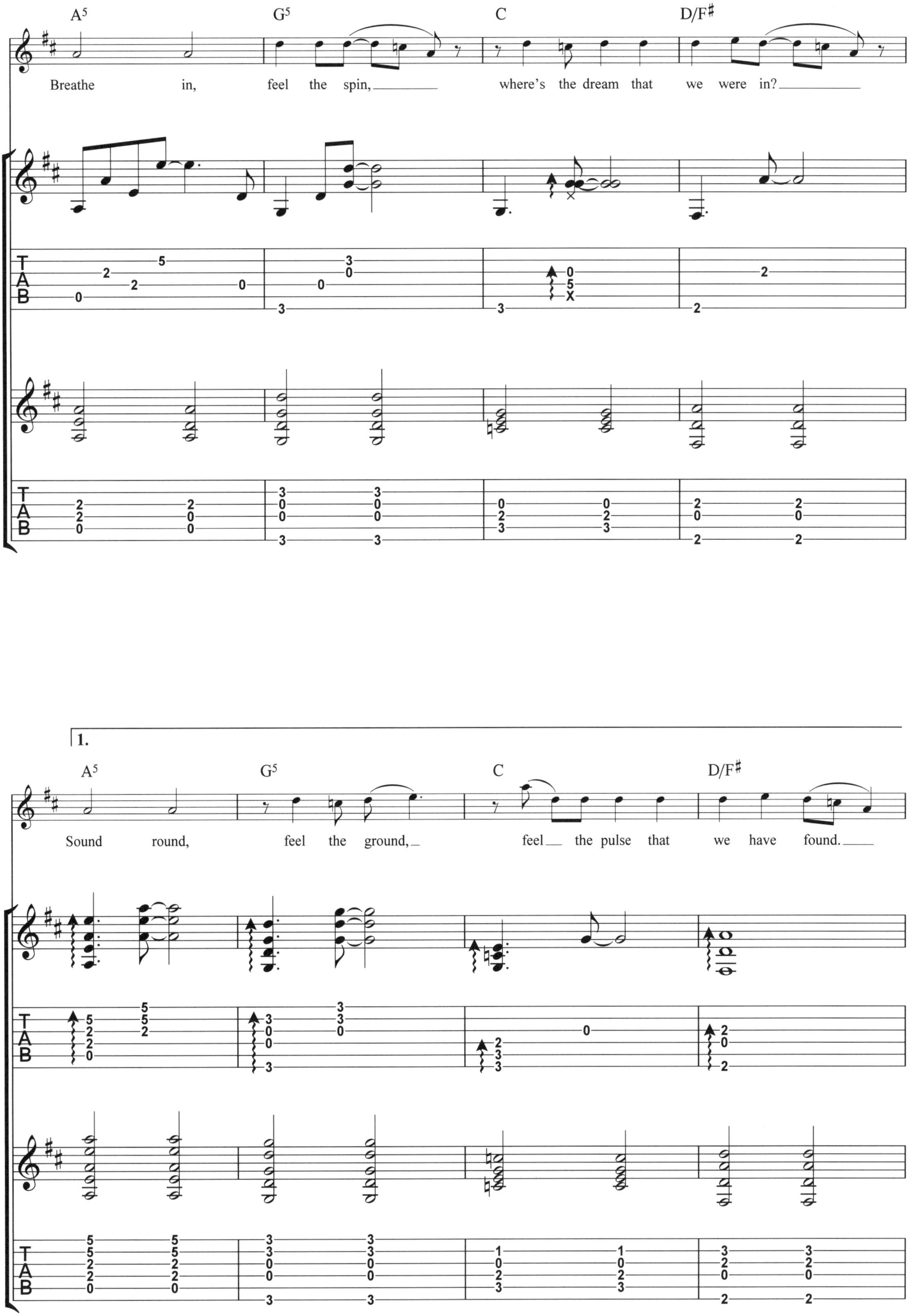
A5 G5 C D/F♯
Breathe in, feel the spin, where's the dream that we were in?
1.
A5 G5 C D/F♯
Sound round, feel the ground, feel the pulse that we have found.

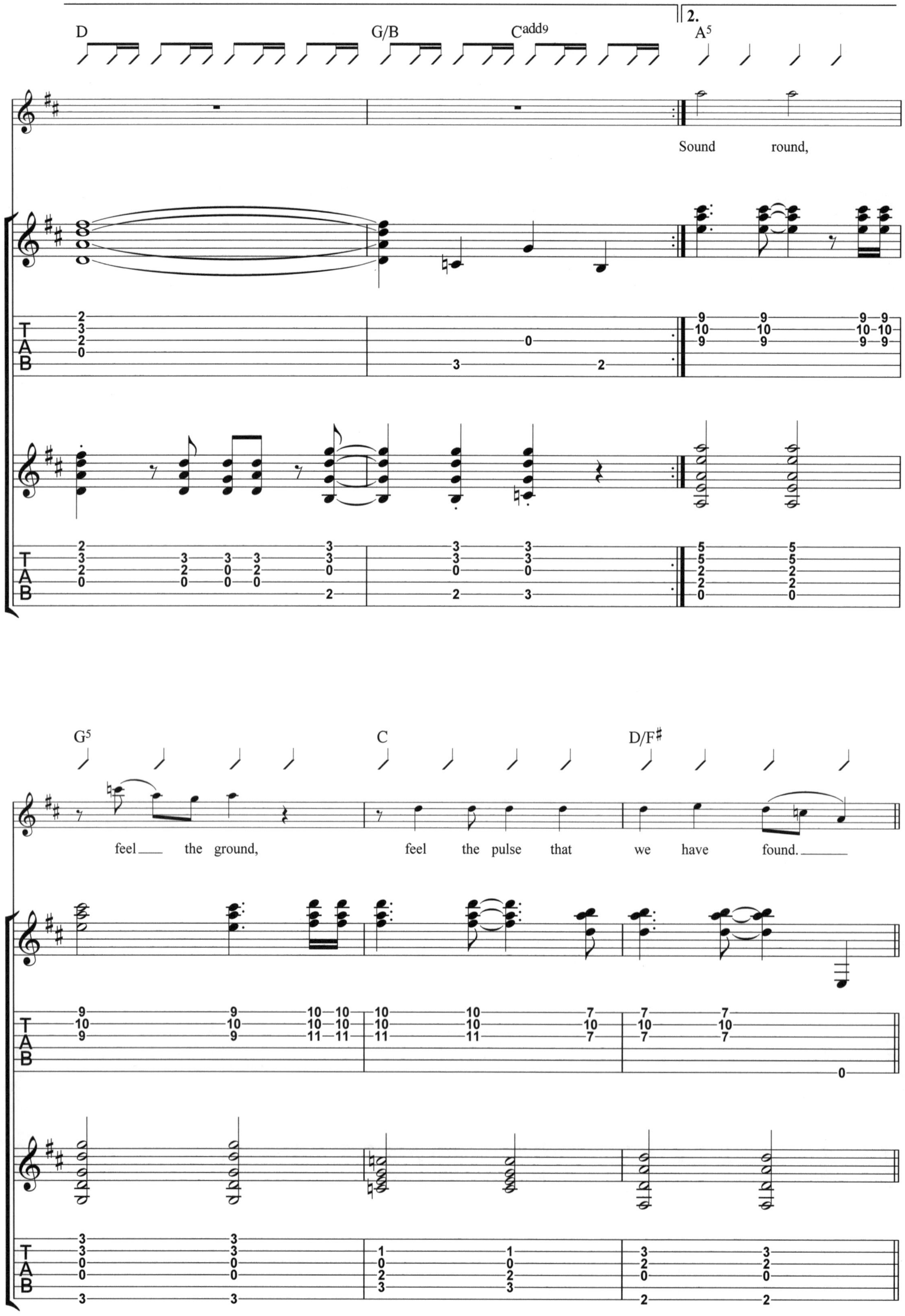
2.
D
G/B
Cadd9
A5
Sound round,
G5
C
D/F#
feel the ground, feel the pulse that we have found.

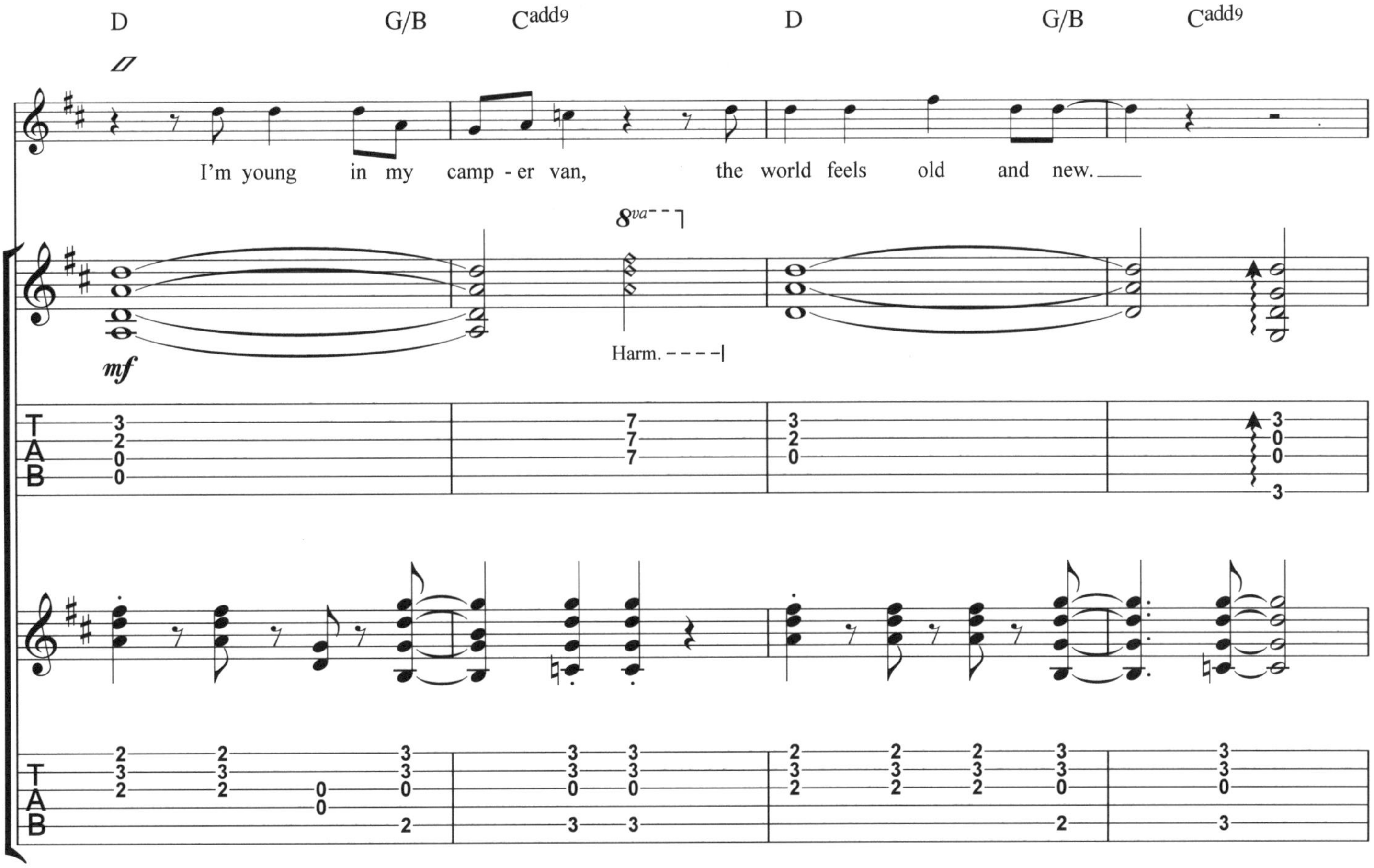

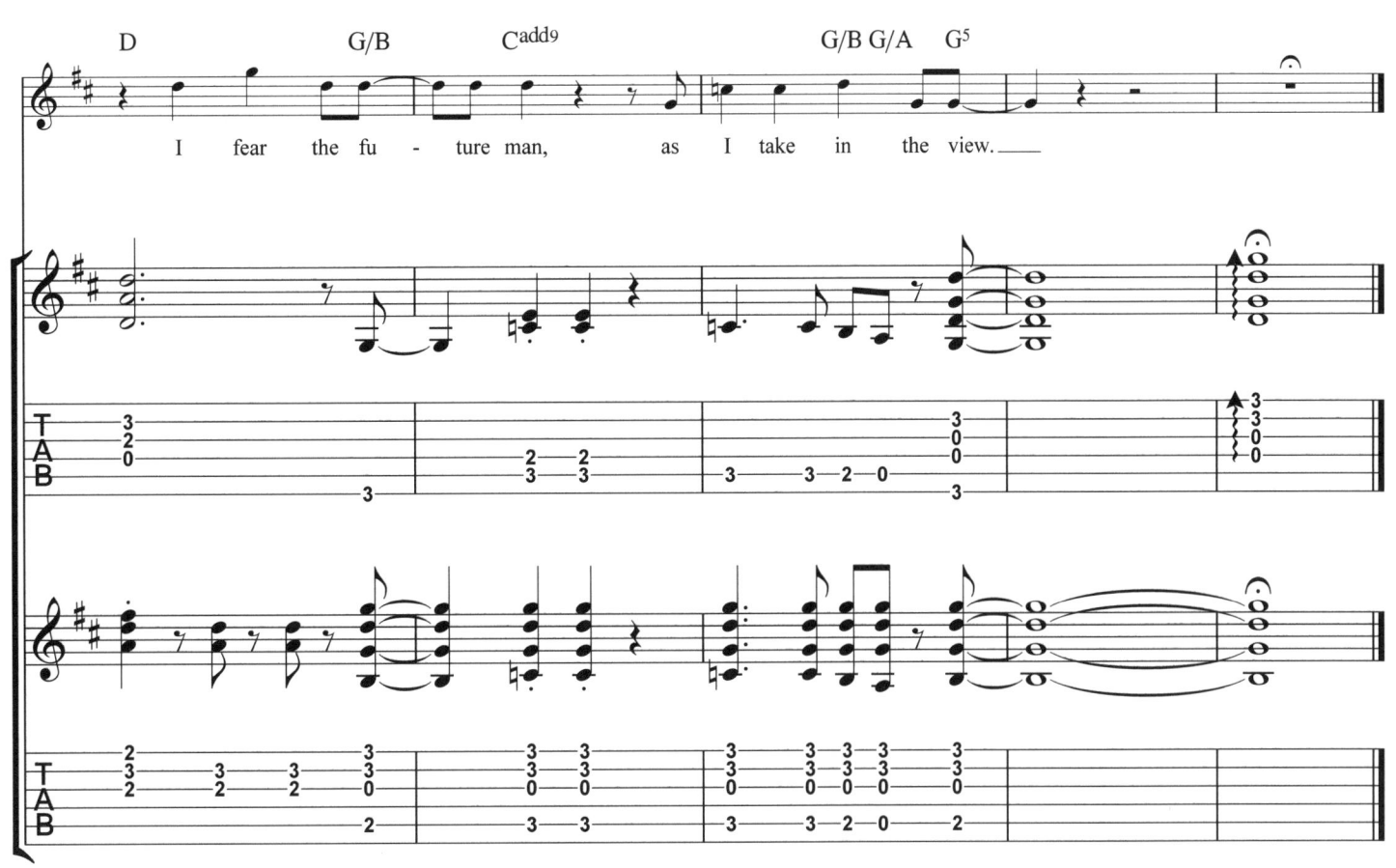

D G/B Cadd9 D G/B Cadd9
I'm young in my camp - er van, the world feels old and new.
8va
mf
Harm.
TAB
TAB

D G/B Cadd9 G/B G/A G5
I fear the fu - ture man, as I take in the view.
TAB
TAB

PICK UP THE PEACE

Words & Music by
Pete Townshend

© Copyright 2006 Eel Pie Publishing Limited.
BMG Music Publishing Limited.
All Rights Reserved. International Copyright Secured.

UNHOLY TRINITY

Words & Music by
Pete Townshend

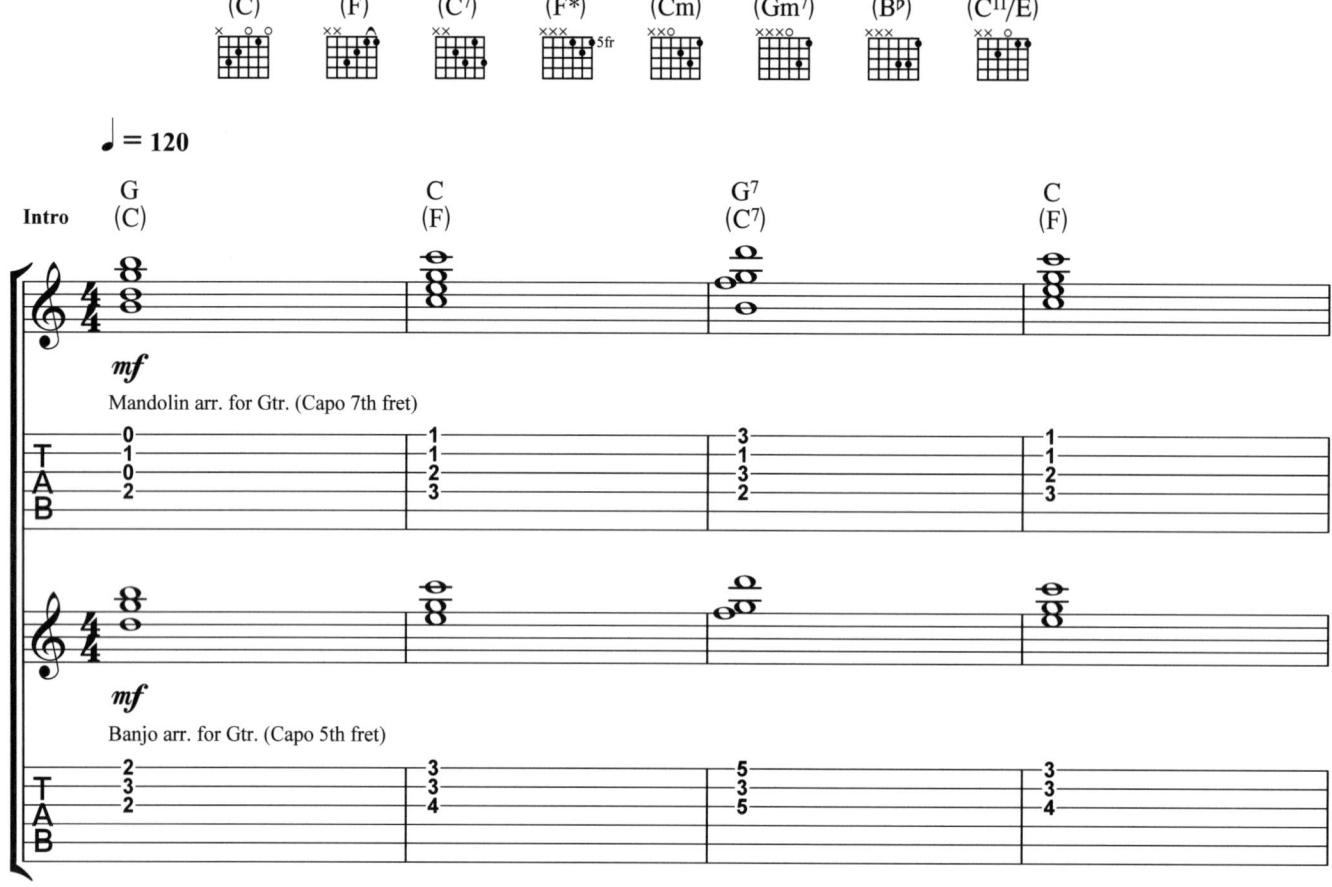

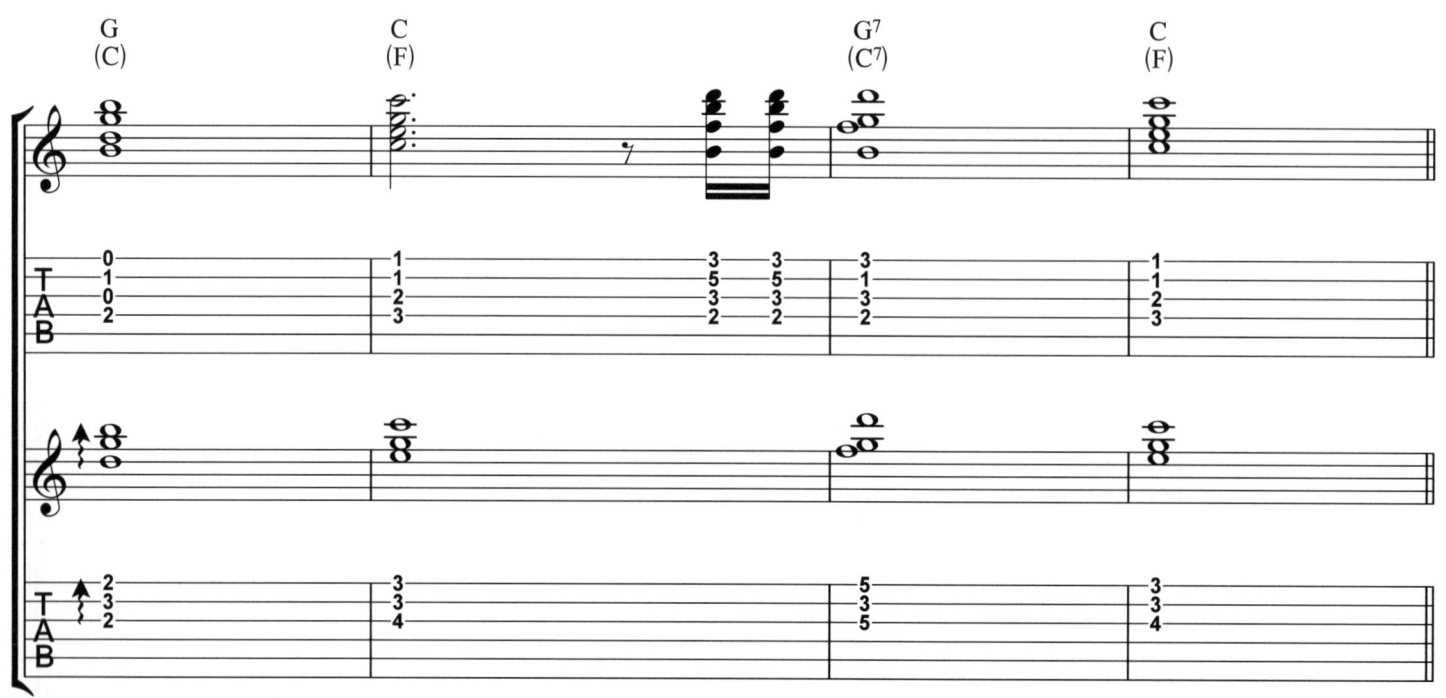

© Copyright 2006 Eel Pie Publishing Limited.
BMG Music Publishing Limited.
All Rights Reserved. International Copyright Secured.

Verse
G
(C)
C
(F)
Three kids from the neigh - bour - hood, three dif - fer - ent
We're not the same, but we can
(𝄋) We watch the tide ebb a - way, car - ry i - deas to the
T
A
B
G
(C)
lives. Three dif - fer - ent ways to be,
talk. We kiss and link our arms,
sea. We hear the mus - ic, re -

three i-den-ti-cal smiles.
we take a walk.
-mem-ber_____ be-ing free._____

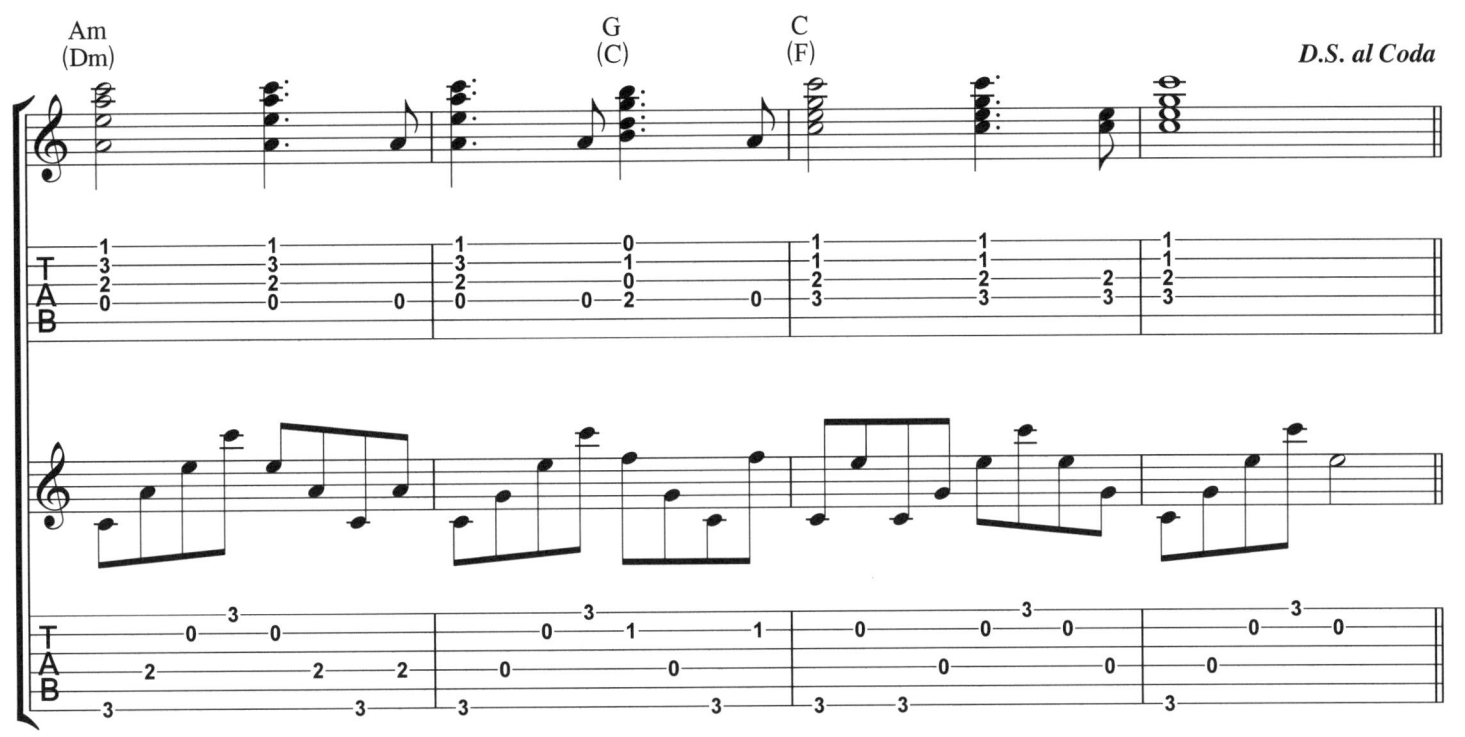

⊕ Coda

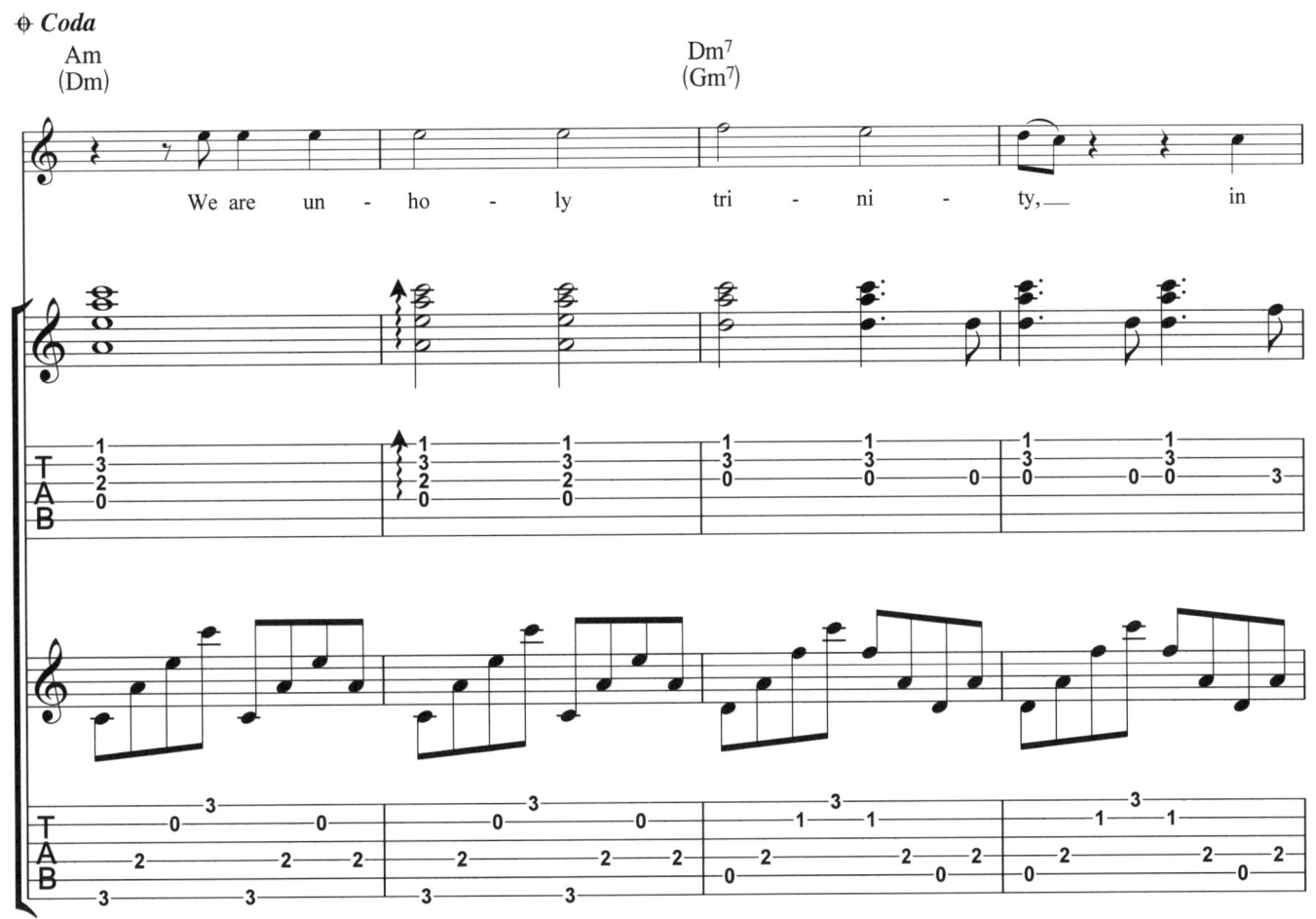

We are un - ho - ly tri - ni - ty, _____ in

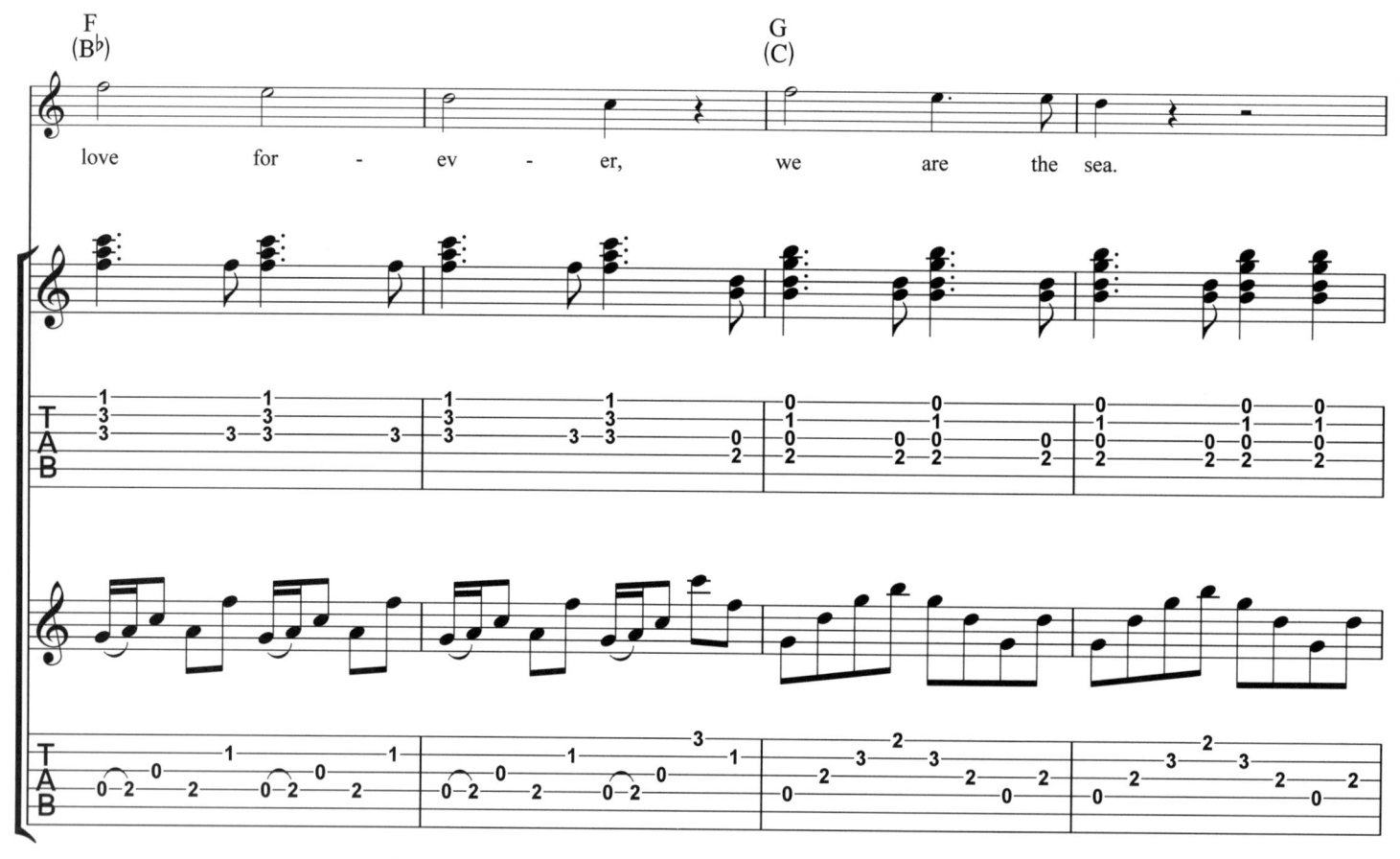

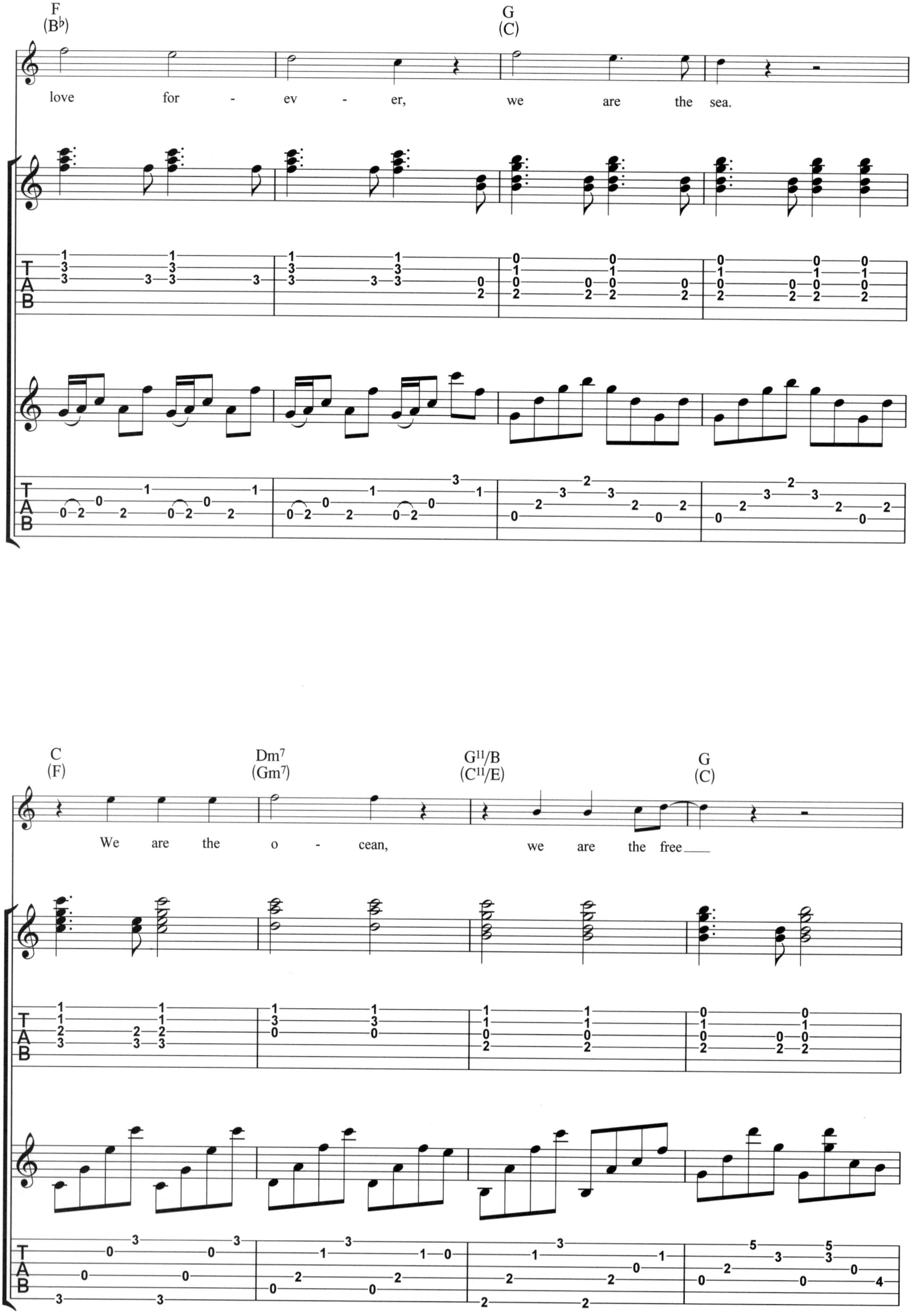
F
(B♭)
G
(C)
love for - ev - er, we are the sea.
T
A
B
T
A
B
C
(F)
Dm7
(Gm7)
G11/B
(C11/E)
G
(C)
We are the o - cean, we are the free
T
A
B
T
A
B

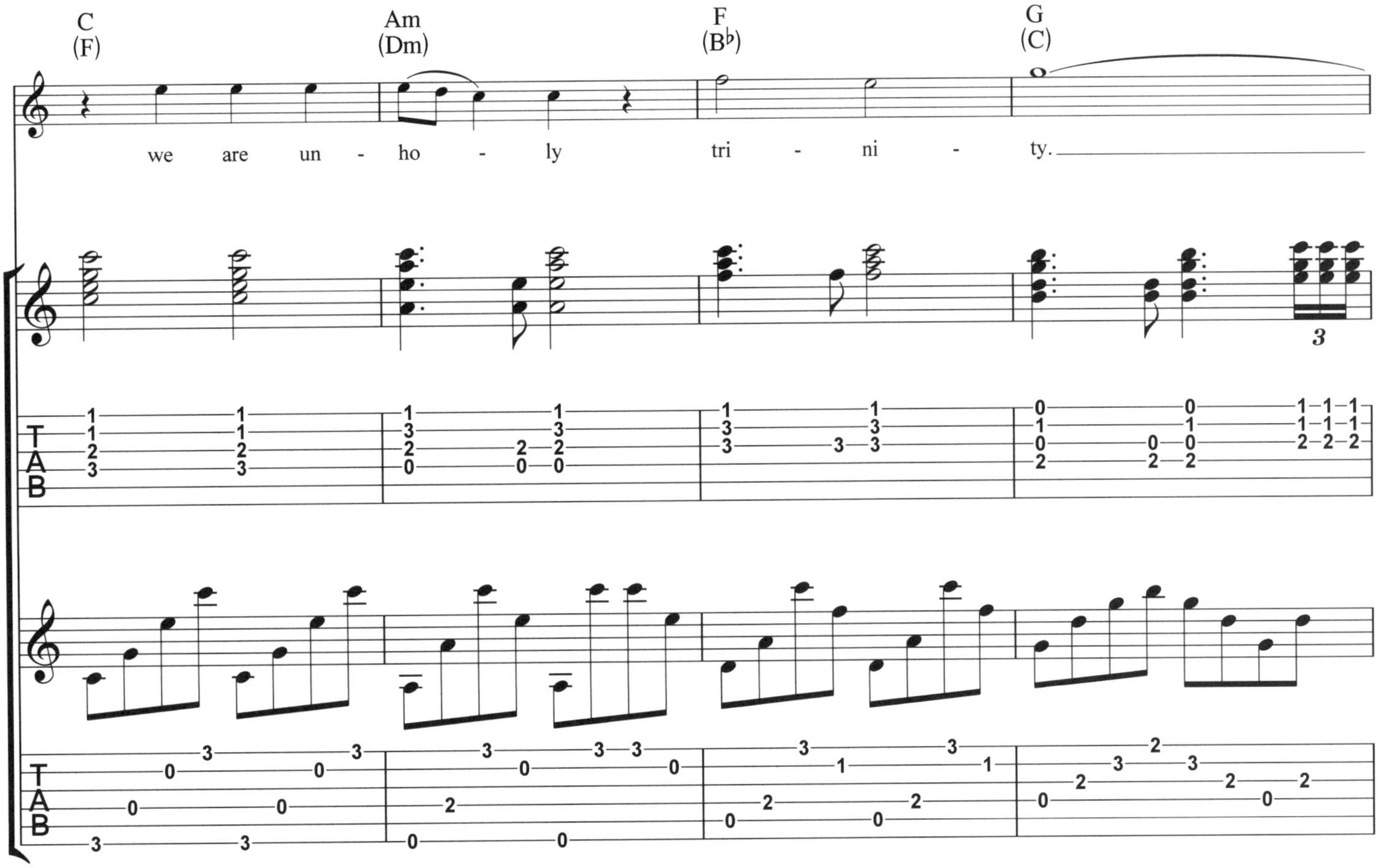
C
(F)
Am
(Dm)
F
(B♭)
G
(C)
we are un - ho - ly tri - ni - ty.
T
A
B
T
A
B

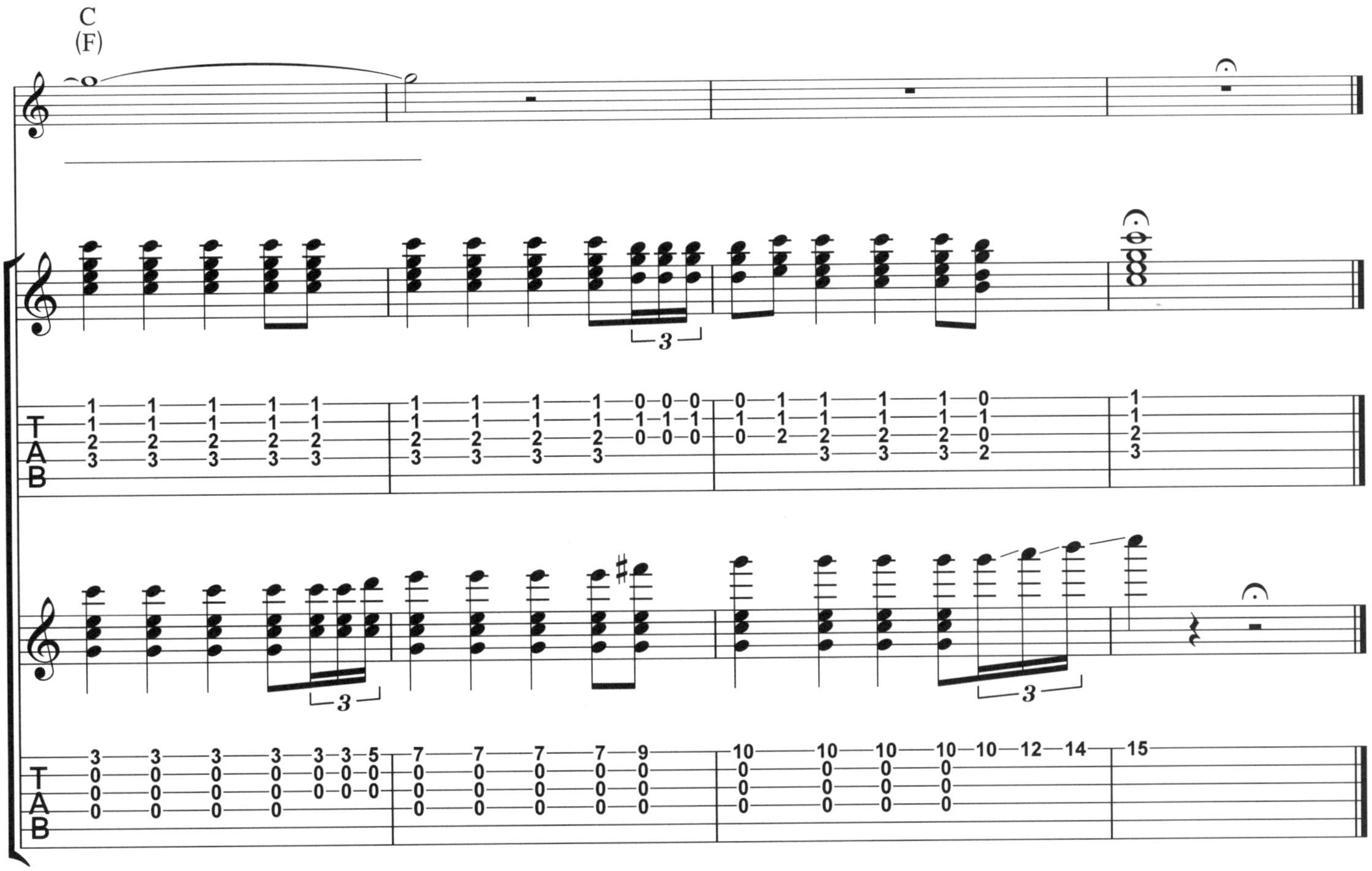
C
(F)
T
A
B
T
A
B

TRILBY'S PIANO

Words & Music by
Pete Townshend

© Copyright 2006 Eel Pie Publishing Limited.
BMG Music Publishing Limited.
All Rights Reserved. International Copyright Secured.

find me such bliss. If you were gone you'd still be here.

Only one Hy - mie.

Why can't they see that life ex - cites me, this boy ig -

88

ENDLESS WIRE

Words & Music by
Pete Townshend

© Copyright 2006 Eel Pie Publishing Limited.
BMG Music Tpublishing Limited.
All Rights Reserved. International Copyright Secured.

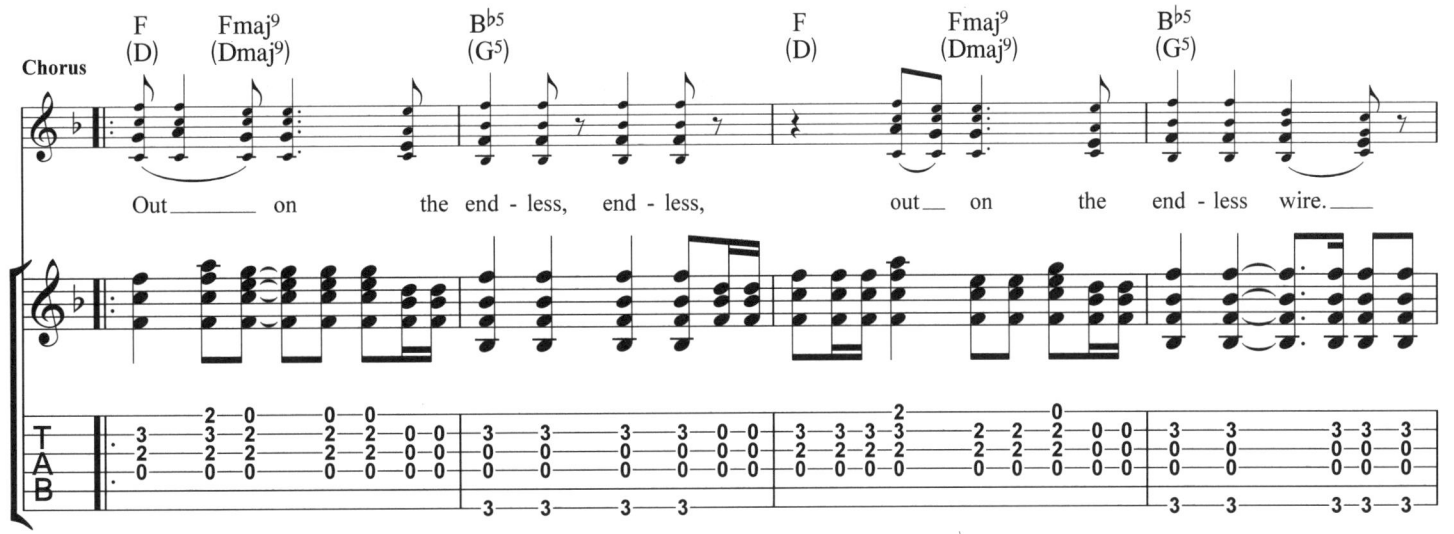

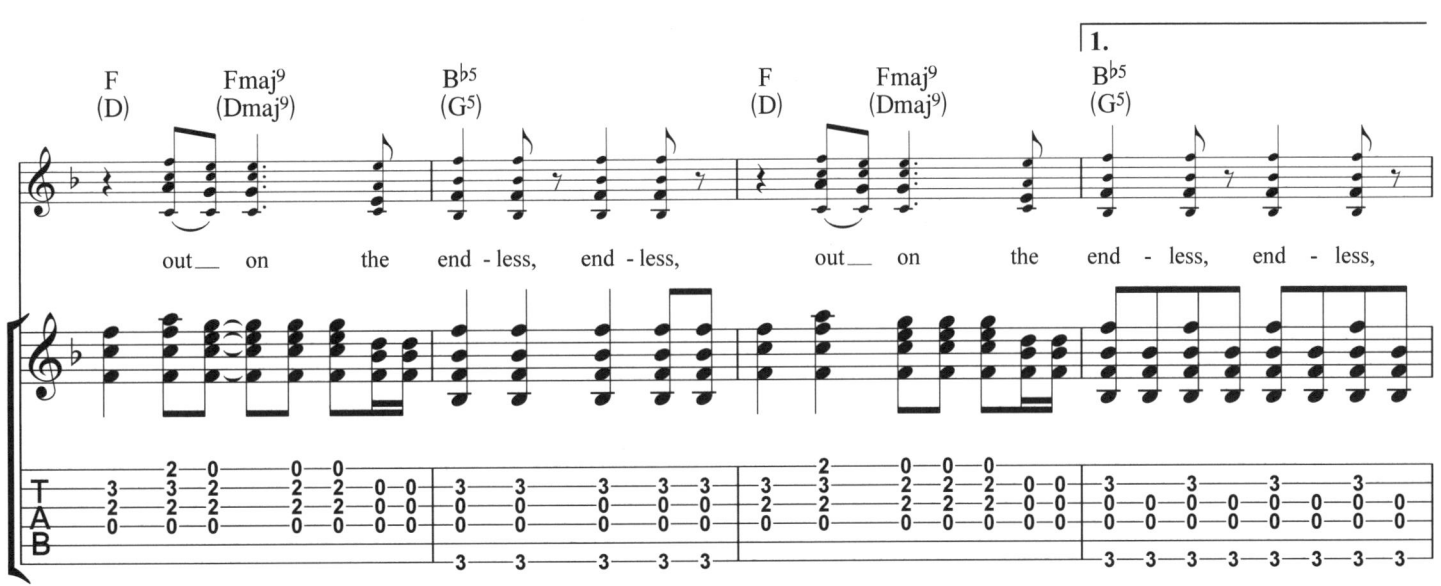

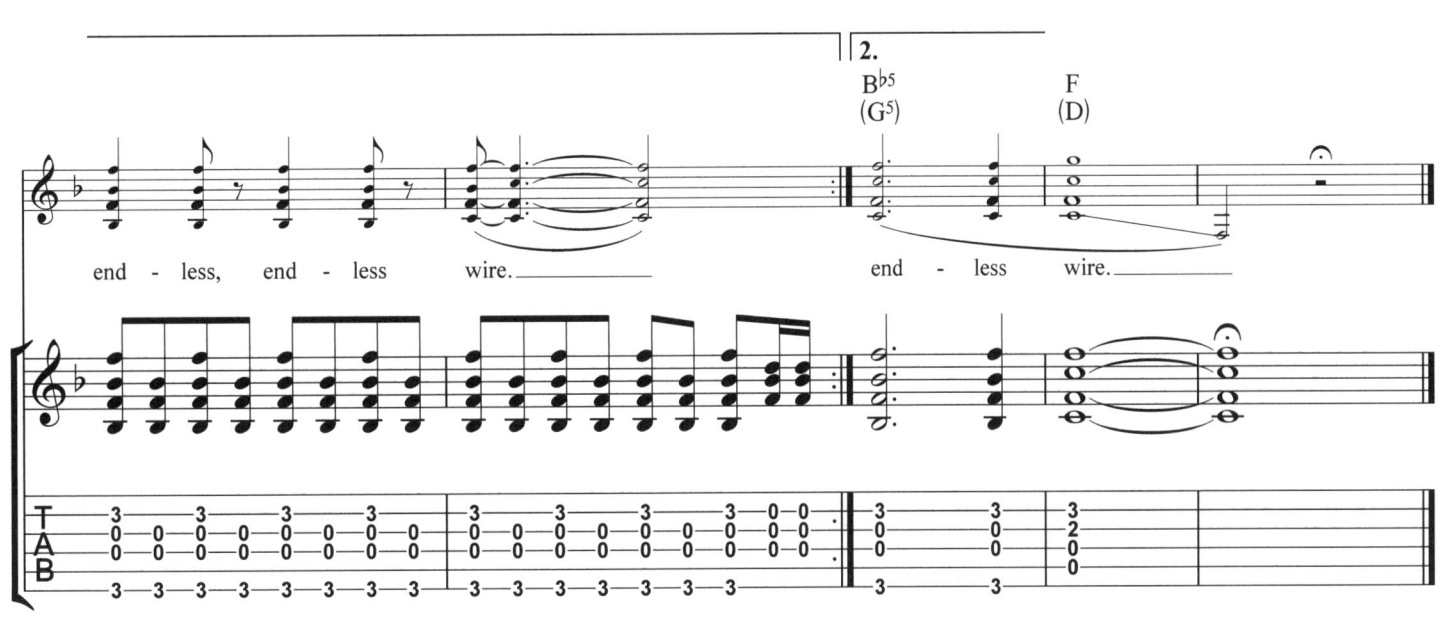

91

FRAGMENTS OF FRAGMENTS

Words & Music by
Pete Townshend & Lawrence Ball

No guitar on this song.
Chord symbols represent suggested keyboard harmony.

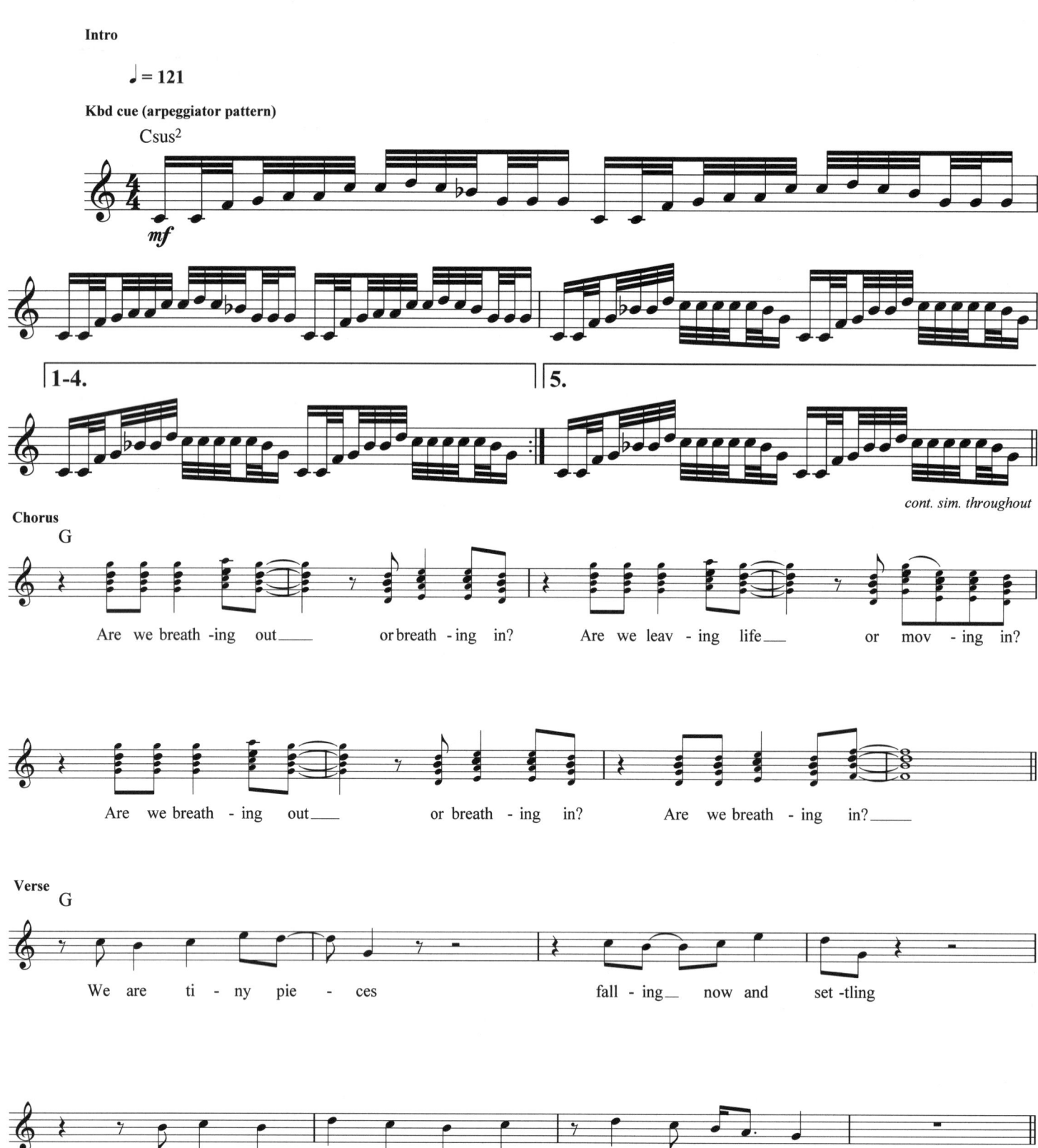

© Copyright 2006 Eel Pie Publishing Limited/Copyright Control.
BMG Music Publishing Limited (75%)/Copyright Control (25%).
All Rights Reserved. International Copyright Secured.

Snow - flakes fall - ing. Snow - flakes fall - ing. Snow - flakes fall - ing.
Snow - flakes fall - ing. Snow - flakes fall - ing. Snow - flakes fall - ing.

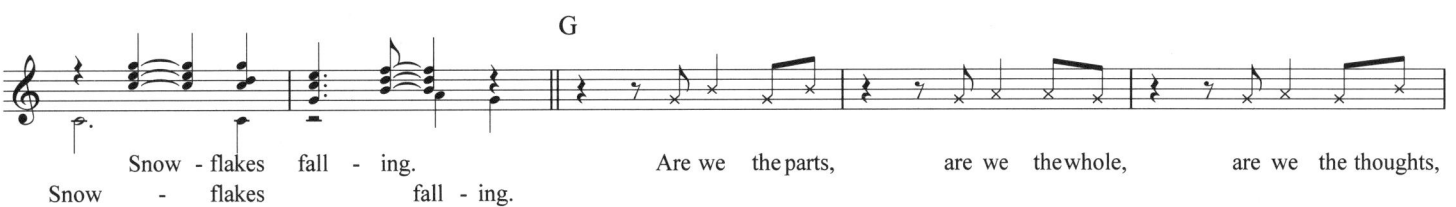

Snow - flakes fall - ing. Are we the parts, are we the whole, are we the thoughts,
Snow - flakes fall - ing.

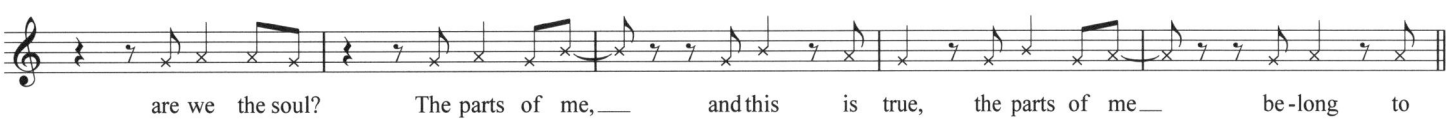

are we the soul? The parts of me, ___ and this is true, the parts of me ___ be - long to

you. Breath ing out, breath - ing ___ in. Breath - ing out, breath - ing ___ in. Breath - ing
Breath - ing out, breath - ing in. Breath - ing out, breath - ing in. Breath - ing

out, breath - ing ___ in. Breath - ing out, breath - ing ___ in. Breath - ing out, Be - long to
out, breath - ing in. Breath - ing out, breath - ing in. Breath - ing out,

you, and you, and you, and you, and you, and

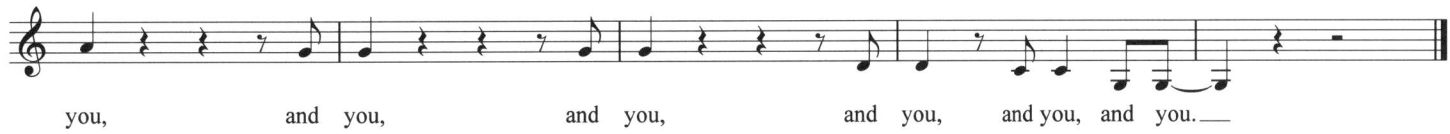

you, and you, and you, and you, and you, and you. ___

WE GOT A HIT

Words & Music by
Pete Townshend

© Copyright 2006 Eel Pie Publishing Limited.
BMG Music Publishing Limited.
All Rights Reserved. International Copyright Secured.

97

THEY MADE MY DREAM COME TRUE

Words & Music by
Pete Townshend

Gtr. 3 capo 3rd fret	
6 = D	3 = G
5 = A	2 = B
4 = D	1 = E

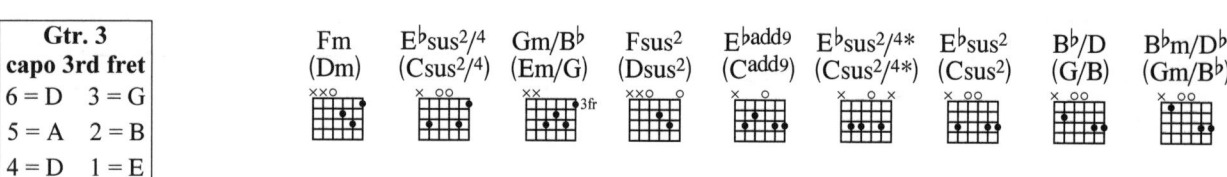

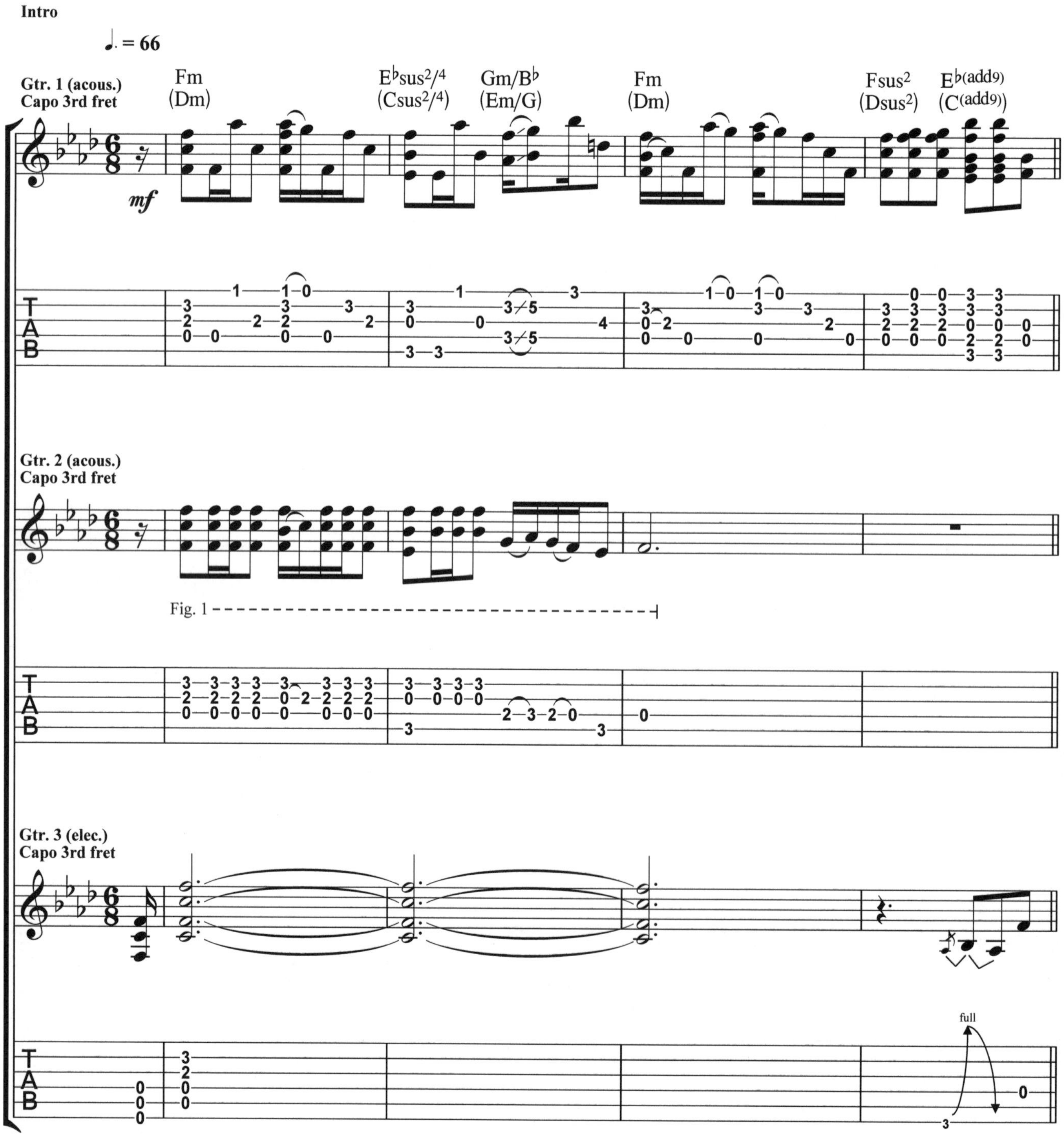

© Copyright 2006 Eel Pie Publishing Limited.
BMG Music Publishing Limited.
All Rights Reserved. International Copyright Secured.

MIRROR DOOR

Words & Music by
Pete Townshend

© Copyright 2006 Eel Pie Publishing Limited.
BMG Music Publishing Limited.
All Rights Reserved. International Copyright Secured.

Verse

If you don't hear me, how can I tell you? If you don't lis-ten, why
A thou-sand an-gels, a mil-lion child-ren, fire and fear in a

should I speak? If you're in-diff-'rent, how can I reach you?
su-i-cide eye. Gold-en stair-way to a Zep-pe-lin hea-ven,

Just 'cos you're an-gry don't as-sume I'm weak.
roll-ing thun-der un-der a New York sky.

...Fig. 1 ends

Gtr. 1 w/fig. 1

Howl-ing Wolf and old Link Wray, Dave Van Ronk and Dor-
Frank n' El-la, Ray 'What'd I Say', John-ny Cash and

-is Day. Bob-by Da-rin, Brown-ie Mc-Ghee,
John-nie Ray. A-ma-de-us and Lud-wig Van,

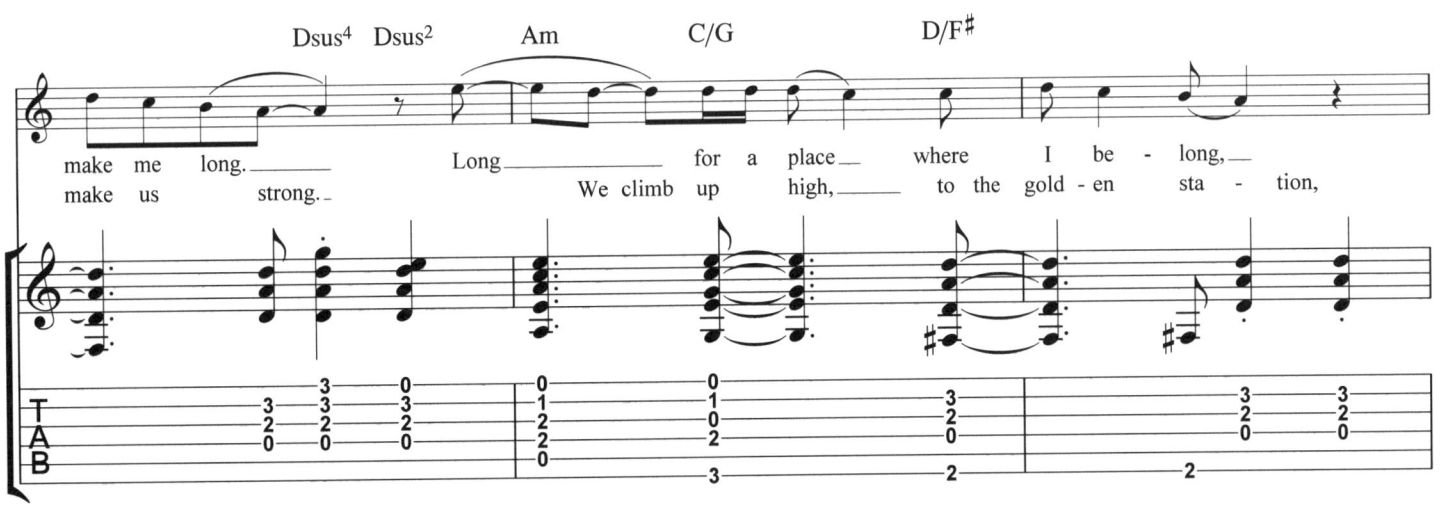

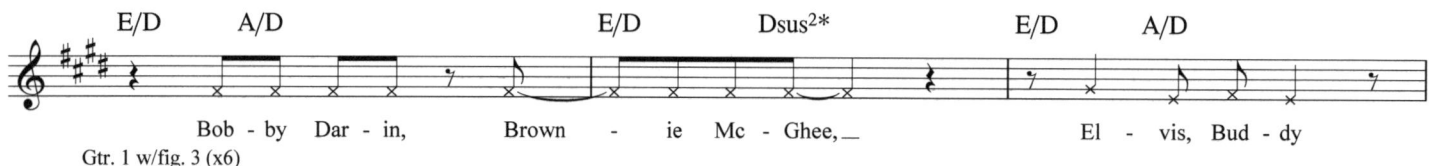

Bob - by Dar - in, Brown - ie Mc - Ghee, _____ El - vis, Bud - dy

Gtr. 1 w/fig. 3 (x6)

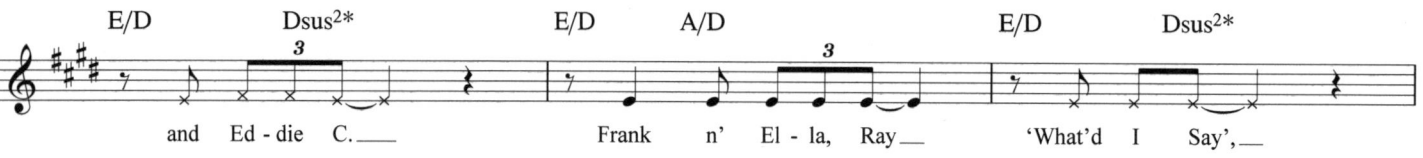

and Ed - die C. _____ Frank n' El - la, Ray _____ 'What'd I Say', _____

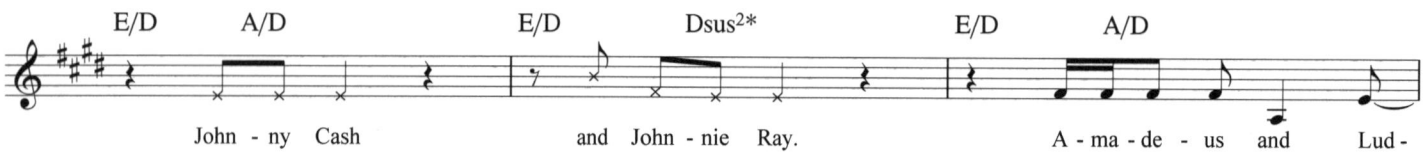

John - ny Cash and John - nie Ray. A - ma - de - us and Lud -

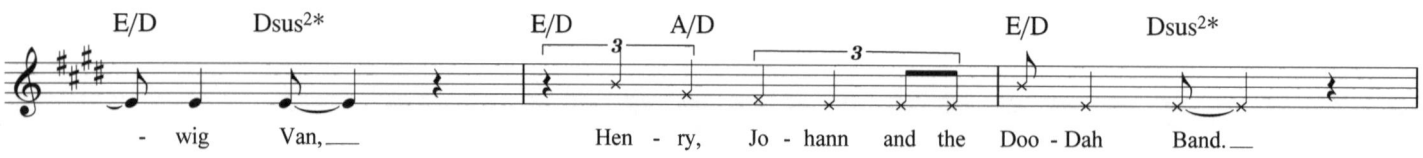

- wig Van, _____ Hen - ry, Jo - hann and the Doo - Dah Band. _____

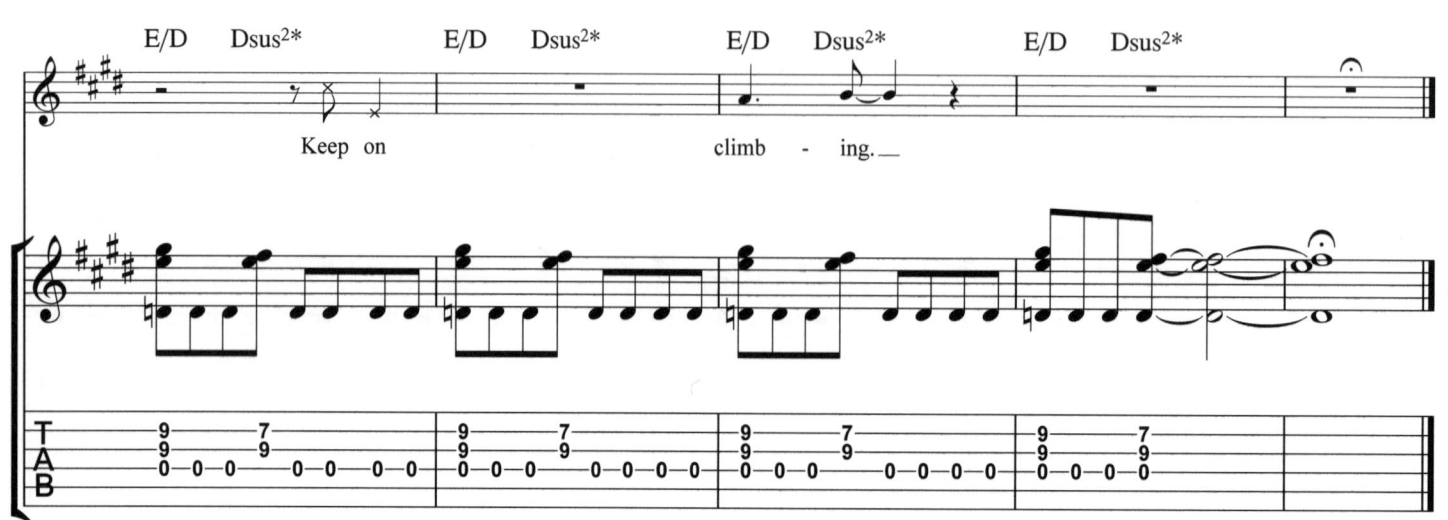

Keep on climb - ing. _____

TEA & THEATRE

Words & Music by
Pete Townshend

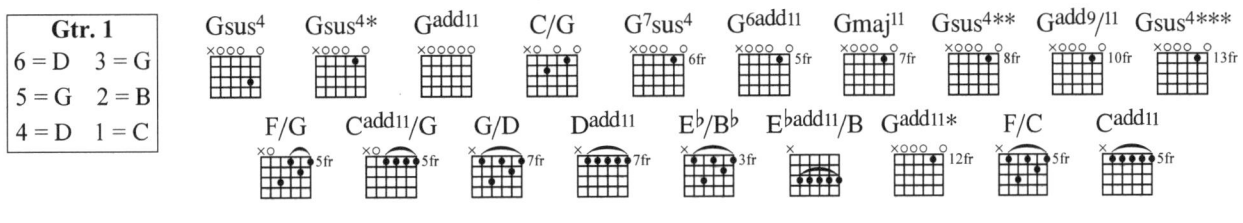

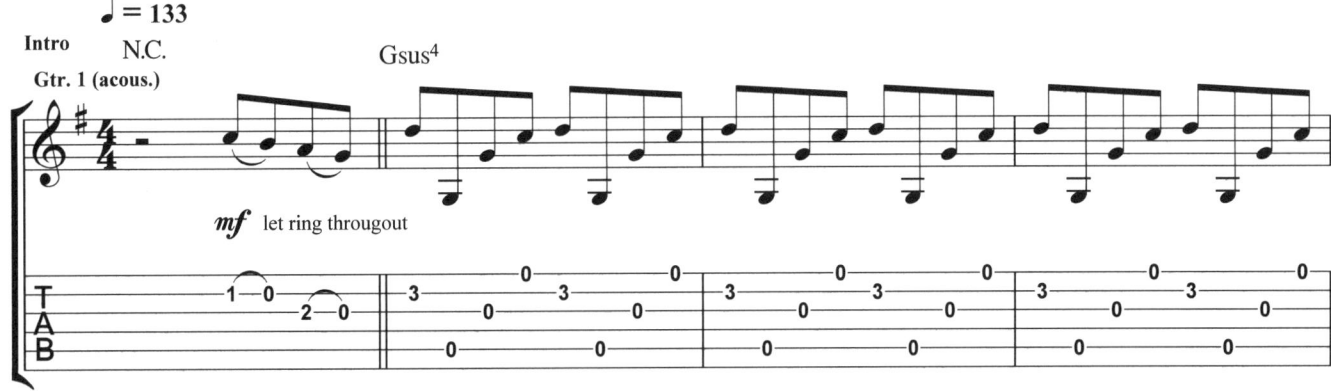

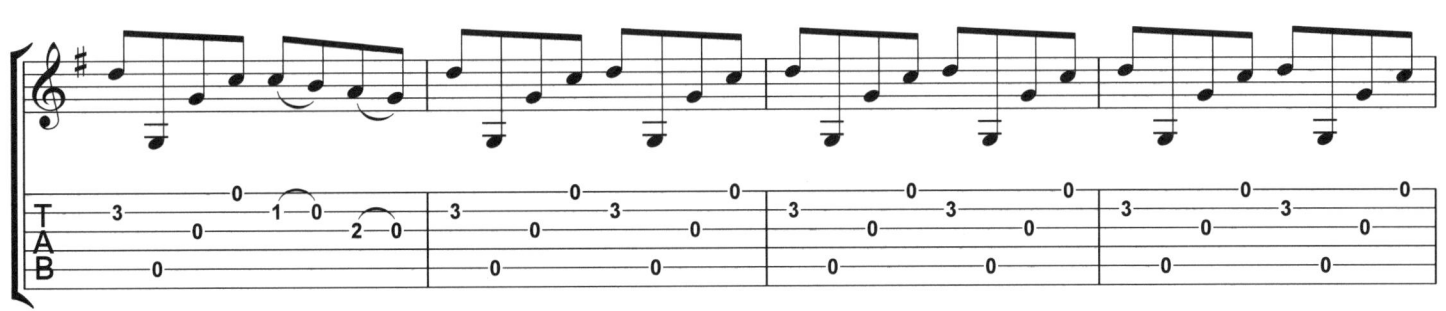

Will you have_ some tea,

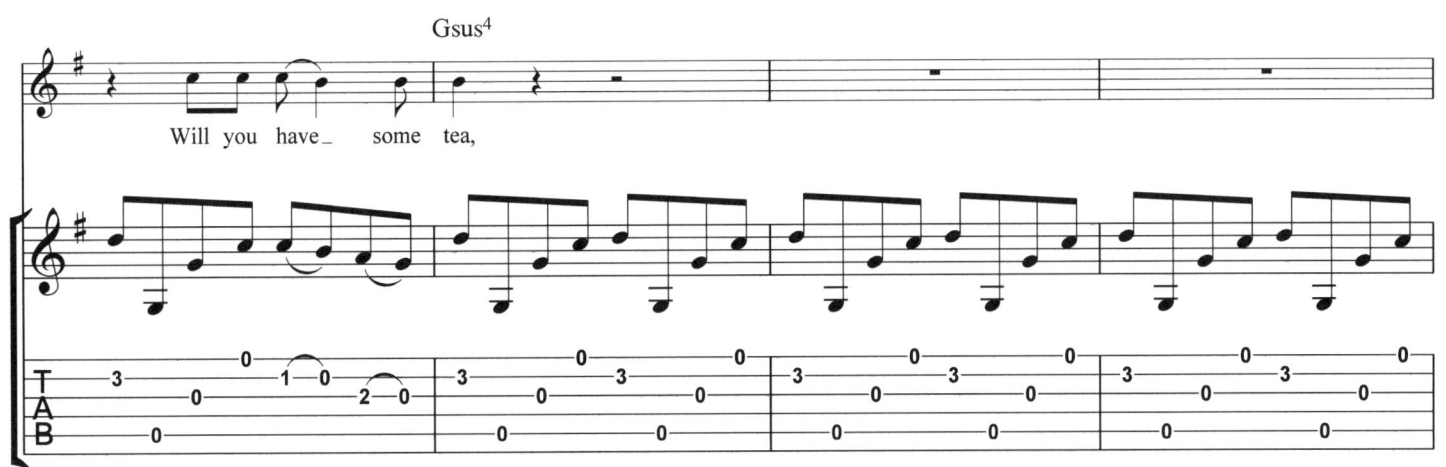

© Copyright 2006 Eel Pie Publishing Limited.
BMG Music Publishing Limited.
All Rights Reserved. International Copyright Secured.

af - ter thea - tre with me?

Verse

We did it all,

did - n't we?

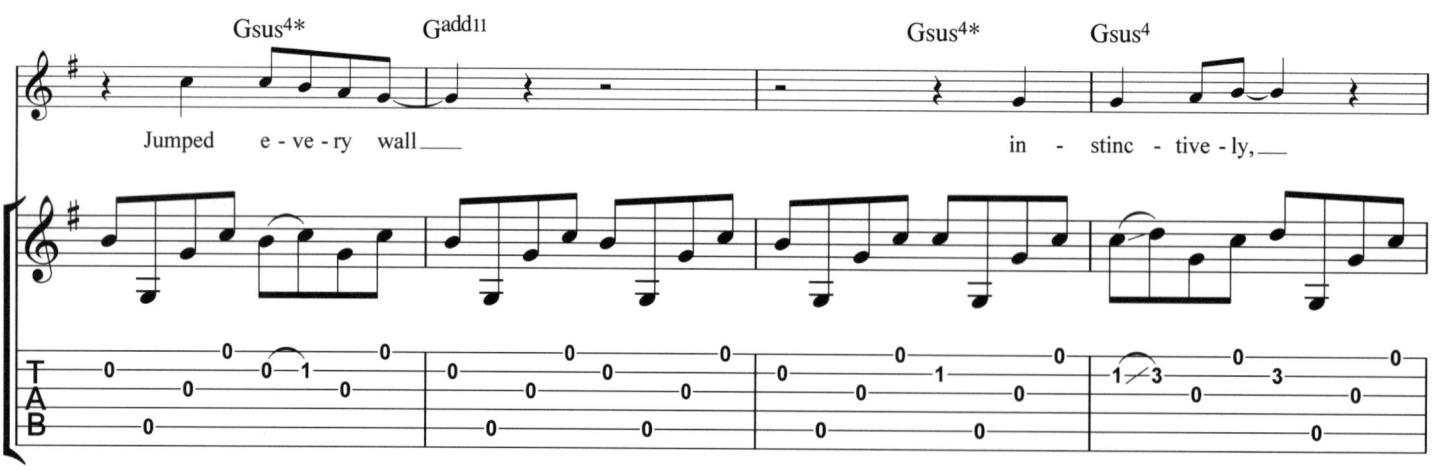

Jumped e - ve - ry wall

in - stinc - tive - ly,

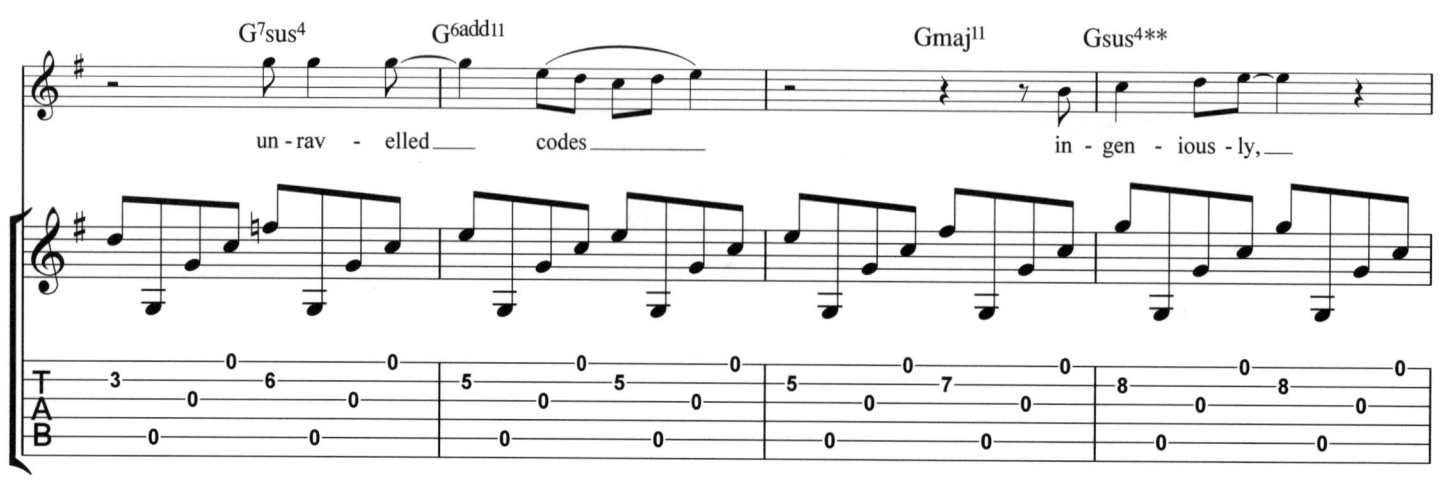

un - rav - elled codes

in - gen - ious - ly,

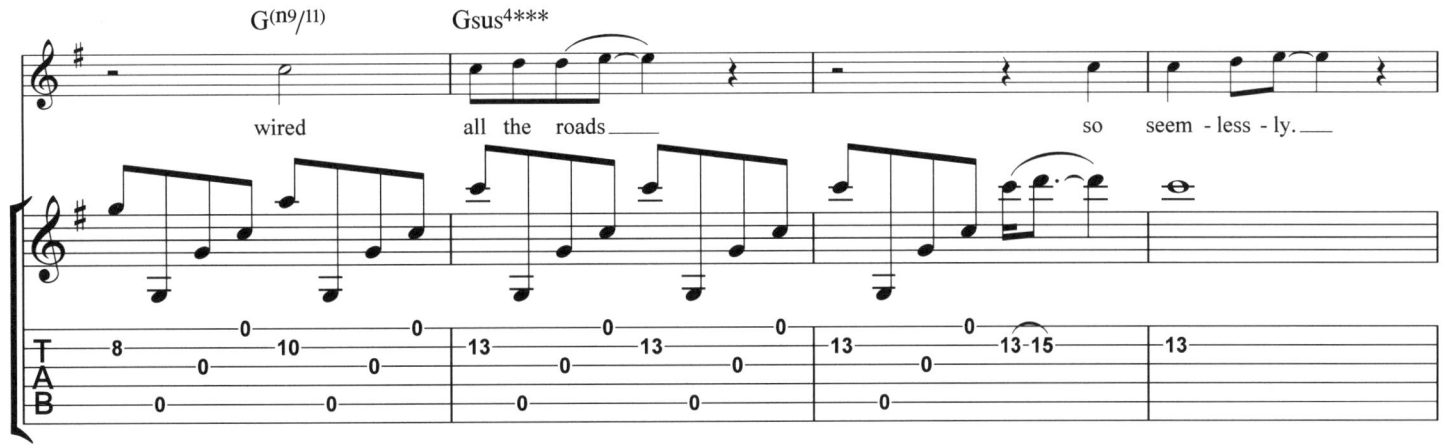

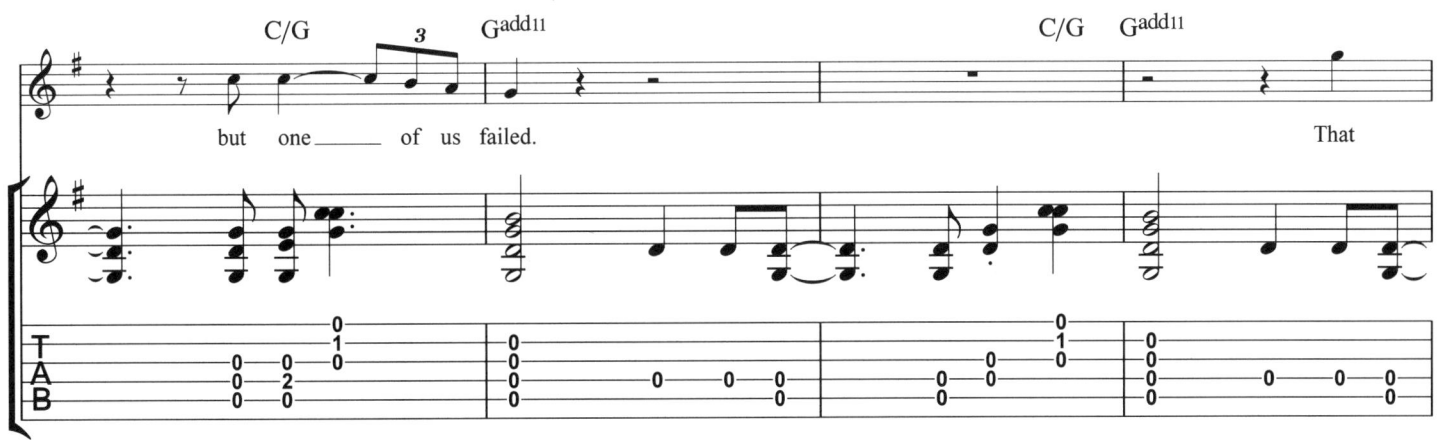

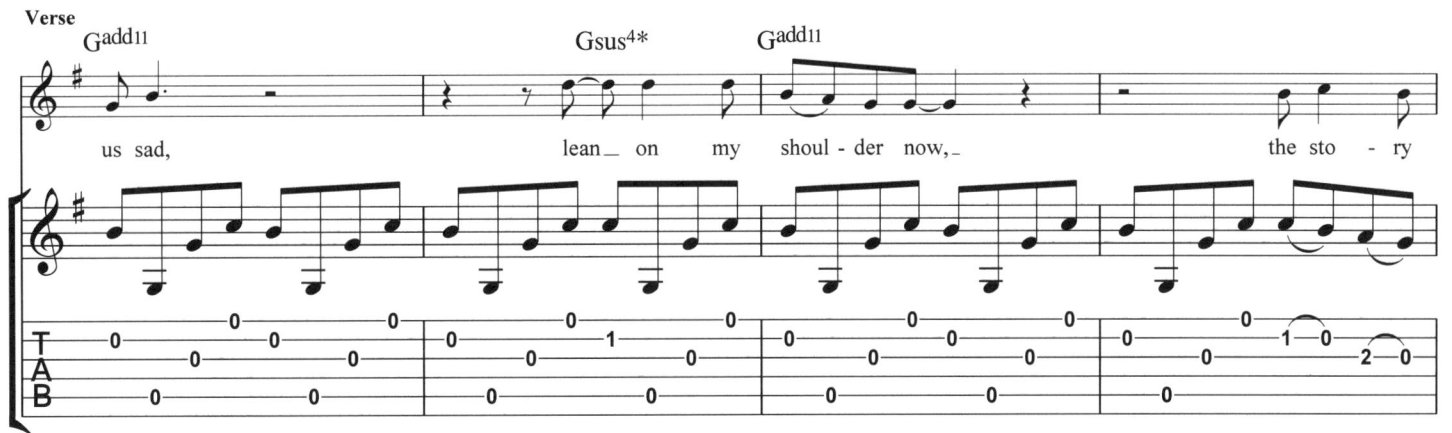

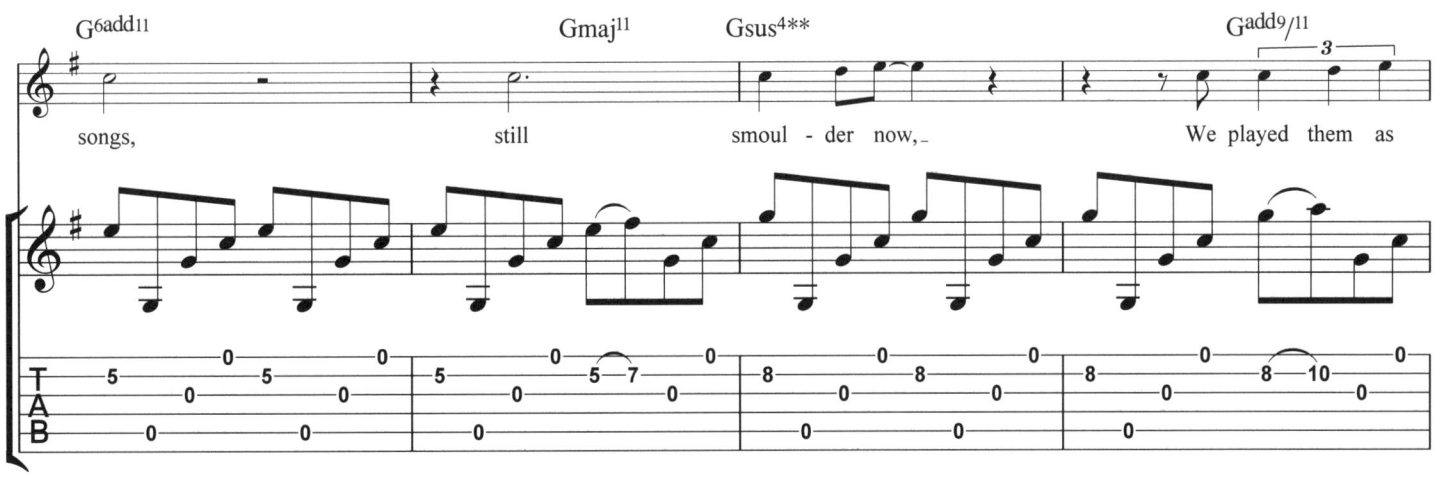

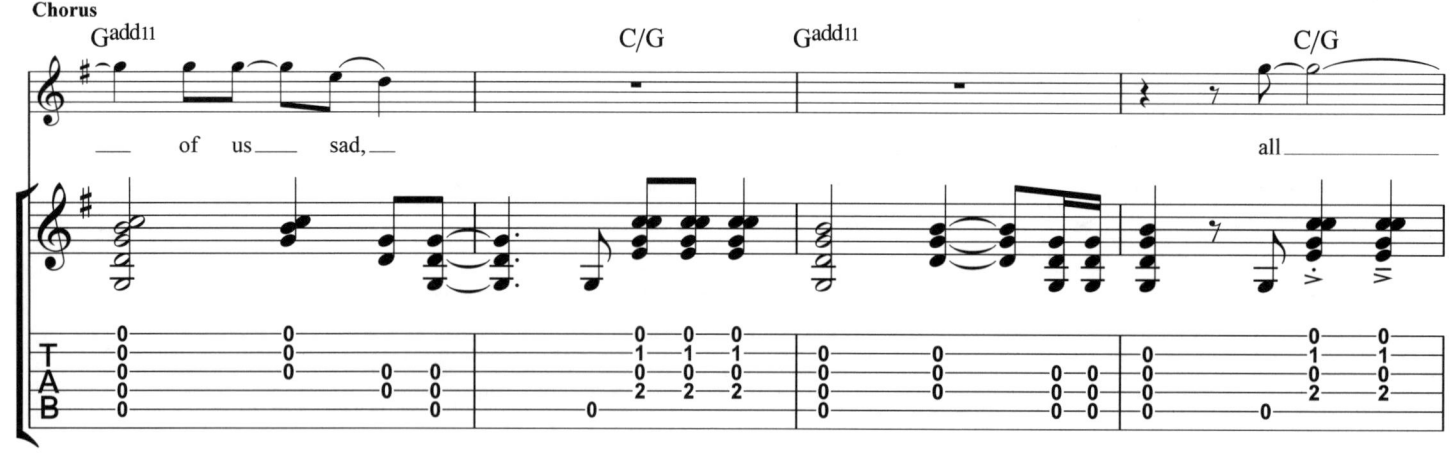

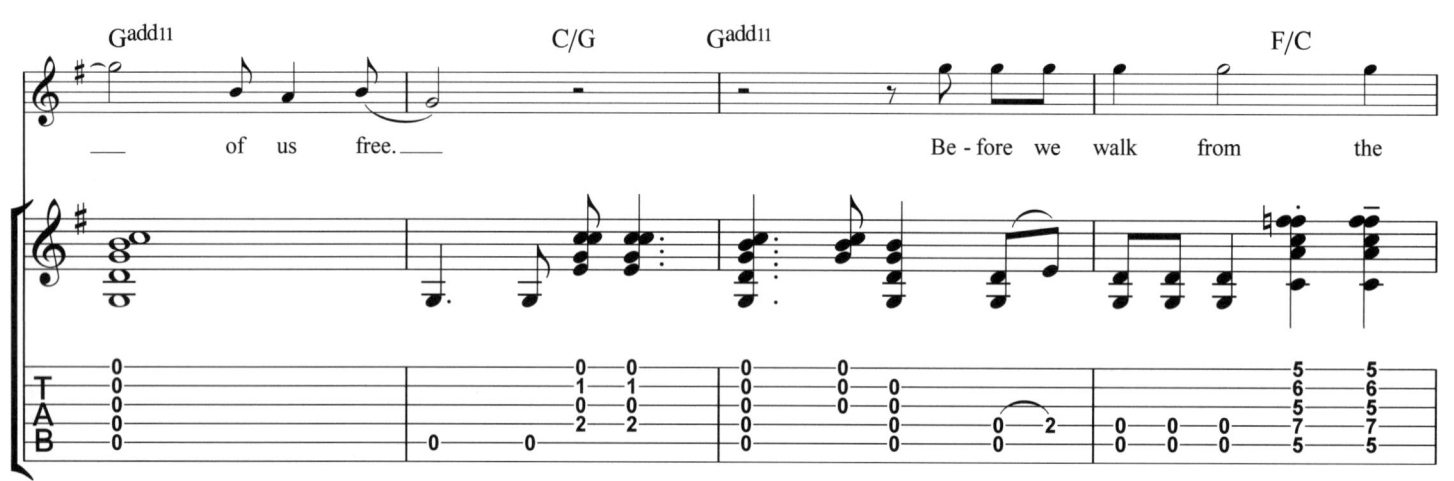

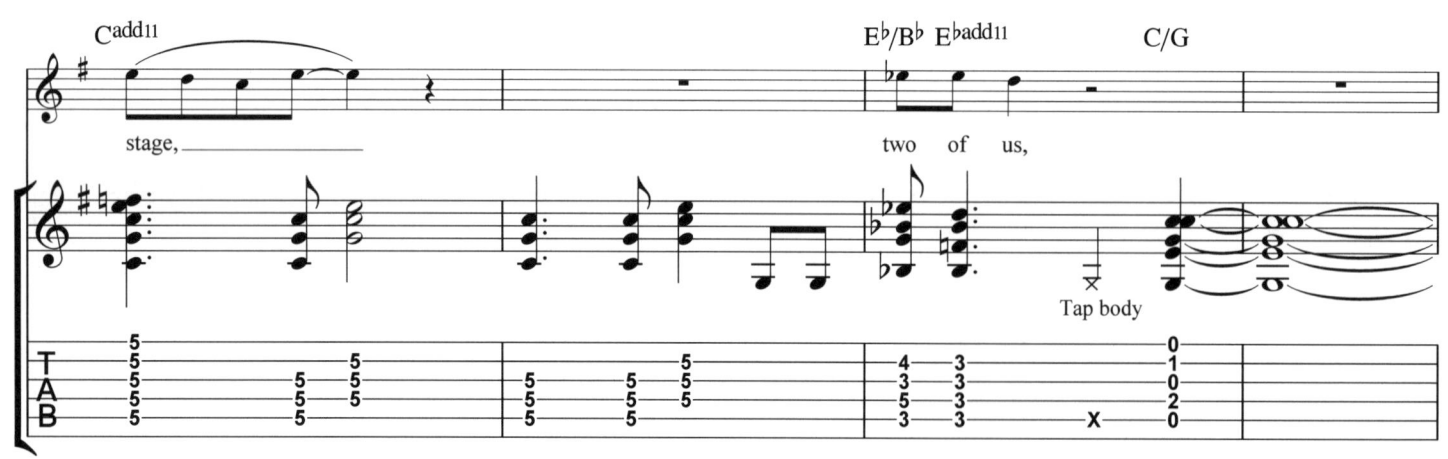

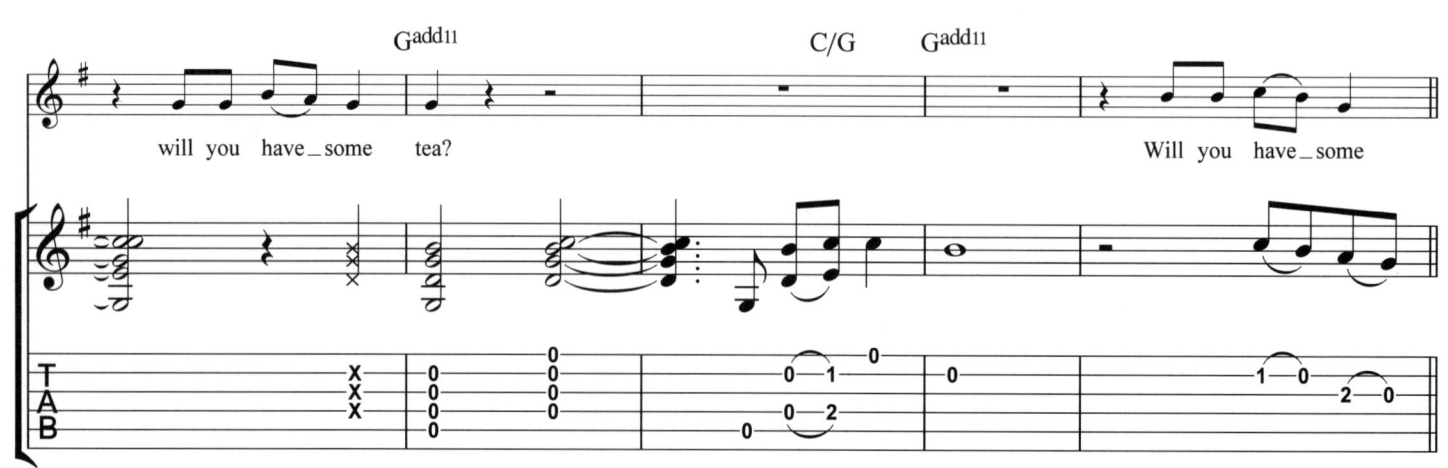

Outro

tea   at the thea -

-tre with me?

WE GOT A HIT (EXTENDED VERSION)

Words & Music by
Pete Townshend

Lyrics:
We got our folks to-ge-ther, we broke down
We came un-der pres-sure, we need-ed time to fly.

© Copyright 2006 Eel Pie Publishing Limited.
BMG Music Publishing Limited.
All Rights Reserved. International Copyright Secured.

114

G
D
bar - ri - ers.
We found a dream to dream,
In - side the case of trea - sure,
8va
Harm.
TAB

Cadd9
G
D
G
cont. sim.
we were the car - ri - ers.
We got rich and fa - mous,
there was an e - vil lie.
And we were bruised and bat - tered,
TAB

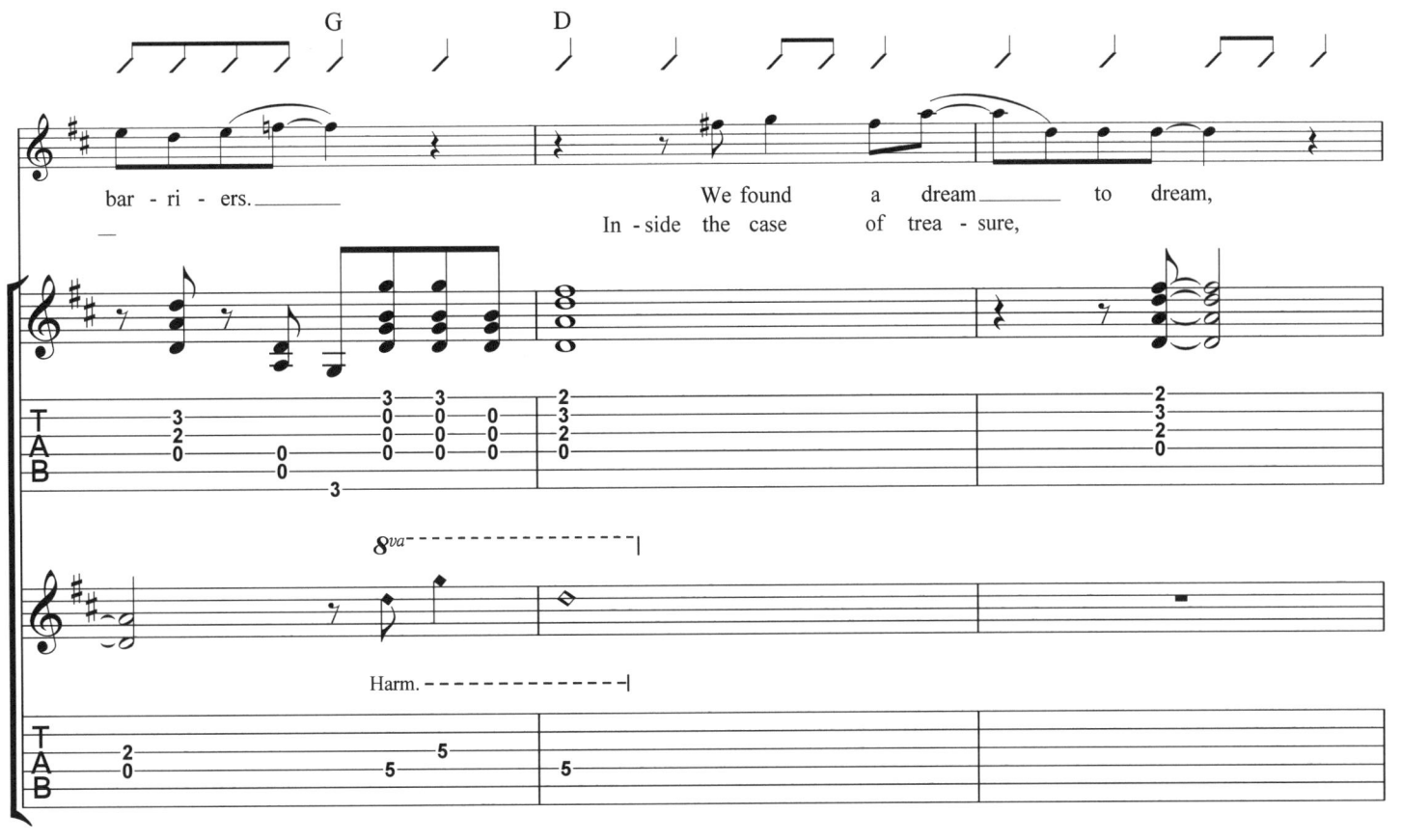

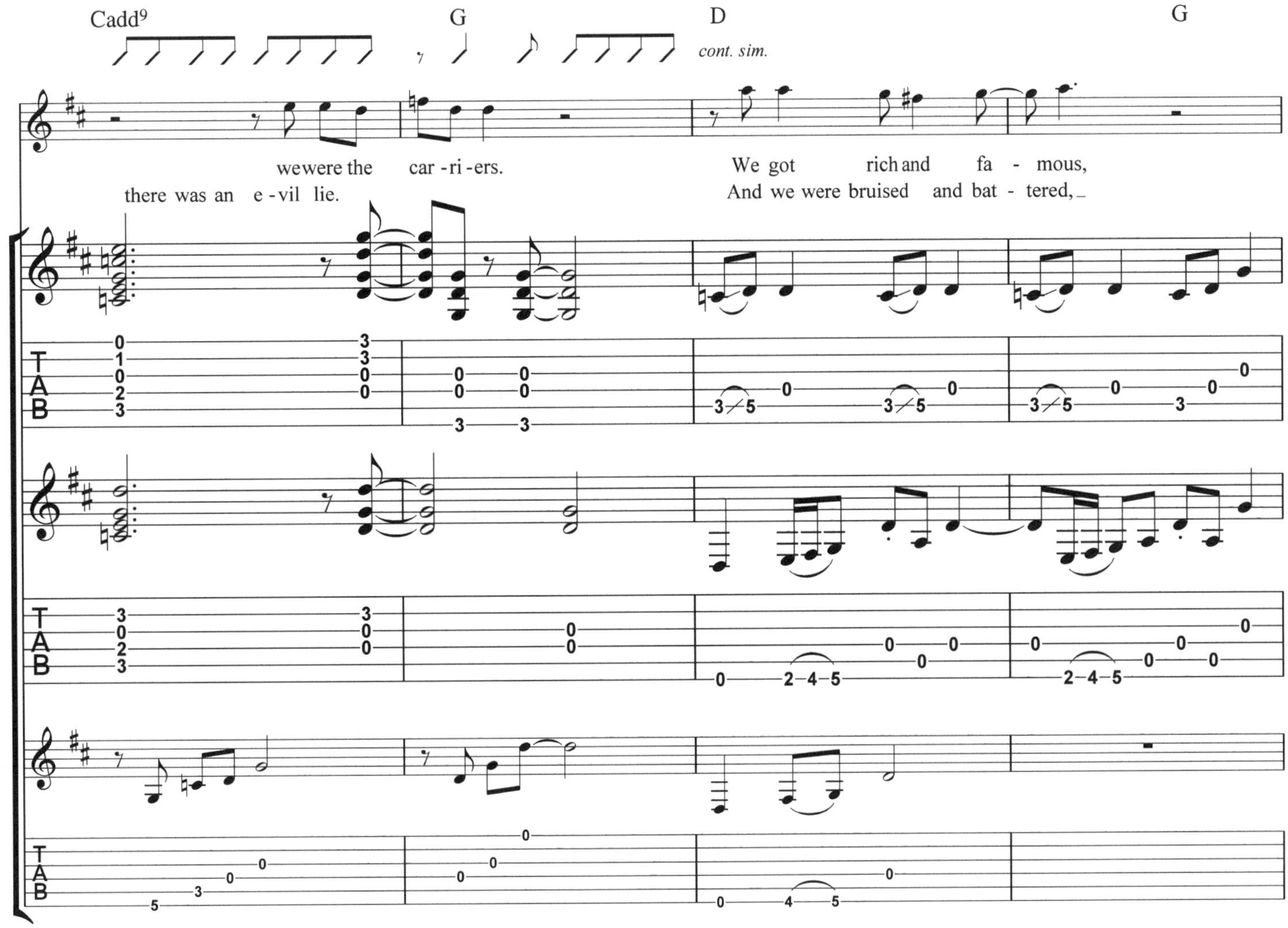

We got our folks to-geth-er, we broke down bar-ri-ers.

D
Cadd9
G
We found a dream to dream, we were the
Harm.
TAB
Cadd9
G
car - ri - ers, we were the car - ri - ers. We got a

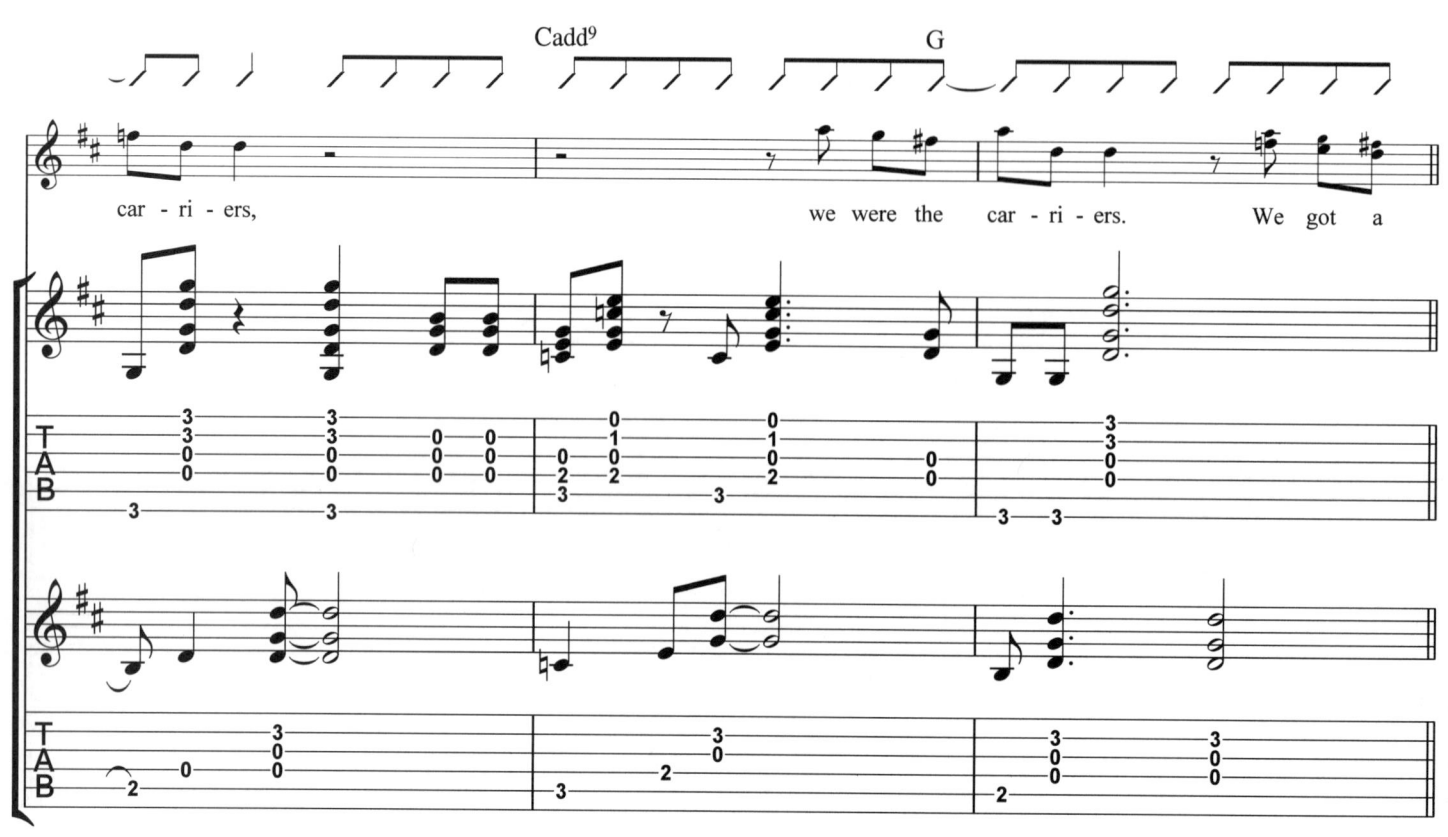

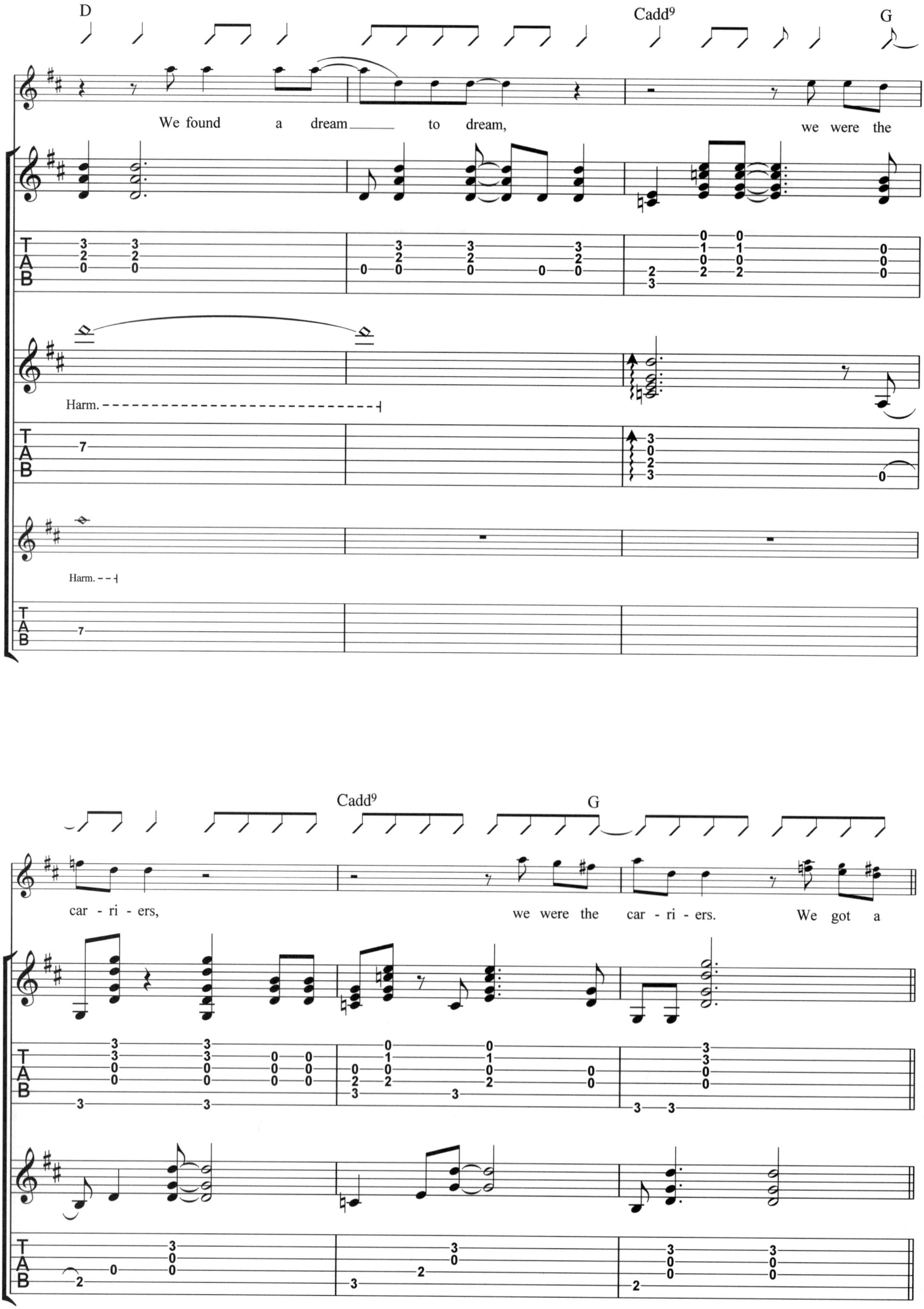

Chorus

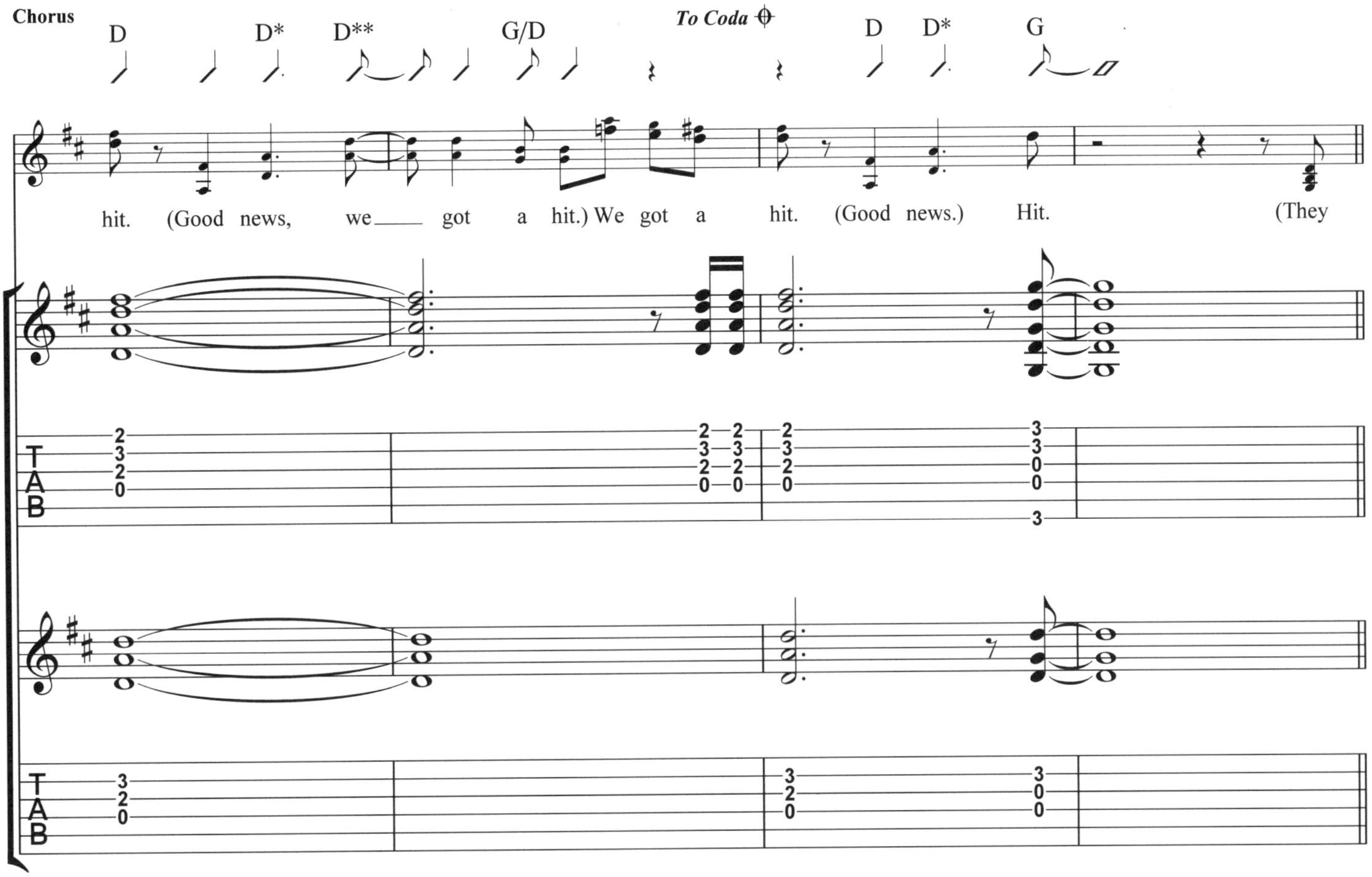

Bridge

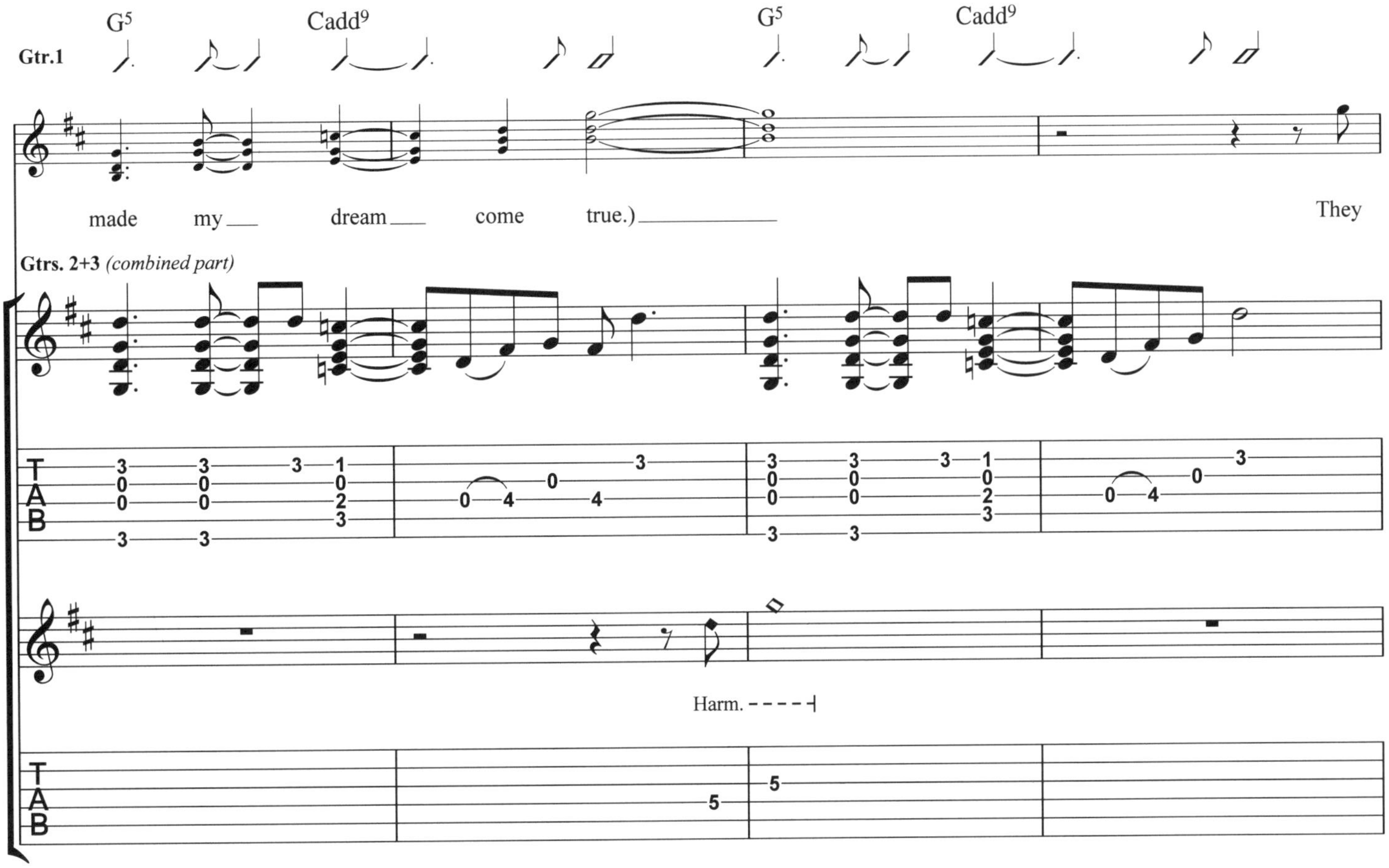

G5 Cadd9 G5 Cadd9
made my dream come true.
They made
Gtrs. 3+4 cont. in slashes
Harm.
D G D
Gtrs. 3+4
my dream come true.
Gtr. 1

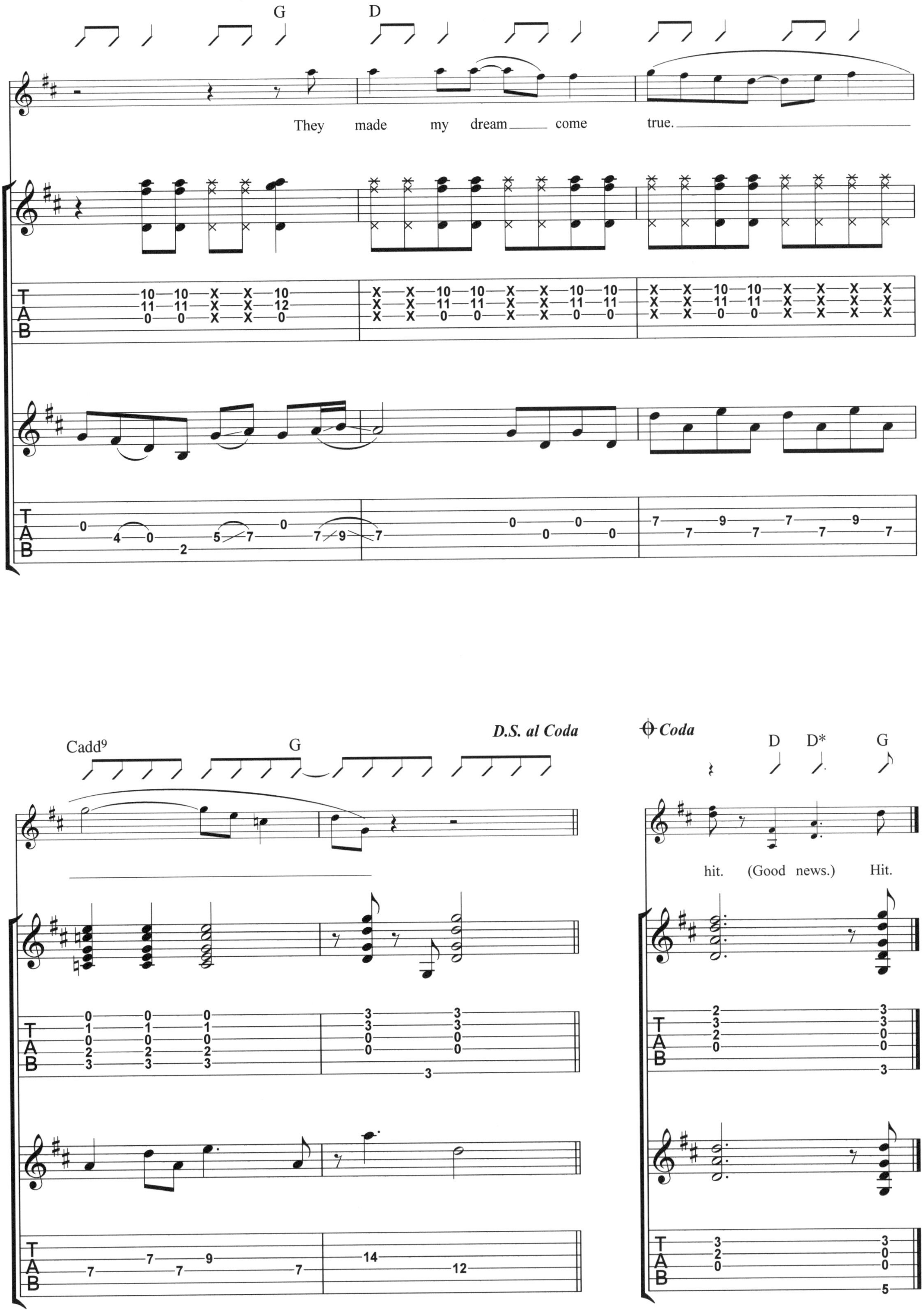
G
D
They made my dream come true.
Cadd9
G
D.S. al Coda
Coda
D
D*
G
hit. (Good news.) Hit.

ENDLESS WIRE (EXTENDED VERSION)

Words & Music by
Pete Townshend

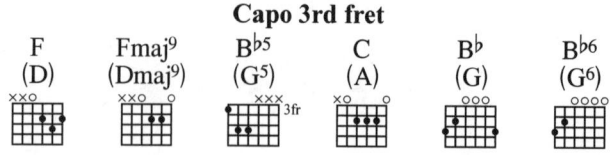

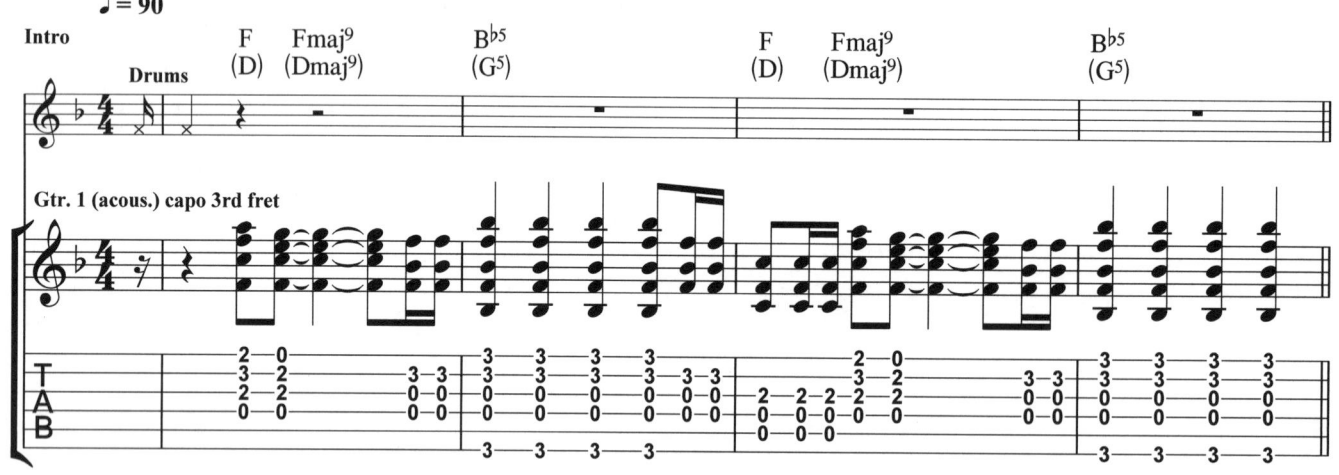

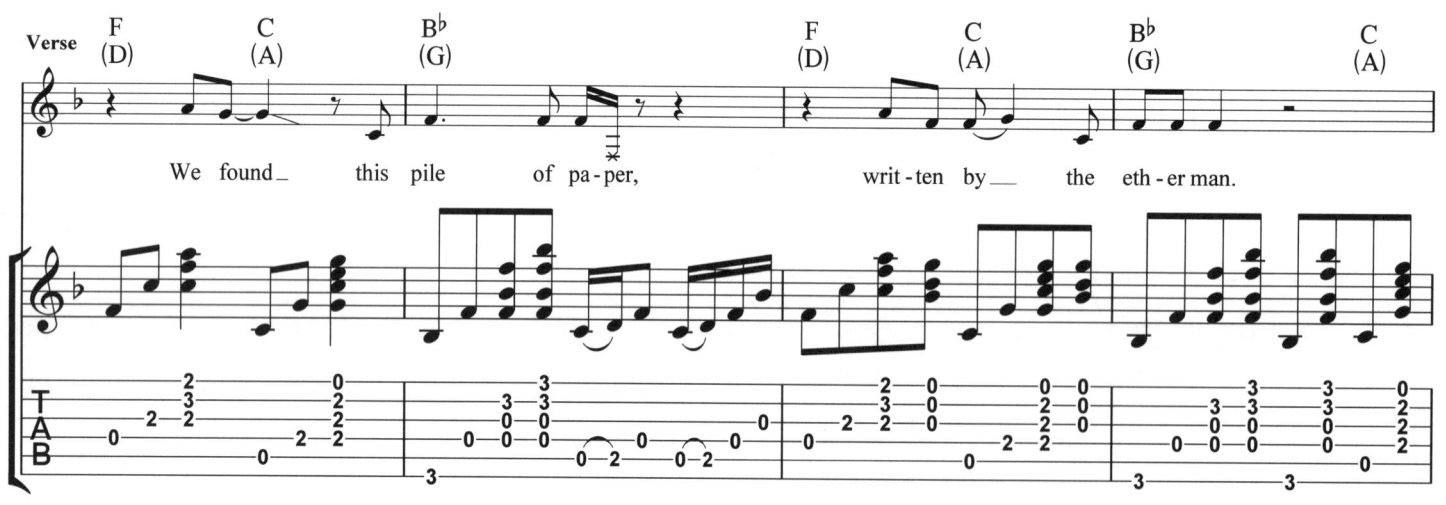

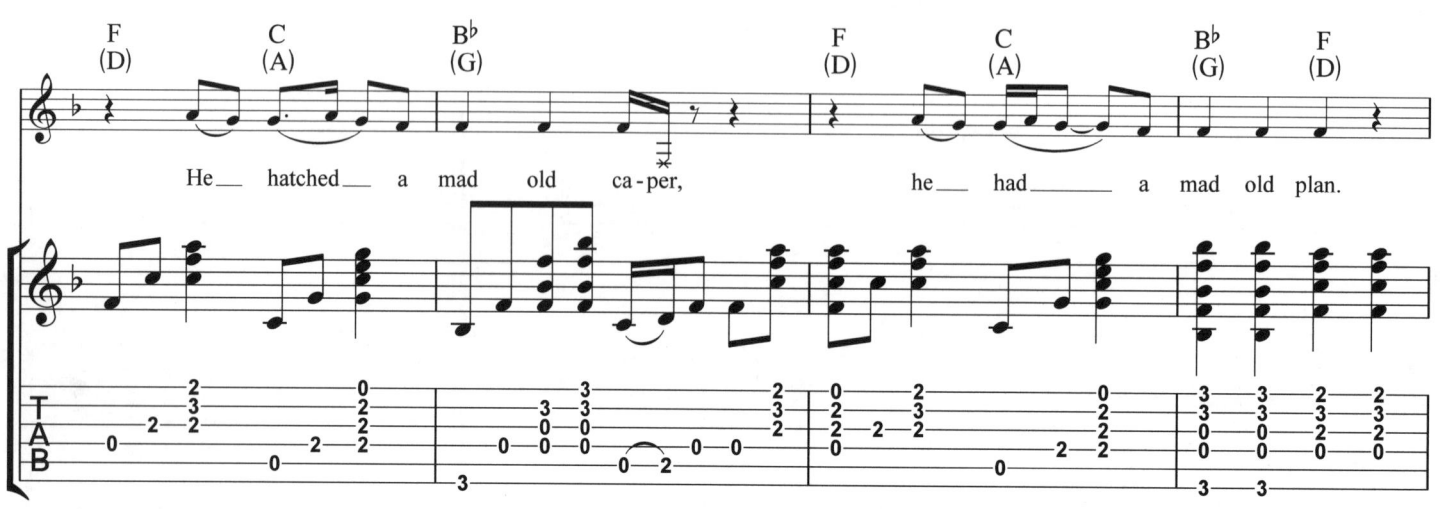

© Copyright 2006 Eel Pie Publishing Limited.
BMG Music Publishing Limited.
All Rights Reserved. International Copyright Secured.

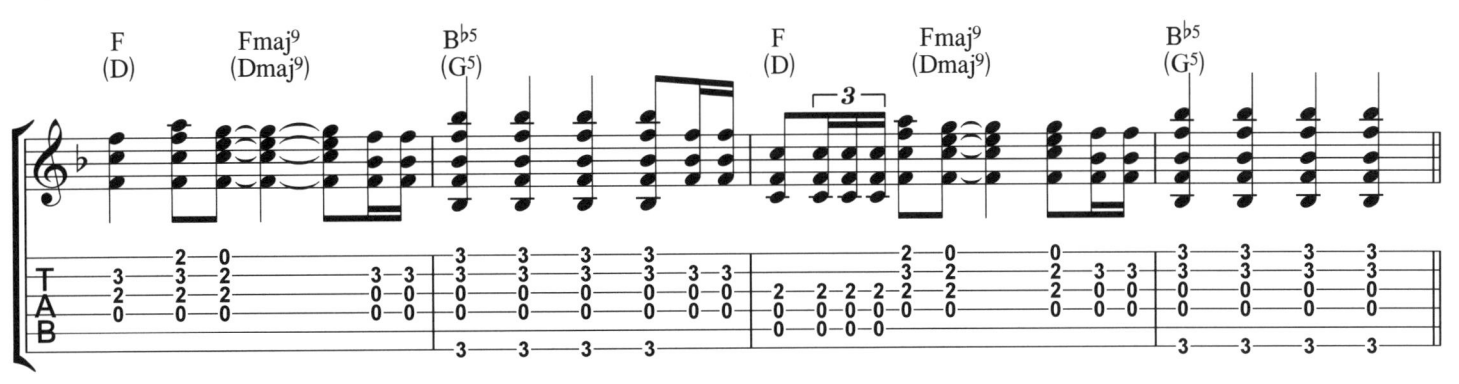

He'd turn us into music, he'd show us to our portals.

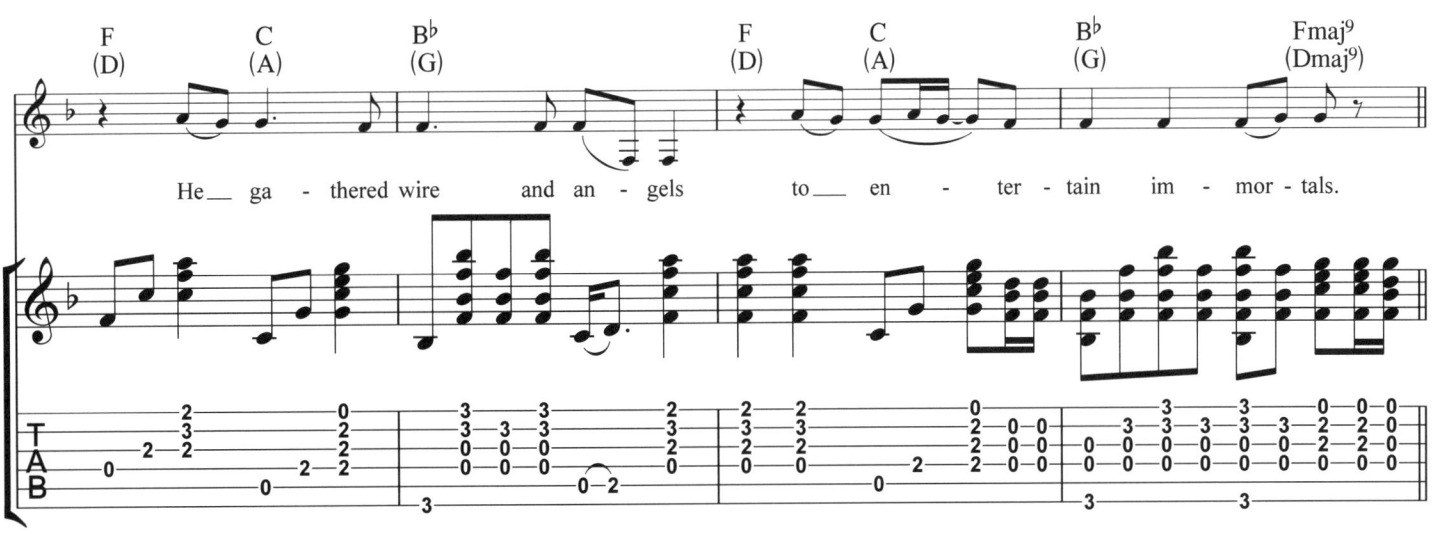

He gathered wire and angels to entertain immortals.

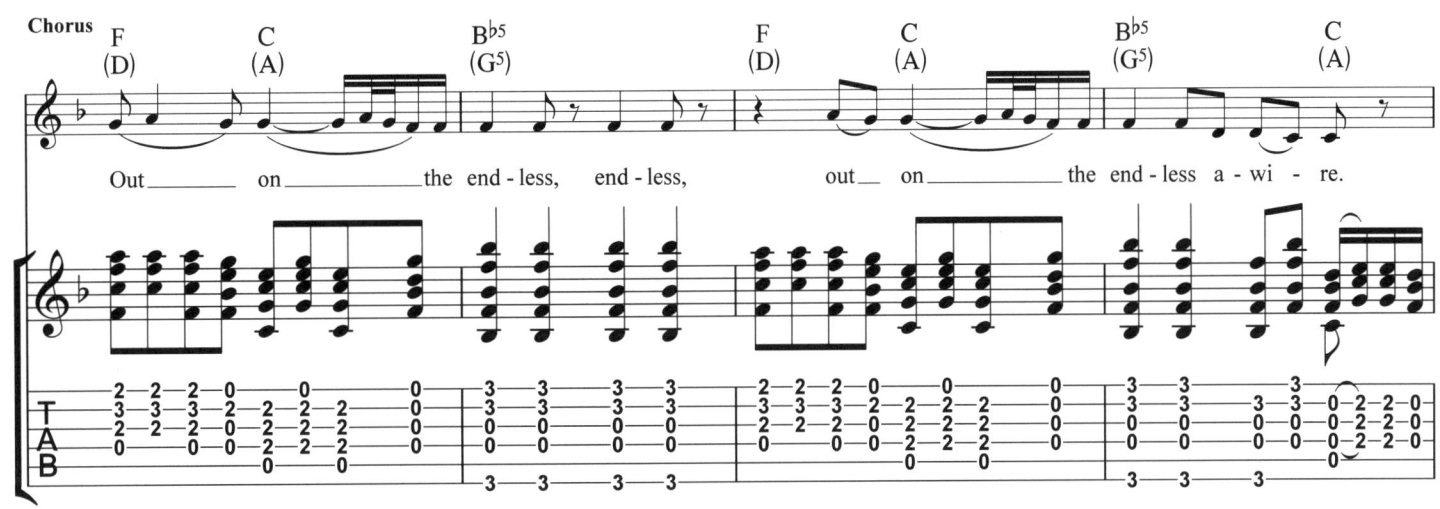

Out on the endless, endless, out on the endless a-wire.

123456789

GUITAR TABLATURE EXPLAINED

Guitar music can be notated in three different ways: on a musical stave, in tablature, and in rhythm slashes.

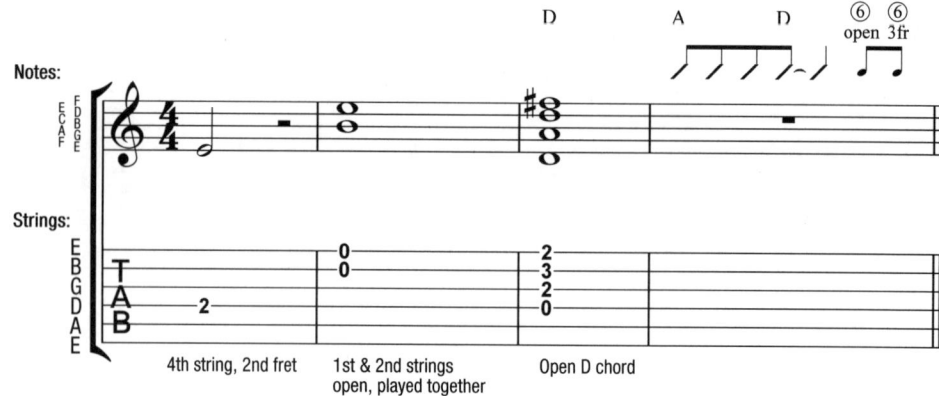

RHYTHM SLASHES: are written above the stave. Strum chords in the rhythm indicated. Round noteheads indicate single notes.

THE MUSICAL STAVE: shows pitches and rhythms and is divided by lines into bars. Pitches are named after the first seven letters of the alphabet.

TABLATURE: graphically represents the guitar fingerboard. Each horizontal line represents a string, and each number represents a fret.

4th string, 2nd fret   1st & 2nd strings open, played together   Open D chord

Definitions for special guitar notation

SEMI-TONE BEND: Strike the note and bend up a semi-tone (½ step).

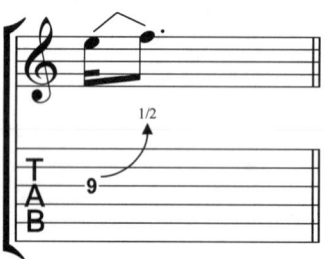

WHOLE-TONE BEND: Strike the note and bend up a whole-tone (full step).

GRACE NOTE BEND: Strike the note and bend as indicated. Play the first note as quickly as possible.

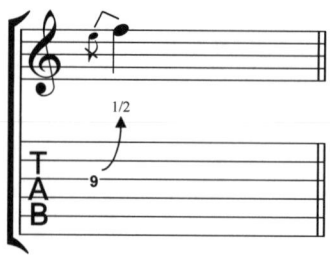

QUARTER-TONE BEND: Strike the note and bend up a ¼ step.

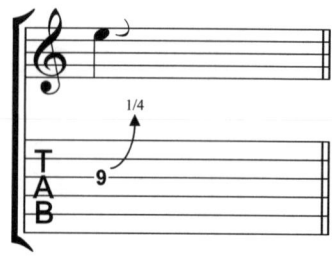

BEND & RELEASE: Strike the note and bend up as indicated, then release back to the original note.

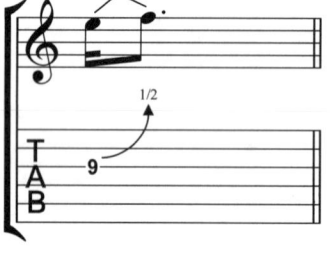

COMPOUND BEND & RELEASE: Strike the note and bend up and down in the rhythm indicated.

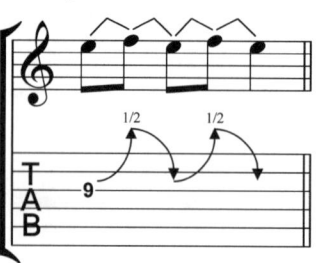

PRE-BEND: Bend the note as indicated, then strike it.

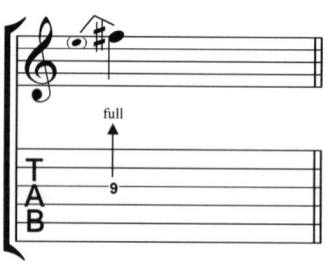

PRE-BEND & RELEASE: Bend the note as indicated. Strike it and release the note back to the original pitch.

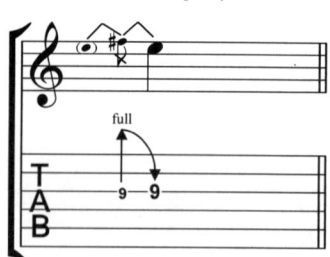

HAMMER-ON: Strike the first note with one finger, then sound the second note (on the same string) with another finger by fretting it without picking.

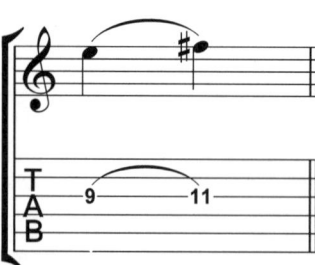

PULL-OFF: Place both fingers on the note to be sounded, strike the first note and without picking, pull the finger off to sound the second note.

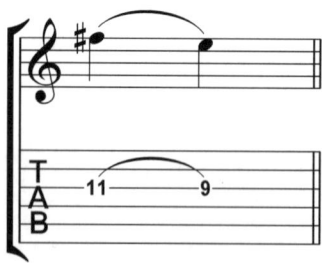

LEGATO SLIDE (GLISS): Strike the first note and then slide the same fret-hand finger up or down to the second note. The second note is not struck.

MUFFLED STRINGS: A percussive sound is produced by laying the first hand across the string(s) without depressing, and striking them with the pick hand.

NATURAL HARMONIC: Strike the note while the fret-hand lightly touches the string directly over the fret indicated.

PICK SCRAPE: The edge of the pick is rubbed down (or up) the string, producing a scratchy sound.

PALM MUTING: The note is partially muted by the pick hand lightly touching the string(s) just before the bridge.

SHIFT SLIDE (GLISS & RESTRIKE): Same as legato slide, except the second note is struck.